BEYOND ORPHEUS

The MIT Press
Cambridge, Massachusetts, and London, England

BEYOND ORPHEUS

Studies in Musical Structure

David Epstein

Arthur Bloom produced the musical notation for this book.

This book was set in IBM Composer Theme
by Jay's Publishers Services, Incorporated,
printed and bound by Halliday Lithograph Corporation in the United States of America.

Library of Congress Cataloging in Publication Data

Epstein, David.
  Beyond Orpheus.

  Includes bibliographical references.
  1. Music—Theory. 2. Musical form. 3. Music—Philosophy and aesthetics. I. Title.
MT58.E67   781.3   78–232
ISBN 0–262–05016–1

To my parents

CONTENTS

Contents

FOREWORD

It is not mere fashionability, for that is by now largely a past fashionability, which suggests that the "normal" and "revolutionary" oscillatory historical paradigm is particularly suitable to situate chronologically and characterize ideologically the fragmented, pluralistic, disarrayed, thus revolutionary, condition of musical creation over the past seven or so decades. This is a period so long—and with no normalcy in sight—that one might be tempted to tamper with the paradigm and declare such an extended reign of coexistent, though almost discrete, revolutionary musics as, finally, the normal music. I do not mean for this lighthearted equivocation to be taken seriously except to lighten our heavyhearted awareness of our complexly delicate musical condition and to heighten our awareness that in music, at least, what further characterizes a revolutionary period is that it reexamines its past, and this by reexamining past and present examinations, "theories," of that past.

It was fervently in that spirit, and not with a view to subtle methodological refinement, that Heinrich Schenker, whose deep contributions are one of the two main sources of David Epstein's present work, step by step—over a quarter of a century—evolved his revolutionary theory of musical explication. As a practicing, "practical" musician, he found the various forms of the "received view" of the music of the past—for Schenker, the only music—crucially incomplete; they were unable to account for those regularities that are the most pervasive of constancies in the music under examination, and yet were, apparently therefore, disregarded and swept under the analytical rug. Schenker gradually realized that such regularities would not be entailed within the normal theory simply by adjoining to it new, independent premises, but demanded for their derivation a different ontologization, an assumption of other bases, compoundable into novel concepts, which particularly are extensible to distinguish those contingencies and dependencies that embody temporal progression. In the "normal" theory Schenker found such dependencies, in the small, represented primarily by a "context-free" notion of intervallic resolution, free of a specific temporal context within a particular composition; free—even—of a particular composition. And, in the large, obscured, even utterly eliminated, by the notion of "modulation," which—if the term were assumed to possess stable reference—denoted a "change of key," thus a view of a movement of a composition as a movement through a succession of, hierarchically necessarily equivalent, and—thus—equivalently stable, tonal areas rather than as a movement within a hierarchically primary area within which there were locations of varying and various emphases, defining hierarchical scopes and ranges. This movable tonic view of modulation permits no distinction between, say, that "key of B flat" of the "second theme" of the Eroica symphony and that of the "first theme" of Beethoven's *Fourth Symphony*, thus sacrificing the relational distinction between that which is contained within an unfolding and that within which the unfolding of an all-embracing single tonality, represented by its scale collection and dispositionally focal triad, occurs. What is lost here is so much that must matter if musical memory is to induce the sense of the entification, the unitization, of a total, temporally directed, movement.

As Epstein points out, explicitly with regard to Schenker's conception of "rhythm" and implicitly in his discussion of "modulation": although Schenker appears to speak relatively little of the specifically "rhythmical," his detailed conceptions of "unfolding" and "composing out" convey dynamisms of direction, embedded and concatenated. And yet it cannot be said that Schenker displays a sufficient awareness of the critical failure of the "normal" view of musical "form" to capture the central property of temporally successive subsumption; for that view postulates the norm of a few acceptable patterns of dimensionally coordinated "repetitions," constituted of concomerations of moments related—or unrelated—simply categorically, nominally. Schenker even apparently attempted to preserve, by renovation, this view of "form," by the voice-leading activation and containment of its formal "sections." But, by so doing, he was seduced into that sadly static, literal, representation of recurrence which permits him, even in his most elaborate analysis—that of the *Eroica* Symphony, which underlies so much of chapter 6 of this study—to terminate his measure-by-measure "graphical" explication of the first movement some 290 measures before its end, at the point of what he labels, resignedly, "Wiederholung." Only in a few inadequate, summary sentences of his verbal commentary does he attend to the radically nonrepetitional nature, beginning just three measures after his "graph" ceases, of this "formal repetition." Nor does he attempt to display what is "recapitulated," a by-now-in-the-work intricate network of dimensional paths which induce new environments of the recurrent "event" and new conjunctions and influences of dimensional recurrences.

Schenker, no doubt unawarely, and Epstein, highly awarely, are engaged in the act of rational, reasoned reconstruction which, while it is not and cannot be concerned to intimate a mode of compositional construction or creation, or the nature of compositional "performance," is emphatically concerned to offer a mode of construal. Therefore, this activity shares with the compositional process the issues raised by the real-time character of perceived musical consecution. For, to convey this quality in what cannot be, for it cannot be controlled to be, "real-time" analytical prose or symbolism poses a problem of representation no less severe in degree than, though considerably different in kind from, that confronting the composer. His creative mental imagery must persist in simulating such a real-time eventuality, while yet conveying these images in notational, transcriptional, non-real-time.

Beyond Orpheus, in its sundry and original examinations and applications of the musically temporal, reflects those current standards of analytical theory which hold that no explanation is satisfactory that does not incorporate time-dependency considerations, considerations complying with the musical event's temporal indexing, both modularly—by metrical orientation locally and periodic position globally—and "absolutely," by the qualitative relations of precedence and subsequence. For only by so formulating can analysis typify the epistemic circumstance, in which knowledge of a musical work is acquired and accumulated as the work proceeds, in compositionally controlled time.

If the second primary source of Epstein's analytical synthesis—Schoenberg's "Grundgestalt"—insinuates only that music theory makes strange, if Viennese, bedfellows, it has become increasingly evident that Schoenberg and Schenker are, multiply, complementary historical figures. Even methodologically, while Schenker made an illicit, irrelevant leap from his analyses to his evaluations, Schoenberg—as a theorist—moved from the normal theory, extended by no more than Riemannian generalizations on which he superimposed and within which he imbedded his motivically derived conception of the "basic shape," to—as a composer—a profoundly innovative, revolutionary position, whose geneses and "justifications"—nevertheless—for him were in concept derivable from and within his "normal" theory. But the move from traditional transformations applied to functionally based or independent "motives" to those same interval-preserving transformations applied to a total ordering of all twelve pitch-classes induced a revolutionary alteration of the hierarchical relations of order and collection, a fundamentally new conception of musical time, of musical structure, of necessary and possible degrees of context dependence.

Only when conjoined with a dynamic theory such as Schenker's, as Epstein has done, does the "basic shape" conception define in time, and individuate beyond the tautological identifications of the thematic. I long have suspected that Schoenberg's asserted concern with those methods of his "middle period" which "made it seem impossible to compose works of complicated organization or great length," when one considers the quantitative complexity and temporal length of such pieces as "Erwartung" and "Die Glückliche Hand" (even without their textual assistance), was a frustration engendered by an awareness of the potentialities of such motivic extensions as those revealed by Schenker's construal of the total "development" of the first movement of the "Eroica." Schenker makes such a construal in just the third figure of his graphical analysis, albeit a correspondingly advanced stage of his reduction, which (as Epstein shows on pages 121 and 127) therefore permits it to be interpreted as an extended inversion of the motive of the celebrated measures 6–11. Such an expansion requires the capacity of a pitch-class to dominate an extended region, by a hierarchization unavailable under simply single dimensional motivic conditions.

If Schenker, thereby, wrought more than he realized or cared to recognize, so Epstein, by his fusion, suggests yet further explicit extensions of its application. For instance, in Schenker's analysis of that Mozart *Symphony No. 40* in Epstein's chapter 7, the complete "development," again, can be interpreted directly as a descending motion, through seconds, of the minor seventh from "G" down to "A," It thus extends to some 38 measures the measure and a half, beginning on measure 3, where the climactic B♮ descends to C in the first violins, and the same pitch classes again represented over 3 measures in the bass from measures 28 through 34. These occurrences may be taken to provide an answer to why, in the sense of what it is doing there, the "F sharp minor" occurs early in the "development" (see page 4), and how a conventionally misplaced root position tonic (G minor) triad dares appear at the beginning of this "development" as, rather, the beginning of a path retracing the "basic shape" of the thematic descent through the seventh.

If Epstein's conflation of construals endows Schenkerian analyses with yet greater powers of individuation, augmenting those provided by diminutional parallelism in the stratified descent from singular foreground to archetypical background, it provides "basic shape" analyses with a capacity for extending what is essentially familiar thematic and motivic individuation beyond and beneath the music's surface. It provides further capacity for investing the varied occurrences of the basic shape with temporal orientation, which not even an apparently plausible a priori can supply otherwise to symmetrically related or derived variants of the "basic shape."

To expose more broadly and deeply the singularity of a musical work, and—correspondingly—to minimize its being understood chiefly as a token of a "formal," even structural, type, is a normative goal of otherwise only casually related analytical approaches of our revolutionary time. Boretz, particularly, penetrates and transcends thematic, motivic, and comparable facets of individuality to discover and uncover uniquenesses of process, internally analogous modes of progression, and means of cumulative containment which themselves yield the characteristic thematic, rhythmic, timbral, and other aspects of the surface, and which depend only minimally on communal attributes. Like those of Epstein's book and the contributions of Meyer, Narmour, Kresky, and Charles J. Smith (among a number of important contributors to this discipline), this concern can be couched in the "revolutionary" assertion that musical surfaces are misleading if they cannot lead one beneath the musical surface.

Epstein is a wise child of his time, not only in that he has acquired and used the wisdom of his theoretical fathers, or in that he has followed the course of such fathers as Rameau and Hauptmann in pursuing and applying pertinent wisdom outside of his immediate intellectual domain, or in that by compounding the methods and results of others he not only has extended imaginatively the applications and explanatory scope of aspects of those individual theories in ways not susceptible to them singly, but in that, through his analyses, he sends us not only to other works of music and about music and to further generalizations of his ideas but to considerations and yet reconsiderations of the most central questions of musical explanation and understanding. Through even the most specific of his observations we are led necessarily back to think again of, and in, musical essentials and fundamentals.

Milton Babbitt
Princeton University

PREFACE

Several times in his career Arnold Schoenberg paid homage to some of his major music teachers—Bach, Mozart, Beethoven, Brahms. In a sense he spoke for all of us, for like Schoenberg we too have "studied" with these men; it is upon their music that we have cut our musical eyeteeth. They have set our standards as well as our basic repertory.

Though we all know this body of music, many of us know it in different ways, for we have been in contact with it through different modes. It is the nature of this contact that often determines how we will think about the music, if we think about it at all. The practicalities and real-time pressures of performance, for example, force perceptions different from those of analysis, or of listening, however casual or intense. At one time or another we have probably assumed all of these roles, but not necessarily with the same music, or with the major portion of the repertory and the musical issues it raises.

Observations on many of the scores discussed here have come through performance, the music approached with both a conductor's perspective and a composer's training and viewpoint. Though not by design or intent, a continual interaction between mind and ear has ensued, in the process raising issues that would nag and persist, at times without offering answers. Sooner or later these issues had to be confronted; a book—predictably, perhaps—has been the result.

Often in this kind of musical engagement it is anomaly that catches the attention, leading one to question why it exists, how it fits an overall design, indeed whose anomaly it is, that of the composer, the piece, the period, the style. A dialogue with the music develops, one that must have some answers at least, those for the practicalities of performance if nothing else—a bowing required here, an emphasis, tempo, nuance suggested elsewhere. Answers may be hard to find, for we work in part by intuition; yet intuition does not always satisfy at these moments. We want reasons, and reasons demand facts, evidence, proof. We begin to theorize. In large part this has been the chronology, in fact the genesis of *Beyond Orpheus.*

A number of the ideas that appear here had their origin in my doctoral dissertation completed some years ago for Princeton University. I was fortunate to profit from the superb graduate education offered by Princeton, and I am grateful for the stimulation, the teaching, and the detailed critical discussions of these thoughts in their original form provided by Milton Babbitt and Edward T. Cone. I also appreciate deeply the teaching and influence of Roger Sessions, who was a profound musical force at Princeton during the years of my graduate work.

Shortly after Princeton I was a conducting fellow with the Cleveland Orchestra under the late George Szell. His work was a living example of the synthesis of musical thought and action, and his influence has remained these many years.

The intellectual climate of Boston has been a privileged one in which to develop this study, enriched by colleagues, friends, and students with whom I have discussed and refined ideas. It is impossible to acknowledge all these people individually, and I hope they will accept my general statement of thanks. I am especially grateful to my musical colleagues at MIT for critical comments: Jeanne Bamberger, John Harbison and his wife Rosemary, Irving Singer of the Department of Philosophy. I would also like to thank Arthur Berger, Edward Cohen, and Seymour Shifrin of the Brandeis University Music

Department for their suggestions, as well as Ray Jackendoff of the Department of Linguistics at Brandeis for his valuable theoretical discussions. My thanks to my former colleague Robert Freeman, now Director of the Eastman School of Music, who, in addition to reading the manuscript in an earlier version, also provided a forum at Eastman for the testing of these ideas through an invitation to teach a graduate theory course there as a guest. Conversations with Arthur Komar and with the pianist Theodore Lettvin have been valuable for their stimulation and their perceptions. I am grateful to Howard Webber, former Director of the MIT Press, for his interest and assistance in the publication of this book.

My further thanks to my students, who over the years have heard these ideas and responded to them. Some in particular have been unusually helpful, and I wish to acknowledge David Breitman, Ronald Cohen, and Nicholas Pippinger for their contributions.

Last, and far from least, my appreciation to all the members of my family, who endured a preoccupied and absent-minded writer during the evolution of this book. That we all survived the experience is a testament to a sturdy sense of humor—a quality worth cultivating if for no other reason than self-protection, should I be tempted in the future to write once again.

Lexington, Massachusetts
August 1974

MUSICAL STRUCTURE

1 INTRODUCTION

Since the Renaissance at least, the arts have been conceived as ways of exploring the universe, as complementary to the sciences. To a certain extent, they create their own fields of research; their universe is the language they have shaped, whose nature and limits they explore, and in exploring, transform. Beethoven is perhaps the first composer for whom this exploratory function of music took precedence over every other: pleasure, instruction, and, even, expression. A work like the *Diabelli* Variations is above all a discovery of the nature of the simplest musical elements, an investigation of the language of classical tonality with all its implications for rhythm and texture as well as melody and harmony.[1]

So wrote Charles Rosen in his study of the classical style. It is a judgment with which few musicians today would disagree, either in its characterization of Beethoven or its broader focus on the arts. Indeed, what may with Beethoven have been an unusual preoccupation with structure has since become a prevalent musical concern. Structure, analysis, the study of systems—these are in large measure the intellectual currency of the twentieth century. Their domain has long since extended beyond "objective" data, the seeming province of physical science, to pervade methodology, even conceptualization, in such "inexact" fields as the social sciences and the arts.

Science has been drafted as a handmaiden in this new world view, various of its modes of perception—linguistics, mathematics, physics—co-opted wherever they might provide the means for more precise definition of concepts, or for greater control and technique in studying the arts. Science's growing awareness of theory itself—its construction, uses, limitations—is reflected in the self-scrutiny of recent music and musical theory. Certainly no music in the past has been subjected to such detailed study or sophisticated modes of analysis as music within our time. Particularly is this true for music *of* our time, most notably for that vein of contemporary musical thought that has evolved from the serial concepts of Schoenberg and his school.

It is curious that with the developed techniques of analysis and with the heightened perception and awareness of musical content that have arisen from the study of contemporary music, tonal music of the eighteenth and nineteenth centuries, particularly of the so-called classic-romantic era, eludes our comprehension on many levels. We still do not fully understand what makes this music "work"—what factors impel its temporal forward motion, what controls the unfolding of its contents, what precisely constitutes its rhythmic structure. Nor is it clear what analytical perspective will best penetrate and reveal these properties. Is stylistic analysis pertinent? Does "form" reside within the "formulas" codified by an earlier generation of theorists—ternary, sonata, rondo? Do Schenkerian analyses satisfactorily account for these questions?

Subtle questions persist on levels more difficult still to come to terms with. How do we explain the musical as well as psychological feeling of unity sensed in the great works of Mozart, Haydn, Brahms, Beethoven? Given, for example, a sonata-form movement from the piano sonatas of Mozart, why can we not substitute in it themes from other of these sonatas, assuming congruence of tempo, key, and meter?—a question Rudolph Reti posed explicitly in 1950 and one on which many musicians have mused before and since.[2] Why, for that matter, can we not alter the given sequence of themes within the same work? What determines the propriety of their order of appearance?

Further, what factors in these works make for coherence? Is the syntax of conventional harmony a major cause, or is it perhaps a surface facade that in its efficiency as a system hides deeper causative elements?

The domain of the unknown is not confined to the abstruse or the ineffable. With respect to the demonstrable in tonal music—for example, to harmony and to tonal relations—how are we to understand events within these parameters that are beyond the normative? What in fact do we mean in describing these events as "nonnormative"? Nonnormative in relation to what? Prevalent practice? A composer's own style (if this can be generalized)? Or nonnormative with respect to the individual work itself? Does a work establish its own norms? If so, can these be unearthed and can musical events in these works be seen as extensions of these guiding principles? Or do these events belong perhaps to that domain which Edward T. Cone has suggested is "beyond analysis"?[3]

These questions do not necessarily refer to extreme harmonic phenomena such as Wagner's "Tristan" chord. They pervade the earlier repertoire. What of chromatic harmony in Beethoven's *Eroica* Symphony, to choose one of many examples? Why the augmented sixth chords in measures 22 and 44? How explain the abrupt harmonic shifts that initiate the coda (measures 551–564)? What thinking lies behind the juxtaposition, beyond normal practice, of tonal regions only distantly related: E minor to E♭ major in the *Eroica;* F♯ minor to G minor in the Symphony No. 40 of Mozart (first movement, beginning of development); the Neapolitan regions of Beethoven's Op. 59, No. 2; Op. 95; Op. 57 (*Appassionata*, first movement); or the numerous similar instances in Haydn, Schubert, Brahms?

Unquestionably, aspects of composition do lie beyond analysis. Are we to assume, however, that events such as those described lie within the domain of the ineffable? On what grounds can we justify such an assumption? Are not these events perhaps manifestations of some manner of systematic thinking, operative in musical realms beyond those to which an older theory paid close scrutiny? Should not this possibility be explored before consigning such striking musical moments to the realm of the beyond?

If the systematic view is tenable, some consequences with interesting implications follow. For one, it would seem that the analytical process must concern itself with systems and their properties. Further, the process must designate and elucidate those musical premises that in part determine systems, as well as designate the hierarchical places of events that occur within systems. If musical events can be convincingly shown as aspects of system, in other words, as deliberate, then the boundaries of the unknowable—that which is "beyond analysis"—will be pushed back to confine a smaller territory. Or perhaps they will mark a different territory, one which contains more intuitive compositional decisions, as Cone has suggested. For instance, why, given methods of treating material, each seemingly of equal value, should one treatment be chosen above the rest?

Contemporary musical thinking has developed perspectives that can provide insight into some of these problems of music from past eras. Indeed, historical demarcations, admittedly artificial time frames, can at times distort a deeper reality—the concern with the past that is a living part of the present: Stravinsky admired and emulated certain features of the classical style, consciously turning them to personal account; Webern transcribed Bach; Schoenberg transcribed Brahms and Monn; Ravel did homage to Couperin; Britten, to Rossini. None of this was mere feasance. Features of the older music were of live interest, providing modes of study for the newer works. The new in turn heightened perceptions of the past, as well as modes of its performance.[4]

Concern with the past offers valuable insight in yet another dimension. For while contemporary music only occasionally and for special reasons may have emulated the past, in a deeper and more general sense it has evolved from past practice. This is particularly important in regard to serial thinking, perhaps the dominant and potentially richest vein of thought to have emerged in this century. The fact that Schoenberg's approach to music had at its roots concepts from studies of tonal music from Bach through Brahms is of more than purely historical interest. It suggests that serial concepts themselves—as explicit viewpoints and procedures—may yield insights into similar viewpoints and concepts of earlier, tonal music.

If so, these ideas provide a special assist to analysis. For classical music rarely formulated its compositional practice into explicit concepts. The concepts lay embedded in the music itself, requiring extrapolation from the internal evidence of a specific work. Some concepts were yet more elusive, for they were in part precompositional, envisioned in advance of the stage where a work assumed concrete shape. As such they exerted a pervasive but generalized influence over the music that came into being, serving a role in compositional thought (as they still do today) analogous to assumptions in verbal thought. The parallel is limited, however. For while we are trained from an early age to sense and to negotiate verbal thought, our training in the conceptual thought of music attains no comparable level. Only lately in fact has even the awareness developed of the kinship shared by the two modes of thought.

Thus we must often grapple with the elusive in dealing with musical structures. If in this process any concept—be it analogical, historical, visual—offers insight or assistance, it is useful. At times it may also be speculative—though this at first may seem a curious choice for a rational process that seeks the specific and the demonstrable. If speculation poses the "right" questions, however, it may lead to a sequence of observations ultimately capable of theoretical statement: verifiable and explanatory of data in a manner more comprehensive than previously possible. Theory, once made, can dispense with the speculation that led to it.

Speculation plays much the same role in creative thinking as it does in theoretical or analytical work. This is hardly surprising, as analysis seeks at ever deeper levels to touch and retrace the creative process. Composition in its early stages often requires extraction of the essential core of an idea from a domain of imprecise impressions. Once caught, the idea can be stated with definition (a rhythm, a shape, a timbre, all of these), hence dealt with. Stravinsky has described the process eloquently in *The Poetics of Music.*[5] Schoenberg's *Grundgestalt* represents a stage in the process, the rendering of the imprecise into the precise. Beethoven's sketchbooks are a view into the process itself.

Upon the arrival of the actual work, aspects of precomposition become its expendable appendages: musical volition, that which sought form-giving shape (Stravinsky's "speculation"), now appears an act removed from its initial creative role. It acquires primarily an aesthetic interest. In the same manner, working sketches become documents of history. An underlying concept of shape (as Schoenberg's) devolves into a historical, or past, element or stage in the compositional process, though analytically it is still relevant.

Given the validity of speculation in theory-building and analysis, speculation would seem valid as well in theoretical writing, provided (and the qualification is essential) it is seen for what it is and not confused with established, demonstrable certainty.

Musical complexity is in general a stumbling block to analysis, for the analytical method often seeks a unitary, if not unified, view of things. Singularity is in some ways an intrinsic analytical necessity, for the act of analysis is by prerequisite selective. It is a species of model-building, by its selective nature deliberately and unavoidably distortive, yet useful for making particular observations. Analysis is at odds, however, with a perceived, total reality. Effective analysis views its object as through a prism, whether its perspective is historical, rhythmic, or harmonic. It places a coherent frame around its perceptions—a beguiling frame, in fact, so clear and so secure it is in the facts it reveals. This may be false security, though, for in reality no such coherent frame exists. The work is a composite of many perspectives, all intertwined and cofunctioning, manifested in differing degrees of prominence at any given moment and on differing levels.

Thus no one analytical perspective can possibly provide all the relevant information about a work, for by its many facets a composition precludes such a singular view. The musical reality and the analytical model must ever stand both in contradiction and in symbiotic relation. It is an uneasy but unavoidable coexistence, its causes lying in the physical and psychological impossibility of viewing simultaneously and with equal attention multiple and differing phenomena.

Recognizing this, it becomes clear that no one analysis can truly "explain" a work, nor can any one analytical perspective suffice. For that matter, neither can any analysis possibly substitute for the rich amalgam of surface and substance that constitutes the work. If anything, the full measure of the work might be the hypothetical composite of all relevant information provided by different analytical approaches. And by the criterion of relevance (though this must be determined), we do not exclude the need for analytical discrimination. Clearly some observations are more discerning than others.

ANALYTICAL
PERSPECTIVES

As with any inquiry, the results of analysis will in part be determined by the assumptions and the frame of reference shaping the inquiry itself.[6] To date, three or four analytical perspectives have characterized the existing literature. For lack of better terms, the first two might be described as the historical-stylistic approach and the formal-descriptive approach. A third is the analytical system developed by Heinrich Schenker; a fourth, less codified to date, is the concept of *Grundgestalt*, or basic shape, as set forth by Arnold Schoenberg.

The first two approaches hardly need discussion here, as they have been widely developed over a period of years and are buttressed by a large existing literature. Historical-stylistic analysis, long characteristic of musicological research, embraces diverse concerns through a basically historical orientation. These concerns may range from accuracy of historical detail or attribution vis-à-vis individual works to styles of performance practice in differing eras. The latter field alone is vast, including matters as varied as Renaissance practice of *musica ficta;* development of instruments and instrumental technique; bowing styles in baroque music; fashions of ornamentation and improvisation in different historical periods, to mention only a few. Clearly all of this is pertinent to an informed approach to music of any time, our own not excepted.

The formal-descriptive view of form has characterized analytical writing for decades and is perhaps best represented by authors such as Sir Donald Tovey, Hugo Leichtentritt,[7] and recently, Wallace Berry,[8] in a perceptive treatment of the subject. The approach is largely descriptive of such things as phrase lengths, harmonic progressions, modulations, and musical character of themes—these in terms of surface information, features of a work presumably apparent to the trained musical mind. In his book Berry tries to avoid these generalities in part by a categorical approach: subclassifications are created within classes of established musical forms to account for idiosyncracies found in individual works. Thus ternary form is broken down into simple ternary, incipient ternary, compound ternary, integrated compound ternary, extended compound ternary, and so on. The method is somewhat akin to botanical studies in their stratification of genera, species, and subspecies. Like botanical classification, its usefulness lies largely in identification.

The shortcomings of the formal-descriptive approach have met their due share of criticism.[9] With its tendency to categorize, and by the very natures of its formulas, formal-descriptive analysis creates models to which actual works conform in only the most general way. It deals primarily with musical surface and lacks the analytical equipment to probe the deeper inner dynamics of music itself or the unique properties of an individual work.

For all its inadequacies the approach is useful, and though some of its spokesmen have in an almost maddening way proffered surface for substance, that information it does provide seems prerequisite to more sophisticated analysis. There are, after all, phrases, cadences, simple harmonic motion, sections, modulations, three-part forms, rondos; one cannot comprehend music without taking such features almost for granted. Even advanced thinkers from Schenker to Schoenberg have accepted the categories and some of the terminology of the approach as conveniences at least, while indicating their limitations.

The studies of Schenker, and the analytical method that evolved from them, offer an approach to analysis of a deeper order. Schenker has suffered unjustly in the past from misunderstandings of his theories and, in the English-speaking world, from the unavailability of translations of his most important works. Fortunately these misunderstandings are receding, and Schenker at long last is beginning to come into his own. The forthcoming English translation of *Der freie Satz* (1935), the last and in many ways most important of Schenker's books, should be a significant contribution to his English bibliography, complemented by a growing list of articles and books on his ideas, that has developed over the last twenty years.[10]

It is not possible to do justice to Schenker's extensive thought within the space of this book. Nor, in view of his expanding bibliography, is this necessary. Familiarity with his ideas will be important, however, in following much of this book, as many of his concepts are assumed herein.

Schenker's contribution to analytical thinking is manifold, its major aspects involving the following points: (1) Structure is clarified through perspective. The small and the large, particularly with respect to melody (line) and harmony, are seen separately. (2) A distinction between structure and embellishment emanates from perspective. Structure determines long-range formal projection. Embellishment does not; its purview is local, that of detail and prolongation. (3) By means of reduction technique, musical structure is revealed in layers (*Schichten*), moving from a foreground of localized surface detail through various middle-ground levels, in which the more far-reaching features of structure are abstracted from surface presence, to the ultimate background—Schenker's *Ursatz*. Here the bass and upper melodic line (*Urlinie*) form a coordinated fundamental structure, the temporal projection of the tonic triad, a phenomenon shared by all tonal works. (4) Harmony, particularly at intermediary points, is shown as resulting from line and from counterpoint. It is put in realistic perspective, removed from the textbook distortions of verticality, inversion, chord labels. Harmonic inversion, concurrently, is seen as the result of melodic flow of outer parts. (5) Harmonic movement in the large, and the key centers other than the tonic that it engenders, are seen in relation to the primacy of the tonic, the only true tonality of a work. The conventional idea of "modulation" is replaced by a view that reveals tonal motion in a broader and richer (and more realistic) perspective. (6) The concept of compositional unfolding (*Auskomponierung*) is introduced, the "essence of music," wherein voice-leading serves "as the means by which the chord, as a harmonic concept, is made to unfold and extend in time."[11]

If there is any secret to the art of composition, surely it lies in this last concept, the often intuitive sense for unfolding a work in time. To do so is more than simply to project a structure through some period of time. It is also to sense, to construct, and to control the manner by which this structure reveals itself, stage by stage, withholding certain of its contents until particular timed moments—and throughout maintaining musical tension and focus until its final moment.

For Schenker this unfolding was essentially a harmonic event, the working out, through line, of the tonic chord. As such it is an inadequate concept, for though it projects harmonic progression in time, it is in itself essentially nontemporal—nonrhythmic. Yet the inner dynamic of this process, the unfolding and the inner control of musical tension, is probably rhythmic at its core.

The concept of unfolding established by Schenker has the potential for further extension. Schenker's graphs, though they cope specifically with rhythm almost not at all, nonetheless are suggestive of rhythmic flow and of the inner dynamics and tensions that accompany this flow. Texture, weight, orchestration, and the many other dimensions of music that contribute to rhythmic definition can be found to coordinate with the harmonic and melodic (phrase) demarcations of Schenker's graphs. (Chapter 5 of this book focuses on this relationship.) No one man can investigate all the implications of his ideas. Schenker himself was aware of the possible extensions of his concepts. With regard to orchestration, for instance, he realized that weight and textural definition by instrumentation were not matters of chance or intuition, but that they explicitly served to emphasize features of structure.[12]

Schenker's conceptual framework, like any framework, leaves certain cogent questions untouched or inadequately answered. Rhythm, in both its local and large-scale roles, is one. So are the more general questions of the unity and the "uniqueness" of a given work—the reasons why, as Rosen has put it, the inner sense of a work should have taken just its specific outer form. How does a work achieve a sense of unity such that all its parts, all its component elements, seem cut of one piece? Could not other lines, other local harmonic progressions, be substituted within a given Schenker graph and equally fulfill the general middleground functions demonstrated by the specific work in question? Or, to refer to a question posed earlier, could not other themes, other motives, be substituted satisfactorily for those of a given work, assuming congruence of key, meter, and tempo? Most musicians, probably by intuition, would answer "no" to these questions. Yet to sense musical unity is not to demonstrate it. An analytical framework is still needed that is oriented toward these concerns.

To answer questions of unity, one must eventually come to grips with the forces that shape thematic material—with motive and its larger implications. Schenker deals with motive on some levels, but tends to see it as a subsidiary force, functioning within a more basic framework of harmony, and seemingly subservient to the primacy of harmony. In passages in his book, *Harmony* (such as pp. 4 ff.), which represents an early stage in the working out of his theories, he recognizes the motive as an organizing force that gains cogency through repetition—repetition that may, but need not, be literal (perhaps a presaging of Schoenberg's concept of "developing variation"; see Appendix A of this book). Oswald Jonas, in his preface to *Harmony* (pp. xvi–xvii and 4–5, fn.), points out that Schenker later, in *Der freie Satz*, recognized the organizing function of the motive as a background force.[13] Indeed graphs from Schenker's later studies, such as *Der freie Satz*, do illustrate motives in this light. Motives are often seen as the linear "filling-in," at various structural levels, of the notes between the extremes of a motivic interval. Almost never are they rhythmic. Thus while the motives in Schenker's later studies provide an illuminating concept, they are not concerned with the full significance of motivic shape to musical organization. This seems to be a matter of emphasis; Schenker's primary concerns lay elsewhere. The compositional concepts of Schoenberg, on the other hand, were deeply involved with motive as a prime form-giving force in music. These concepts provide the basis for much of this book.

Although Schoenberg's thinking was oriented almost to an extreme toward motive, the concept had considerably different meaning for him than for earlier writers like A.B. Marx or Hugo Riemann, for whom motive was in the main seen in its local, contiguous note-to-note perspective. (Riemann at times indicates awareness of more general and large-scale formal manifestations of motive, such as the *Hauptthema* in Beethoven.) For Schoenberg, the term "motive" itself was really a subsidiary concept, a subspecies of the much broader concept of *Grundgestalt*, or basic shape, as it has come to be known in English.

The *Grundgestalt* concept was not a simple idea, though it was central to Schoenberg's thinking and lay at the base of his conceptualizing about music. He made it more difficult for his followers by never addressing the idea directly in print, despite his extensive articles on musical subjects. Apparently he only discussed it with his students. It is from their accounts, then, that we must construct his exact meanings, aided by the numerous indirect references to the idea in his articles and his instructional books. These matters are pursued in the following chapter.

The structural views of Schoenberg and Schenker are, if anything, complementary. They share important features in common, though the emphases and viewpoints differ. Both, for example, recognize musical surface as foreground projection of background ideas. Both recognize the "composing-out" or "unfolding" process as the essential inner life of a work, though the conceptions of the process itself are at some variance. Both view musical structure on various levels. Both see harmony, distant tonal regions, and the so-called process of modulation in relation to the primacy of an overall tonality. (Schoenberg's *Harmonielehre* makes this quite clear, as do Josef Rufer's accounts of his teacher's views on harmony.)[14]

Further, both are keenly aware that harmony is a prime motivating force in tonal music. (Rufer's discussion of Schoenberg's *Grundgestalt* shows that harmony played a large role in this concept. See Rufer, pp. 56 ff.) If there are significant differences between the two approaches, they lie in the degree of emphasis upon the formative roles of shape and motive, and of rhythm. In this respect, the reference frame of Schoenberg broadens that provided by Schenker.[15]

The following chapters are in part concerned with Schoenberg's *Grundgestalt* concept and its broader implications for musical structure. Some of these implications are suggested by the serial ordering of pitch to which the *Grundgestalt* gave rise in twelve-tone music, and by the extension of properties related to the *Grundgestalt* found in total serialism. The relevance of shape to rhythmic structure, as well as its further implications for pitch in the domains of localized harmony, and of tonal relations in a larger perspective are studied in subsequent chapters. Nuances of phrase, dynamics, and articulation are also studied in terms of their structural importance.

These studies build upon previous work in this area, including Schoenberg's writings; the efforts of those within his circle to clarify some of his ideas; and studies by Rudolph Reti,[16] Hans Keller,[17] Alan Walker,[18] and Charles Rosen.[19] Rosen's work, unlike that of the others cited, avoids a singular orientation to shape as the fundamental formative influence. He touches upon this viewpoint and its ramifications, however, and with insight.

The studies by Keller and Walker deal primarily with pitch shape, particularly with respect to themes. Rhythmic shape to date has received less attention—though Keller and Walker have touched upon it—and little systematic treatment. The harmonic and tonal implications of shape, as well as nuance, are mentioned in various places but have yet to be extensively developed.

Reti's studies were among the first to appear concerning thematic shape and process. To them must go much of the credit for initially exploring a new terrain; to their failure, unfortunately, must also be attributed some of the skepticism that greets subsequent studies of thematic relevance.

Reti's studies are characterized by a largely intuitive approach, and by an almost total absence of methodical proof. Thus while he has some valid insights, his presentation often marshals dubious evidence, with the effect of weakening the credibility of his contributions. Terminology is only minimally defined; neither are criteria presented for discerning the structural from the ornamental within themes. Little or no account is taken of structural levels; nor of the roles of stress, accent, syncopation, or rhythm in general; nor of harmony. The scale degrees upon which structural notes may rest are often left undistinguished. Thus two themes in different keys may be seen as congruent, where the same note in one rests on the tonic and in the other on, perhaps, the submediant, with different accompanying harmonic implications. Much of the writing simply asserts, equating conjecture with proof, or stumbles upon the intentional fallacy. This is particularly true of the chapter on thematic key relations in *The Thematic Process in Music,* where the mere existence of two notes relevant to a theme is given as proof that they generate key relations on the same roots, with no further demonstration.

Schenker's *Ursatz* and *Urlinie* and Schoenberg's *Grundgestalt* with all its larger implications, can be viewed from a different and still broader perspective. Both are species of compositional premises, perhaps the most significant and determinative of such premises.[20] They are not, however, the only premises operative in composition. Subsequent chapters in this book examine others, ones more properly viewed as sub-premises functioning within the larger confines of the structural concepts outlined above. Ambiguity in the rhythmic and pitch properties of basic musical materials is seen as such a subpremise. Procedure itself in some works constitutes another manner of subpremise. So do some local events—a small pitch motive, for example, which may generate manifold harmonic structures, making of a piece a virtual exploration of these derived harmonic possibilities.

All the foregoing analytical systems can also be classed together, within a still larger perspective, as essentially "static" as opposed to "dynamic." That is, they view a work in its already-composed, fully laid-out structure, shifting the focus of attention among various parts for purposes of comparison, demarcation, quantization. (Schenker's approach, as will be discussed, is less oriented this way than others. Yet, while it in-dicates the forward *direction* of a work, it is not fully concerned with its *dynamics* of forward motion.) This observation suggests that the next analytical perspective needed is one which concerns itself with the inner motion of compositional growth—in brief, with the internal mechanisms by which a work unfolds in time.

As suggested earlier, this unfolding is primarily a rhythmic phenomenon. Rhythm itself, though, is not a parameter that is fully defined by its own internal elements. We identify rhythm and its articulation as much (or more) by harmonic progression, linear contour, texture, and weight—criteria from other musical domains—as we do by accent, stress, metrical emphasis, and agogics. The large-scale role of rhythm in formal articulation may perhaps be determined by factors within these other domains. This view and its usefulness as an analytical perspective are explored in Chapter 10.

It would be well to review the limitations imposed upon the studies that follow. First, they are concerned with music written within the era commonly known as classic-romantic, in effect from Haydn and Mozart through the middle nineteenth century, as delimited by Brahms.

Second, these studies are restricted to music written in what might be called the German-Viennese tradition—the most seminal body of music that emerged during this broad period.

Third, they are confined to absolute music. Our understanding of structure is still sufficiently unclear that it seems advisable to avoid the further complications of words and/or dramatic action—implicit or explicit—and their relations to structure, or their effects upon it.

A fourth and final limitation: the matter of "expression" in music is beyond the confines of these studies. Statements like this may offend readers who assume thereby that "expression" (the imprecise term is indicative of the problem itself) either does not exist in music or is considered unimportant. This is not the case. The limitation here is a practical one alone; the question of what music "says" is vast and complex and demands separate study. Nor is the question divorced from interests discussed here. The old dichotomy between form and content has long since been recognized as false, with the consequent awareness that much of what a work has to "say" is in-timately intertwined with the manner in which it wields and transforms its materials. For its materials are the means as well as the medium of its communication. Indeed, in attacking this problem it is first of all essential clearly to perceive, to recognize, and to comprehend what it is we hear, free of external or misconstrued meanings. It is this multiple task that is the central focus of this book.

The question for which many listeners seek answers about music and its expression is basically one concerning the personal message communicated by a work. This must remain a separate study, one which in fact has amassed a broad and even ancient lit-erature. Interested readers might pursue work by Suzanne Langer,[21] Leonard Meyer,[22] and Nelson Goodman[23]—among the more perceptive contemporary treatments of this subject.

Ultimately these concerns about musical expression may never be answered in the verbal manner that some would hope for. For the question itself is framed at variance with the realities of musical communication. Whatever "expression," values, or personal interior world is communicated by music, however compellingly it is communicated through a medium—sound and time—that is unique, intrinsic unto itself, and incapable of translation. Were this not so, we should long ago have seen more success in the many attempts to relate musical essence through metaphor, poetic description, analogy, and image. The medium tempts translation: it is in some respects a language itself, in many ways parallel to spoken language, possessing grammar, syntax, inflected meaning, levels of structure, styles of usage. Yet within its property of nontransmutability lies much of the compelling quality of music.

To summarize: analysis can be viewed as a species of model building, by nature selective and thereby (deliberately) misrepresentative of the whole, by means of which certain properties can be studied in isolation from their context. No one analytical perspective or approach can be expected to explain or reveal all the significant properties of a work, as such results would be incompatible with the analytical process itself.

To date analysis seems to have unsatisfactory answers to questions such as what factors in music make for coherence, unity, uniqueness; or how to comprehend musical events seemingly beyond the norms of convention.

Four analytical perspectives are prevalent: the historical-stylistic, formal-descriptive, Schenkerian, and that of basic shape as intuited by Schoenberg. The Schenkerian and Schoenbergian have much in common and, in their differences of viewpoint and emphasis, are complementary. Other more recent approaches, often cross-fertilized by scientific disciplines, have been mentioned: approaches associated with mathematics (set theory in particular) and information theory, as well as with linguistics and physics.

This study begins with an examination and clarification of Schoenberg's *Grundgestalt* concept, an idea which lay at the base of his serial thinking but about which he did not write directly, though he discussed it with his students. Its ramifications for structure with respect to rhythm, harmony, tonal relations, and possibly nuance and dynamics, are subsequently examined—their relevance suggested by the explicit recognition of these implications in total serialism.

The foregoing perspectives can be seen in another light as musical premises, that is, as bases, either stated or assumed, upon which musical reasoning proceeds. While they may in fact be the most pervasive of musical premises, they are not exclusive. Others will be examined in this book, such as ambiguity, the generative properties of local events, and procedure itself.

Finally, within a still larger perspective, all these approaches can be seen as essentially static. They view a work in its laid-out dimensions for purposes of localized study, comparison, and demarcation, free of the active influence of time. A dynamic perspective, as a complement to these others, may be valuable as an insight into the mechanisms by which music unfolds its properties in the dimension of time.

NOTES

1. Charles Rosen, *The Classical Style* (London: Faber & Faber, 1971), p. 445.

2. Rudolph Reti, *The Thematic Process in Music* (London: Faber & Faber, 1961), ch. 1 (first edition released in 1950). Alan Walker has also studied this question in his book, *An Anatomy of Musical Criticism* (London: Barrie & Rockliff, 1966), to the extent of an experimental "rewriting" (really, a reordering) of the sequence of themes in Mozart's Piano Sonata in F Major, K. 332, first movement. See pp. 60–64.

3. See Edward T. Cone, "Beyond Analysis," *Perspectives of New Music* 6, no. 1 (Fall-Winter 1967): 33–51.

4. This concern with the past is continually evident in the thinking, talking, and writing of contemporary musicians. Two examples:

... contemporary music of each new period gives that period a new point of view about the musical past . . . . Important new compositions not only affect how older ones are heard by the public, performers, composers, even critics, but also affect their interpretation and performance . . . . When the focus of 20th-century composition changed from neoclassicism to a great concern for structure—the Webern fragmentation of the Bach ricercare into tiny motives illustrates this clearly—the inner organization of Bach, Mozart, Beethoven and many others became a matter of greater concern than it had been and affected performers and, through them, listeners. For the musical works of the past cannot fail to be reheard and re-experienced in the light of present musical experience . . . .
　　—Elliott Carter, from a letter to the *New York Times*, music page, Sunday, 20 October 1968.

... It is a lack of seriousness to think of tradition as something that merely conserves. The first thing that happens is that performances become dusty and unimaginative. After our orchestra has been working on something very different and very new and very difficult—like Stockhausen, Ligeti, Kagel, Berio or my own music—then, we suddenly approach Beethoven's Fifth as though the ink were not yet dry . . . a quality suddenly comes into the Beethoven which, in a sense, shows up our own work . . . it [Beethoven's music] somehow turns out to be more modern than what any of us do today . . . .
Tradition is one of those misunderstood words. People keep thinking that it means the past. Tradition is actually a dynamic concept which moves from past to future. Without a preoccupation with the laboratory of the contemporary artist, you could not possibly get a real peek into the laboratory of a Beethoven, a Brahms, a Mozart, or a Bach . . . .
　　—Lukas Foss, excerpts from remarks on a panel discussion, reported in the *Newsletter* of the American Symphony Orchestra League, August-October 1968, p. 11.

5. Igor Stravinsky, *The Poetics of Music* (Cambridge, Mass.: Harvard University Press, 1947), ch. 3.

6. Contemporary writings on musical theory, whether dealing with new or with tonal music, show an increasing awareness both of the need for disciplined theoretical construction and the great problems of developing strict modes of examination in a field that has lacked such discipline in the past. Increasing attention is being devoted to the examination of theory itself, its properties, modes of construction, usefulness, and limitations. Understandably, scientific disciplines are being turned to for whatever assistance they may offer. The interested reader may find it worthwhile to pursue some of this literature.

Thomas Clifton, "Training in Music Theory: Process and Product," *Journal of Music Theory*, Spring 1969, pp. 38–63, examines many of the above points, drawing upon the philosophy of science and upon linguistics for models. Clifton's comments regarding the elementary stages of theory construction, the accompanying roles of feeling and perception, and the matter of detachment from observed phenomena (pp. 62–63) are relevant to the foregoing discussion of speculation.

Arthur Berger, "New Linguistic Modes and the New Theory," *Perspectives* 3, no. 1 (Fall-Winter 1964), especially pp. 6–9, draws upon linguistic concepts to make important distinctions in musical inquiry between theory and analysis, analysis and description, technique and structure, structure and form, form and conventional formula, form and style, concept and percept. Leonard Meyer is also concerned with these questions. In *Music, the Arts and Ideas* (Chicago: University of Chicago Press, 1967), ch. 11, he distinguishes between "perception" (the physiological reception of data through the senses) and "cognition" (the mental act of discerning patterns and relationships among perceived data). He notes that these two processes also interact.

See also Benjamin Boretz, "A Note on Discourse," *Perspectives* 4, no. 2 (1966): 76–80.

Boulez's comments on analytical method are also apposite:

... let us define what may be considered the indispensable constituents of an 'active' analytical method: it must begin with the most minute and exact observation possible of the musical facts confronting us; it is then a question of finding a plan, a law of internal organization which takes account of these facts with the maximum coherence; finally comes the interpretation of the compositional laws deduced from this special application. All these stages are necessary; one's studies are of merely technical interest if they are not followed through to the highest point—the *interpretation* of the structure; only at this stage can one be sure that the work has been assimilated and understood.
　　—Pierre Boulez, *Boulez on Music Today* (London: Faber & Faber, 1971), p. 18.

7. Hugo Leichtentritt, *Musical Form* (Cambridge, Mass.: Harvard University Press, 1951).

8. Wallace Berry, *Form in Music* (Englewood Cliffs, N.J.: Prentice-Hall, 1966).

9. The introductory pages of Felix Salzer, "Tonality in Medieval Polyphony," *Music*

Forum 1 (1967): 35 ff., contain cogent comments on stylistic, historical, and purely "formal" (in the present sense) analysis, in particular on their value and shortcomings.

10. David Beach, "A Schenker Bibliography," *Journal of Music Theory* 13 (1969): 2–37, provides an extensive list of Schenker's writings, as well as articles about Schenker. Important among the latter for the reader seeking condensed information about Schenker's concepts is Allen Forte, "Schenker's Conception of Musical Structure," *Journal of Music Theory* 3, no. 1 (April 1959): 1–30. Felix Salzer, *Structural Hearing: Tonal Coherence in Music*, 2 vols. (New York: Charles Boni, 1952; Dover, 1962), is also a valuable organization of Schenker's ideas into textbook form. The book should not be considered, nor was it intended, as an authentic version of Schenker's thinking, for Salzer introduces in it ideas of his own and others adapted from Schenker. A helpful appraisal of this book is found in Milton Babbitt's review, *Journal of the American Musicological Society* 5, no. 3 (Fall 1952): 260–265. Other pertinent articles concerning Schenker are indicated in footnotes 20 and 21 of Beach's article (cited above), p. 35

11. Heinrich Schenker, *Harmony*, ed. and annotated by Oswald Jonas, tr. Elizabeth Mann Borghese (Chicago: University of Chicago Press, 1954), p. ix.

12. Cf. Forte, "Schenker's Conception," p. 26. Schenker's work reflects awareness of rhythm and its function in structure, though he did not develop these thoughts into a coherent theory. For him rhythm did not really exist in the fundamental structure (*Ursatz*), but it did manifest itself on middle- and foreground levels, emanating from counterpoint and making itself most felt in the activity of prolongation on these levels. Forte touches on this problem, pp. 20 ff. Grosvenor Cooper and Leonard Meyer, in their book *The Rhythmic Structure of Music* (Chicago: University of Chicago Press, 1960), somewhat apply Schenker's view of structural levels to the study of rhythm. The question is also discussed later in this book.

13. Jonas, ed., *Harmony* (Schenker).

14. Cf. Josef Rufer, *Composition with Twelve Notes Related Only to One Another*, tr. Humphrey Searle (London: Rockliff, 1954).

15. Although the four approaches to analysis discussed here are perhaps the most widely prevalent with respect to tonal music, it would be misleading to imply that they are the only ones, or even the only ones of value to analysis in general. As indicated in an earlier note (n. 6), contemporary analytical approaches have in part turned to various scientific disciplines, such as linguistics, for assistance in theory construction; some approaches have in fact modeled themselves upon such disciplines. Thus, the mathematical branch of set theory has been of both practical and conceptual significance in regard to aspects of serial thinking, particularly the more recent developments in total serialism. The writings of Milton Babbitt and David Lewin have been most notable contributions in this respect. Likewise physics, particularly the physics of electronics, has been essential to developments in the use of the electronic medium in composition. Numerous articles in *Die Reihe, Perspectives, The Electronic Music Review*, and other journals are exemplary.

Information theory, originally developed in the 1950s in connection with telecommunication, has also presented an attractive corollary to music. Leonard Meyer's book *Music, the Arts and Ideas* offers an extensive example of its use. Music is viewed here as taking place in a world of stylistic probability: the greater the probability, the greater the certainty of future events, and the less the "information" (in the technical meaning of the theory) communicated. The extreme of certainty, for example—tautology—would communicate no information. Deviations in the course of probable events create resistance to probabilities and thereby increase the amount of information, at the same time lowering the index of probability itself. Resistance is thus a correlative to information.

Deviation, in this system, gives rise to uncertainties both desirable and undesirable. Desirable uncertainty is that which arises as a result of the structured probabilities of a musical style. Information is a function of such uncertainty. Undesirable uncertainty arises when the probabilities are not known, due either to irrelevant habit responses in a listener with respect to a given style ("cultural noise") or to external interference ("acoustical noise") that obscures the structure of a given situation. A distinction is drawn between "art" music and "primitive" music (the latter term has precise referents in Meyer's thinking; it does not refer to the music of so-called primitive societies, but rather to music of low-level organization, such as much "pop" music or the music of Ethelbert Nevin) with respect to their speed of tendency gratification (quicker for primitive music). Such speed of gratification reduces uncertainty, which the (musically) immature primitive cannot tolerate.

After designating three aspects of musical enjoyment—the sensuous, the associative-characterizing, and the syntactical—Meyer establishes a relationship between the stimulus "input" and the actual informational "output" of a work. According to his "principle of psychic economy," we compare the ratio of musical means invested to the informational income yielded. "Good" works yield a high return: they are elegant in their use of information, economical in means.

This is but a partial summary of the fundamental information-theory thinking that forms the opening basis for Meyer's book, which subsequently extends these concepts in several directions.

All theoretical systems used for music and

their analytical counterparts must ultimately face the question of utility and the implied corollary question of paraphrase. The ultimate usefulness of any analytical system is its ability to be related in some precise fashion to musical materials themselves—pitch, rhythm, timbre, pulse, time.

Not all systems can deal with these musical materials directly, that is, within their own musical terminology or even their own musical concepts. Some may require translation into the musical domain. Information theory presents such a case. In these instances the question arises whether such a nonmusical system essentially constitutes paraphrase, or whether it enables one to organize and to view musical materials and relations on a higher level of abstraction. Paraphrase alone is of little value. If anything it adds the burden of translation into a musically indigenous frame. If the theory abstracts, however, its value is considerable, as it provides a more concise grasp of elements and interrelations.

16. Rudolph Reti. *The Thematic Process in Music.* Previously cited.
——. *Thematic Patterns in Sonatas of Beethoven.* Edited by Deryck Cooke. (London: Faber & Faber, 1967).

17. Hans Keller. "Strict Serial Technique in Classical Music." *Tempo,* Autumn 1955, 12–24.
——. "K. 503—The Unity of Contrasting Themes and Movements." Part I, *Music Review* 17 (1956): 48–58; Part II: 120–129.
——. "Functional Analysis: Its Pure Application." *Music Review* 18 (1957): 202–206.
——. "Knowing Things Backwards." *Tempo,* Winter 1958, pp. 14–20.
——. "The Chamber Music." Chapter in *The Mozart Companion.* Edited by H.C. Robbins. Landon and Donald Mitchell (London: Faber & Faber, 1965), pp. 90–137.

Keller in the late 1950s carried his work further, creating what he called "Wordless Functional Analysis." This took the form of broadcast tapes for the BBC in which the analytical examples, organized into hierarchies in a programed presentation, were played in the work's indigenous instrumentation (string quartet, orchestra, etc.), followed by a performance of the piece itself. The structural associations were thereby presented through music's proper medium of sound, avoiding the second-level removal from the work caused by words or even by notational graphs.

18. Alan Walker. A *Study in Musical Analysis.* (London: Barrie & Rockliff, 1962).
——. *An Anatomy of Musical Criticism.* (London: Barrie & Rockliff, 1966).

19. Rosen, *The Classical Style.*

20. "Premise" is used here in the sense of a basis, stated or assumed, upon which reasoning proceeds. This raises the question whether music is a system to which the term "logic" (of which premise is an element) can apply. The question is an entity unto itself, beyond the scope of this study. However, a case could be made that music is a form of logic, if logic is understood as a system of principles of reasoning applicable to any branch of knowledge or study. If this is so, it follows that there are a plurality of logical systems; also, that the components, terminology, procedures of reasoning of each individual system are likely to be *sui generis.*

21. Suzanne Langer, *Philosophy in a New Key* (New York: Mentor Books, 1951).
——. *Feeling and Form.* (New York: Scribner, 1953).

22. Leonard Meyer, *Emotion and Meaning in Music* (Chicago: University of Chicago Press, 1956).

23. Nelson Goodman, *Languages of Art: An Approach to a Theory of Symbols* (Indianapolis: Bobbs-Merrill Co., 1968).

2   THE CONCEPT OF SHAPE

Schoenberg formulated the concept of the *Grundgestalt* in the early years of the period in which he was developing twelve-tone theory. The term has acquired a generally accepted English translation of "basic shape" and denotes the fundamental concept underlying a musical work, the features of which influence and determine specific ideas within the work itself.[1] The "ideas" in which the basic shape is reflected have for the most part been seen as thematic, that is, as pitch configurations, though there is nothing inherent in the *Grundgestalt* concept that should restrict its influence to a particular musical domain. It is likely in fact that basic shapes are manifested in other domains and are pervasive in their ramifications.

A basic shape was considered by Schoenberg as a unifying force of great magnitude; he saw the surface features of a work—its themes, lesser configurations, and other structural aspects—as varied representations of this underlying concept. As he pointed out, the concept of a basic shape, though not recognized or termed as such, had been an operative, unifying feature in the music of earlier periods. Schoenberg had come to recognize its significance through studies of the music of the great composers from Bach through Brahms.[2] It was fundamental, furthermore, to twelve-tone music, for a basic shape was a work's elemental basis; indeed it was the primal motivation that in later stages gave birth to tangible shape via the particular order of notes that constituted a tone row.

Schoenberg found in the *Grundgestalt* concept an underlying link between musical tradition, especially that of the classic-romantic Viennese school, and his own compositional theories, which he saw as growing out of this tradition. Thus it was the *Grundgestalt* concept to a large extent that confirmed for Schoenberg the rightness of his evolving musical theories—their musical validity and their historical connections—during those years in particular when the marked surface differences between his music and that of tradition brought upon him so much derision from the public at large, undoubtedly causing self-examination as to the direction of his musical thinking.

In view of the basic importance of the *Grundgestalt* concept to the composer, it is remarkable, even enigmatic, that the term appears very little in Schoenberg's writings and that it is never really defined in precise fashion. To understand fully what he meant by it, one must adduce information and in effect formulate the concept from the many passages in Schoenberg's writings that are relevant to its general aspects, though lacking use of the term itself. Further insight can be extrapolated from the analyses of classical works that Schoenberg made and from his generalized procedures for compositional training set forth in other writings. These primary sources are complemented by the writings and discussions of the concept by others within the original Schoenberg circle.[3]

Perhaps the fullest and most direct discussion of the *Grundgestalt* concept, and one that substantiates the impression of its broad perspective, is provided by Josef Rufer, Schoenberg's assistant at the Prussian Academy of Arts in the 1920s, in his book *Composition with Twelve Notes*.[4] The information is found not so much in the book itself, originally published in Germany in 1952, as in the preface to the English edition by its translator, Humphrey Searle. Searle had difficulty in finding the proper term with which to translate *Grundgestalt*. As he noted, "Some writers have equated this with the *Grundreihe*, i.e., the basic set or series of twelve notes (also known as tone-row or note-row) on which each twelve-note composition is based. However, it is clear that Schoenberg used the term *Grundgestalt* (literally, basic shape) in a rather wider sense than this."[5] Searle discussed this problem with Rufer, who clarified the *Grundgestalt* concept and elaborated upon it in a letter to the translator in 1954, which is reproduced in the preface:

In his composition teaching, Schoenberg formed the concept of the *Grundgestalt* (basic shape) as early as 1919 and used it with the exact meaning which it has in my book—as being the musical *shape* (or phrase) which is the *basis* of a work and is its "first creative thought" (to use Schoenberg's words). Everything else is derived from this—in music of all kinds, not only twelve-note music; and it is not derived merely from the basic *series* which is contained in the basic shape, but also from *all* the elements which, together with the series as the melodic element, give it its actual shape, that is, rhythm, phrasing, harmony, subsidiary parts, etc. In this connection it is especially important to note that Schoenberg, who in those days was working out his method for the first time, applied the results of his composition with twelve notes to composition in general from the outset, by choosing the concepts he used for the theoretical formulation of his method in such a way that they could also apply to music of any kind (tonal, classical, etc.). This happened at a time when he was not yet *able* to teach twelve-note composition, as its formulation was not yet complete. And for this reason he did not need to teach twelve-note composition as a special subject later on, nor in fact did he ever do so: he only taught *Composition*, and it did not matter whether this was tonal, atonal, polytonal or anything else. In one of his articles which I saw after 1945 he mentioned himself that in his teaching of that period he quite consciously absorbed the newly-born perceptions drawn from twelve-note composition in analyses of Mozart, Beethoven and Brahms, but in a camouflaged form. In my very full notes of his teaching between 1919 and 1922 I find these definitions: a *motif* is the smallest musical form, consisting of at least one interval and one rhythm. The next sized form is the *Grundgestalt* of phrase, "as a rule 2 to 3 bars long" (the number of bars depending on the tempo, among other things), and consisting of the "firm connection of one or more motifs and their more or less varied repetitions." The next sized form, the *theme*, "arises from the need to connect several shapes together" and consists of "the connection (here he expressly does not say *firm*) of the *Grundgestalt* (basic shape) with its more or less varied repetitions."
It is quite clear from this that Schoenberg invented and used the term *Grundgestalt* as a concept which is *universally* valid in music, especially in analyses of classical music. So far as I know he never tried . . . to analyse a whole work showing its derivation from a *Grundgestalt*. But he certainly spoke of the possibility of doing this . . . .[6]

Rufer makes clear in the early part of this quotation that the *Grundgestalt* was for Schoenberg a broad concept, inclusive of motivic rhythm and of harmony, as well as of configurations of pitch. The point is important, for it suggests the extensive germinal influence of shape. It is also important because, paradoxically, these broadest manifestations of shape receive the smallest amount of attention from Schoenberg in his writings. Even in the early twelve-tone literature of Schoenberg and others, rhythm, for one, received less discussion than pitch properties of the set or the operational implications of pitch. Thus it is significant that serialism in its origins had a larger purview and that this was recognized, if not extensively discussed, by the author of the theory itself.

Rufer makes this point clear in a subsequent discussion of the *Grundgestalt* concept:

In tonal music two fields of force are at work. One of them is, so to speak, of dual power, for its energies arise from the combination of the melodic and the rhythmical elements and create motivic and thematic (melodic) shapes. The other field of force is that of tonality, which is preponderantly harmonic. Each of these fields of force produces energies out of itself; the latter by the perpetual variation of harmonic formations and sequences of chords with differing degrees of tension, the former through changing combinations and variations of the melodic (the intervals) and the rhythmical elements.

The very varied interplay of both fields of force acts as the motive power of the course of the music. The way in which this interplay takes place represents the musical idea which is the basis of the piece . . . the *basic shape* (*Grundgestalt*) . . . [containing] in its disposition both the fields of force, between which the work "plays"—the basic tonality and the basic motivic content. Everything else arises from these, so that one can truly say: the original conception (= the basic shape) contains the *law* of the whole work and is the first precise formulation of it . . . this applies both to tonal and to twelve-tone music . . . .[7]

Schoenberg further delineates the integral relation of harmony to shape and "idea" in his *Treatise on Harmony:*

In composing, my decisions are guided by what I sense: my sense of form . . . . Each chord I introduce is the result of a compulsion; a compulsion . . . exerted by a remorse-less, if unconscious, logic in the harmonic construction . . . the harmonies set down . . . are components of the idea . . . one may not alter anything about them.[8]

Reflecting a still broader purview in the article on "Folkloristic Symphonies" in *Style and Idea,* Schoenberg describes a work and its growth in terms that are virtually genetic:

A real composer does not compose merely one or more themes, but a whole piece. In an apple tree's blossoms, even in the bud, the whole future apple is present in all its details—they have only to mature, to grow, to become the apple, the apple tree, and its power of reproduction. Similarly, a real composer's musical conception, like the physical, is one single act, comprising the totality of the product. The form in its outline, characteristics of tempo, dynamics, moods of the main and subordinate ideas, their relations, derivations, their contrasts and deviations—all these are there at once, though in embryonic state. The ultimate formulation of the melodies, themes, rhythms, and many details will subsequently develop through the generating power of the germs.[9]

Throughout Schoenberg's writings there are numerous discussions of details that comprise musical ideas. These statements focus largely upon three successive and interrelated matters: first, upon motive, which played a pervasive role in his thinking; second, upon the extension of motive to make motive forms; and third, upon the concept of developing variations, whereby motives (and other shape ideas) continually transform and grow.

These statements give insight into Schoenberg's views upon features of music that by their very nature seem basic parts of the broader *Grundgestalt* concept. As the latter concept must in part be inferred from his writings, it is valuable to study the clear explications of these details.[10]

From these writings and their analyses, and from the accounts of Schoenberg's teaching and thinking provided by those close to his circle, a core of central concepts emerges that in effect constitutes a description of the *Grundgestalt* concept. We see from this description that the *Grundgestalt* denotes a configuration of musical elements that is significant to the form and structure of a work and is manifested throughout the work in differing guises and on various structural levels. In these appearances certain intrinsic features are retained, but are varied or disguised by means of embellishments, elaborations, interpolations, and/or contractions of elements; by inversions, augmentations and diminutions, and other compositional procedures.

This description is vague with respect to "musical elements." Are these elements pitches, rhythms, harmonies, nuances of phrasing, or what? The question is not fully clarified in Schoenberg's own writings. While his primary attention as theorist and composer was devoted to developing structural systems in the domain of pitch, Schoenberg included passages in his books[11] indicating that the *Grundgestalt* concept exerts a structural influence in other musical parameters as well.[12] It is with these other ramifications of a basic shape that this book deals in large part.

The notion of shape raises a number of ancillary matters. It could be asked, for instance, whether a basic shape is an abstraction, several levels removed from the reality of musical surface; or whether it is itself a flesh-and-blood reality, that is, a foreground presence heard in note-to-note configurations of pitch and rhythm. The answer is multifaceted, for shapes in this sense are found on many levels of abstraction, from foreground- to- background, and in a variety of guises.

Foreground shapes, essentially motives in the usual sense, are numerous. The opening movements of Beethoven's *Eroica* Symphony and Brahms's Second Symphony, studied here, are prominent examples. On a more abstract level, the basic thematic shape of Mozart's Symphony No. 40, first movement, is an interesting case, also studied later. Regardless of their initial level of abstraction, however, shapes of major formative scope influence a number of structural levels beyond the foreground, particularly with regard to large-scale tonal plans. The procedure of extending these musical premises into a network of structural associations is in effect an application to music of axiomatic method from other fields of abstract thought. Note how relevant the following description is, particularly its final sentence: "Axiomatic method allows the construction of purely formal theories which are both networks of relationships and tables of the deductions which have been made. Hence, a single form may apply to diverse material, to groups of differing objects, provided only that these objects respect the same relationships among themselves as those present among the undefined symbols of the theory."[13]

A sense of compositional unity characteristic of the *Grundgestalt* concept has been expressed by a number of composers. Schoenberg reflected this not only in his writings, but in his early compositions. Looking back upon the development of his music, as he did in the concluding chapter of *Structural Functions of Harmony,* he mentioned his awareness of unity while composing such pre-twelve-tone works as *Pierrot Lunaire* and *Die Glückliche Hand:* that vertical and horizontal pitch structures both derived from the same basic set of notes.[14] René Leibowitz has demonstrated Schoenberg's sense of unity in works as early as the songs of Op. 1–3 and the programmatic *Verklärte Nacht,* Op. 4.[15] Schoenberg in his middle and later years was interested in the similar unifying procedures he found in Brahms and Wagner.[16]

Schumann seemed aware of this unifying sense when he wrote, "It is most extraordinary how I write everything in canons, only detecting the imitation afterwards, and then finding inversions, rhythms in contrary motion, etc."[17] Hindemith, in the Norton Lectures at Harvard in 1949–1950, expressed much the same idea in metaphorical fashion.[18] Wagner suggested a similar concern with a unified totality in his statement: "Before I go on to write a verse or plot or scene I am already intoxicated by the musical aroma of my subject. I have every note, every characteristic motive in my head, so that when the versification is complete and the scenes are arranged the opera is practically finished for me; the detailed musical treatment is just a peaceful meditative after-labour, the real moment of creation having long preceded it."[19] So did Sessions and Stravinsky.[20,21] Thomas Mann has commented upon this same fact, as it applies in music and literature.[22]

In summary, the *Grundgestalt* was a fundamental concept for Schoenberg, one from which subsequent ideas would emerge. Its usefulness to him was mostly that of a background influence for the more precise and systematic compositional procedures that evolved as twelve-tone theory. Indeed the major portion of his theoretical work, pressed by compositional needs, was concerned with the formulation of twelve-tone theory. Moreover, as suggested earlier in this chapter, it was with pitch and pitch relationships that Schoenberg was most preoccupied in twelve-tone theory, despite his awareness that many aspects of a work must contribute to musical unity.

It could hardly have been otherwise in view of the times. For pitch and its organization were the foremost concerns not only of Schoenberg but of his generation, emerging into musical maturity as they did at a time when the tonal system of Western music was disintegrating as a result of the expansively chromatic practices of their predecessors.

TOTAL SERIALISM

Perhaps the most significant extension of Schoenberg's twelve-tone theory to emerge during the post-World War II period has been so-called total serialism. What Schoenberg achieved in the organization of pitch, total serialism sought to extend in analogous fashion to all or most other parameters of music, such as duration, timbre, and dynamics.

Total serialism can be seen as a further, perhaps ultimate, stage in the evolution of musical concepts emanating from the *Grundgestalt* concept. It represents the extension *in extremis* of certain systematic principles of organization derived from interpretations of the concept itself. To be sure, a *Grundgestalt* was not primarily a systematized concept in Schoenberg's mind, as we have seen, nor apparently in the musical imaginations of many classical masters in whose music Schoenberg originally observed it. Yet there were aspects of systematic thinking evident in the procedures by which shapes underwent transformations and "developing variation" in this older music. Although with many composers of the classical Golden Age these procedures may have operated on a less than conscious level, the results are nonetheless present and demonstrable, as Schoenberg was able to show in his analyses. In Schoenberg's music itself these aspects of systematic thinking were also present from his early works, often, as with his predecessors, emanating from intuitive associations.

One can view Schoenberg's later twelve-tone procedures, in the domain of pitch, as making explicit and systematic relationships among musical ideas that formerly were implicit. Total serialism in turn extended to musical parameters beyond that of pitch this same explicit concern, and a conscious awareness of the wider range of formative relationships. Viewed in this way, total serialism has its roots not only in Schoenberg's methods of serializing pitch but, in a more general way, in the concept of a *Grundgestalt* that gave rise to twelve-tone theory itself. That the relationship of total serialism may validly extend back one step, to the music of the classic-romantic era in which the *Grundgestalt* concept was itself embedded, reveals an interesting perspective from which this earlier and familiar repertoire might be viewed.

The term "total serialism," though it has attained general currency, is distortive. For one thing it misrepresents the extent of successful serialization that has been achieved. A more accurate term might be "multiple serialism," for certainly not *all* the components of this music have come under as exacting control as has pitch. Nor are the musical problems or the quality of thinking with respect to multiple serialization as one-dimensional as "total" serialism would imply.

Milton Babbitt, perhaps the most rigorously methodical theoretician and composer involved with serialism, has applied his extension of serialization largely to rhythm and duration.[23] In defining rhythm as a more independent element than in tonal music, freed of the harmonic weight by which it was often effected within tonality, Babbitt has predicated a deeper structural role for rhythm in his serial schema. Other musical properties—texture, timbre, accent, and dynamics—while coordinated in the articulation of large primary contours, are integrated and interrelated with rhythm in an ordered, quantifiable manner.[24] Thus out of their supportive, secondary roles these properties through systematization attain a more formidable, indeed a more primary, structural significance. This is in keeping with Babbitt's general assertion that the permutative operations applicable to invariant properties in the domain of pitch, if applied to nonpitch elements, must be applied in such a way that the rules of correlation be susceptible to musically meaningful interpretations in these other dissimilar domains.[25]

By contrast, Pierre Boulez has expressed his discontent over the mechanical and mathematical manner in which serialism was applied to components of sound other than pitch in the early stages of this movement, leading to music that disregarded such things as realizable metric relationships, as well as the inherent timbral and registral properties of instruments.[26] Viewing the matter from a later vantage point, he concludes that pitch and duration are the prime musical components, related by functions of *integration*, thus forming the basis of a compositional dialectic. Intensity (dynamics) and timbre belong to secondary categories, related only by functions of *coordination*, thus being unable to claim the same rigor in their morphology as pitch and duration, especially in music based upon natural sounds.[27]

Criticism of recent serialism has come from several vantage points. Meyer, for one, distinguishes two types of total serialism: one, a dependent variety in which the parameters of sound are treated as dependent analogues or variables of one another (as in Babbitt's time-point series, or in Stockhausen); the second, an independent variety in which parameters vary independently, if simultaneously, with one another (as in Boulez's *Structures Ia*), regardless of whether originally related or independently invented.[28] Meyer questions the validity of both types on several grounds. The first objection is based on the nonphenomenological quality of duration, as opposed to pitch. (Time events are only relational, whereas pitch events are both relational and phenomenal.) Operations on time events, therefore (retrograde, inversion), cannot be perceived as variants of a model given earlier, particularly of a model in the pitch domain, but only as new events in themselves.[29]

Whether this is fact or assertion is not clear. Certainly some operations upon temporal events are easily and readily perceptible and have long been so recognized. Augmentation and diminution are the most familiar of these. Likewise, retrogrades with some rhythmic shapes can be perceived (e.g.,). How complex or extensive these shapes may be, or on what level of structural abstraction, before cognition declines is not certain.

Drawing upon experimental evidence, Meyer further claims that the amount of information the mind can perceive simultaneously in different parameters is limited. Thus total serialism is questionable because various of its intrinsically important structural perspectives cannot be grasped in the perceptual moment of performance. Older music avoided this problem (the "masking" phenomenon) by limiting the complexity of some parameters (such as harmony and rhythm) if others were complex (such as melody, or its extension through counterpoint).[30]

While the evidence regarding perception may be true, the musical conclusions drawn from it are uncertain. It is a commonplace that great works of art of our time or earlier, of Western culture or other origins, simultaneously present us with complexities not only within different parameters but even within one parameter itself. Bach's melody, for instance, is often multivoiced, the lines harboring manifold harmonic implications resolvable only within differing temporal limits. All this information is presented within one voice and at one time. Brahms's orchestral textures are frequently complex at the same moments that his harmonic, contrapuntal (and rhythmic) features are also complex (if not ambiguous as well).

These situations can be seen in ways different from Meyer's. Great works of art present us with matrices of information—on many levels, via many perspectives. In music, the complexities are perceived only partly at any one hearing, wherein lies the fascination of these works. True familiarity with great works demands continual re-association, each contact allowing fresh perceptions on a conscious level, as other features absorbed from previous experience recede beyond a conscious plane.

If the perceptual problem is relevant to "totally" serialized music, then it is likewise relevant to other music. The question becomes one of degree of complexity, rather than generic difference from musical antecedents.

Probably the most fundamental criticism of total serialism lies in the fact that the analogy by which its parametric isomorphism is achieved is an extrinsic one. This point has been touched by Meyer and extensively developed by Cone.[31] As Cone points out, the seeming unification of a totally serialized work, the serialization of whose multiple parameters arises from a common denominator of order, may be basically unmusical, since this denominator itself—arithmetical order—lies outside the province of music. If the serialization of a durational row, for example, is to be an expression in a temporal domain of relationships among pitches in a tone row, the correspondence depends upon the arithmetic characterization of the pitch row with reference to pitch class and order number, and upon the application of this arithmetic expression to the temporal parameter. Perception of serial relationships among different parameters thus depends not upon intrinsically musical properties, perceptible as such, but upon extrinsic analogy— an arithmetic conversion factor.

The richness of ideas and suggestive associations generated by total serialism has led to extensions of previous systematic premises, though the question of valid morphological identity remains unresolved. Babbitt's basis for structural ordering of texture, timbre, accent, and dynamics, discussed earlier, is one such extension. Boulez has provided others: (1) through his concern with transposition of the temporal chronometric;[32] (2) through his new look at questions of harmonic functions and vertical phenomena in general (he sees them as transient and nonfixed, partially affected by other domains, such as tessitura); and (3) through his view of linear, horizontal functions[33] and his conceptions of musical space.[34]

Two points in Babbitt's outlook provide a significant link with the precedents of earlier serialism, as realized in twelve-tone practice, and in fact with works of the classic-romantic era. The first is his awareness that rhythmic structure may integrate with tonal structure, the two functioning in tandem "without harm to the individuality of either one."[35] The second is his view of texture, timbre, accent, and dynamics as functions fundamentally of rhythmic articulation, despite their systematization at higher levels in his structures.[36] These views are likewise reflected in the music of

Schoenberg and Berg, as well as in that of Brahms, Haydn, and others, as will be seen in future chapters. They indicate how closely linked are the concepts of serialism, "total" serialism, and past practice.

Independent rhythmic and pitch shapes functioning concurrently were features of the music of past ages. Each shape might be unique, intrinsic to its domain, analogically unrelated, appearing, transforming, and developing in changing association with corresponding shapes of other domains. Thus rhythm A might initially be heard with pitch shape A, and later be implanted upon pitch shapes B and C. In this manner a network of interrelations emerged as the piece unfolded, all emanating from different aspects of shape.

Schoenberg's Fourth String Quartet reveals the same thinking. In its opening movement the tone row, first heard as a melody in the first violin, contains rhythmic motives as well as a pitch sequence. In markedly audible ways these rhythmic motives are restated—sometimes literally, at times with small alterations—both in connection with their original pitch subsets of the row and with other subsets as well. The accompaniment in measure 4 is a rhythmic augmentation of the first violin part in measure 3, and uses pitches 1–6 of the original row. At measure 17 the cello sounds row pitches 1 and 2 inverted and transposed up a fourth. In both examples the pitch and rhythm shapes of the original row are already functioning separately (Ex. 1). Thus the rhythmic motives function independently of the pitch subsets (which are motivic units in this movement), at the same time creating new relationships and interconnections among the shapes in these two domains.

A similar procedure is found in Schoenberg's *Accompaniment Music to a Film Scene*, Op. 34, whose tone row, combinatorial by inversion at the perfect fourth above, is shown in Ex. 2. (Some symmetrical properties of this row are bracketed.) An accompaniment figure is found in measures 9–12. As can be seen, the same basic rhythmic motive is used in all cases, though each new version uses different pitch segments of the original, untransposed row.

A more subtle use of variants of fundamentally similar rhythms is shown in measures 1–3. These motivic fragments are heard in the tense, atmospheric opening of the piece (measures 1–5), which comprises two phrases and two statements of the tone row. Again, different segments of the row are heard, in fact are somewhat paired in their succession of statements, the pairs being subtly related through their rhythmic shapes.

Other examples abound in Schoenberg's music. For instance, the three tetrachords (or six dyads) that comprise the inner shapes of the tone row of the *Klavierstück*, Op. 33b, are phrased in such a way that these dyad pairings (A, B, and C) are quite evident (Ex. 3). Moreover, the rhythms are all variants of one another, largely through diminution. Thus two versions of a rhythmic motive function symbiotically with different pitches of the tone row. This approach persists throughout large sections of the piece. George Perle has shown similar interchanges between rhythmic and pitch shapes in Berg's *Lyric Suite*.[37]

The view of these shape relationships is admittedly different from that we have come to know as total serialism, in method at least. Philosophically, however, the two approaches have an important premise in common: namely, that a work in its totality stems from basic musical ideas whose identities and characteristics lie in different parameters; further, that the work reflects these interrelationships among ideas. In this sense, total serialism is truly a descendant of Schoenberg's thinking, for this sense of relationship was one of his cardinal principles. Though he did not pursue all his

Ex. 1. Schoenberg: *String Quartet No. 4*, **first movement**

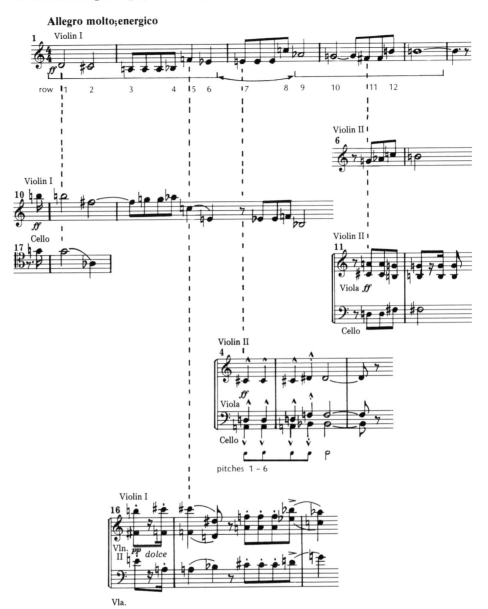

The Concept of Shape

Ex. 2. Schoenberg: *Accompaniment Music to a Film Scene,* **Op. 34**

row   1   2   3   4   5   6   7   8   9   10   11   12

pitches 4–6   pitches 7–9

pitches 10–12   pitches 1–3

pitches 4   5   3   6

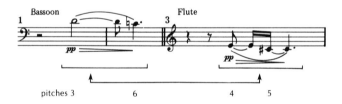

pitches 3   6   4   5

pitches 7   8   11   12

Ex. 3. Schoenberg: *Piano Piece,* **Op. 33b**

Mässig langsam (♩ = 64)

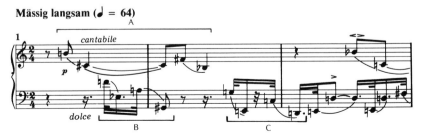

ideas to their ends, he made clear numerous times the conviction that musical unity is a total entity, found in all aspects of a piece.

There is at the same time a basic difference between Schoenberg's approach to unity and that of what might by now be called "classical" total serialism. For Schoenberg a *Grundgestalt*, which underlay any explicit appearance of shape, was a "flesh-and-blood" idea, experienced with an inner intensity and conviction that gave birth to subsequent ideas. As Cone has pointed out, some of this presence of musical reality has been lost in the successive levels of abstraction by which shape concepts have been adapted to the practice of total serialism. Yet abstraction is no stranger to musical thinking. It is certainly the essence, for one, of Schenker's reduction techniques, themselves valid reflections, in a reverse order, of abstraction in creative thought.

It would seem to be a matter of balance: between the sounds and pulses of musical experience—the physical roots of music—and the structural power gained by conceptual distance from these roots. As in many matters of art, there are no final arbiters, no ultimate values. Nor is the matter resolvable on purely rational grounds. The tension between the two poles is ever kinetic, dialectical.

SHAPE IN CLASSIC-ROMANTIC MUSIC

If serialism is relevant to classical music, the relevance lies in its suggestion of the wide range of musical domains wherein significant shapes may lie and of the characteristics these shapes may possess. Serialism has paid explicit attention to musical events that more commonplace views of music, particularly views of pre-twentieth-century music, often leave unexamined. The norms of style, of conventional context and procedure, of harmonic syntax, of rhythmic flow, of tonal relations, of nuance, are so easily heard as the ordinary, the usual, that their inner contents may be accepted at face value.

Was it ever thus? Did the classical ear hear—and conceive—of these events in an equally uncritical way? The question is, of course, ultimately unanswerable. However, the antecedents of total serialism and its connections with classical practice suggest that these musical domains may have been subjected to specific compositional thinking in this earlier music. Total serialism can be seen in historical perspective as systematizing and extending, perhaps to the ultimate degree, certain musical concepts emanating from the *Grundgestalt* idea—concepts developed through the intermediary stage of twelve-tone practice. Yet the *Grundgestalt*, with its implicit premise of unity, was itself based largely upon music of the classic-romantic era.

Thus there is a historical chain of evolution over two centuries concerning concepts of shape and their bases for musical organization. To view earlier music through the frame of reference of present-day serialism—to reverse the historical perspective, in other words—prompts a provocative question: Are earlier works unified by aspects of shape beyond those of thematic (pitch) contour that are so often the main focus of study? Can it be, for example, that formative shapes influence rhythmic properties of classical-romantic music? Further, that harmonies, harmonic progressions, key schemes, tonal relations may derive from a basic shape—a point of particular importance where these relationships exceed the norms of conventional practice or seem the result of arbitary decision? Do dynamics, register, other secondary characteristics of phrase also control formal order to some degree? Are they more, in other words, than purely local events?

It would be unrealistic to approach classic-romantic music as if it were as tightly organized as totally serialized music—where virtually each note, rhythm, texture, timbre, accent, and dynamic fits into a formal scheme. Without doubt the formal schemes of totally serialized music exceed the prevalent assumptions of homophonic music. However, music of the classic through middle-romantic era did embrace a system of harmonic syntax, tonal relationships, and rhythmic practice sufficiently common to form conventions that constituted both boundaries and lines of orderly musical thought.

In many of the great works of the classic-romantic era, moreover, there lie within these conventions subtleties of organization that cannot be accounted for by the context of common practice alone. They must be perceived in their relationship to ideas germane to a particular work. Lying beyond these conventions are events still more enigmatic, events seemingly incoherent unless viewed in relation to their formative germs.[38]

A case in point concerns the matter of tonal relationships in classic-romantic music and the contemporary serial practice of row transposition. In their derivations of transposition levels by means of row rotations or by combinatoriality, Babbitt, Krenek, and Stravinsky extend the structural referents of intervallic properties of a set (set being loosely viewed here as a basic shape) to a domain of wider and more long-range pitch implications. In rotation procedure it is the local interval alone, basically a thematic and motivic phenomenon, that exerts this broader influence.[39]

This prompts the question whether similar thinking about local and long-range relationships of motivic intervals may be reflected in Beethoven, Mozart, and Brahms. One answer is that such thinking was not necessary, that harmonic conventions of tonality generally indicated the transposition (or, in this context, modulatory) areas for long-range progression. This is true enough as far as it goes. It fails, however, to explain progressions and tonal relations that lie beyond these conventions.

The acceptance of convention as structural definer masks other important questions. Is it reasonable, for instance, to assume that Beethoven, Mozart, and other masters were unaware of the structural implications of anomaly? Were context and custom so strongly directive or formative? Did an artist rely upon them so greatly for general solutions to specific problems? If so, how can evolution and extension of musical thought or style be explained?

Similar questions arise from the idea in serial thinking that the pitch contents of a set or subset (again, a shape) determine harmony through their vertical disposition. Can this thinking have played some role in tonal harmony, despite the pervasive influence of normative syntax?

All of this is germane to a further issue—that structural growth in music is more complex than can be sustained by purely "thematic" development. In other words, it is multidimensional growth. Thus analytical procedures that concern themselves primarily with theme—even with basic shape as theme—fail to touch other areas where structure may be deliberate, unique, intrinsic to a particular work, for example, harmony, tonal relations, duration, phrase, register.

Questions like these have prompted the following analytical studies. They have led to the conclusion that basic shapes in classic-romantic music are manifest in many domains.[40] Prior to presentation of analyses of works from this period, it would be well to examine the various musical domains themselves, to consider their general properties and characteristics, and to establish criteria for their determination.

Musical domains have been isolated into the following categories:

1. Pitch, with reference to thematic shape, harmony (structure and progression in a local sense), tonal relations (harmonic progression and key schemes on larger structural levels).

2. Duration, with reference to tempo; rhythm and meter (in their small-scale roles as they bear upon thematic shape and in their larger ramifications).

3. Phrasing and nuance.

The third group is a catchall group, inclusive of dynamics, timbre, register, styles of phrasing, and other aspects pertaining to the surface character of musical passages. Finer discriminations could be made. It is not likely that they would yield greater insights, though, since these secondary aspects of structure act largely in a coordinative and supportive capacity, assisting the articulation and projection of primary elements. There are instances, however, when these musical features achieve a greater degree of autonomy.

Although the examinations of the domains of pitch, tonality, and duration that ensue serve mainly as preludes to forthcoming analyses—setting the ground rules, as it were, and the criteria for analytical judgments—the discussions of these domains are in themselves studies in depth, enhanced by examples and largely analytical in method.

Nor are analytical judgments purely objective, relying as they do upon perceptions and discriminations concerning significance, validity, and relevance of observed data. Criteria, models, modes of thought—these constructs assist in a process intrinsically based upon subjective impressions. For better or worse, musical analysis rests upon no final absolutes, has no single "truth." As Babbitt has well put it, "there is no authority of ultimate validity beyond the formed, informed, and intelligently experienced musical perception."[41]

NOTES

1. This translation of *Grundgestalt* has been used by Erwin Stein in the article "New Formal Principles," translated from the German original by Hans Keller, which appears in Stein's book *Orpheus in New Guises* (London: Rockliff, 1953); and is used by Humphrey Searle in his translation of Josef Rufer, *Composition with Twelve Notes Related Only to One Another* (London: Rockliff, 1954).

2. This autobiographical quote is illustrative of the influence of older composers on Schoenberg's thinking: "From Bach I learned (1) to think contrapuntally, i.e. the art of inventing musical figures that can be used to accompany themselves; (2) the art of producing everything from one thing, and of relating figures by transformation . . . ." (The article further attributes to Mozart, Beethoven, Wagner, and Brahms other insights along these lines, gained from studying their works.) From the 1931 draft of an article entitled "National Music," quoted in Willi Reich, *Schoenberg: A Critical Biography* (London: Longman Group Ltd., 1971), pp. 175–176.

3. This process will not be without contradictions. For example, in one of the few discussions of consequence that the *Grundgestalt* receives in Schoenberg's writings, in the book *Structural Functions of Harmony*, the term is translated as the equivalent of tone row, basic set, or note series. Schoenberg's pupil Erwin Stein, in his article "New Formal Principles," uses the term in the same sense, making clear that a basic shape lies exclusively in pitches and in the intervals between them, free of rhythmic control. See Arnold Schoenberg, *Structural Functions of Harmony* (New York: Norton, 1954), p. 193, and Stein, "New Formal Principles," p. 62.

Yet it would seem from much of the writing and teaching that have emanated from the Schoenbergian tradition that the *Grundgestalt* concept had a wider significance. There are passages in Schoenberg's writings that confirm this impression and indicate also that the general concept of a basic shape connoted more than a pitch series exclusively.

4. See note 1.

5. Rufer, *Composition with Twelve Notes*, p. vii.

6. Ibid., pp. vii–ix.

7. Ibid., pp. 56–57. Rufer further discusses the role of rhythm in Schoenberg's basic shape concept on pp. 136 ff. The rhythmic, as well as pitch, roles of shape are also reflected in his analyses (after Schoenberg) of Beethoven's Op. 10, No. 1, first movement, pp. 38 ff.

8. Excerpted from a quotation from the *Treatise on Harmony* in Reich, *Schoenberg*, p. 52. (Original source: Arnold Schoenberg, *Harmonielehre* [Vienna, Universal Edition, 1922], p. 502.) In a similar vein, in his *Fundamentals of Musical Composition*, Schoenberg speaks of the inherent harmony usually implied in the shape or contour created by the intervals

and rhythms of a motive. Cf. Arnold Schoenberg, *Fundamentals of Musical Composition* (New York: St. Martin's Press, 1967), p. 8.

9. Arnold Schoenberg, *Style and Idea* (New York: Philosophical Library, 1950), p. 201.

10. Foremost among these sources are three pedagogical books, all steeped in the musical styles of the so-called common-practice era: Arnold Schoenberg, *Models for Beginners in Composition* (New York: G. Schirmer, 1943).
——. *Preliminary Exercises in Counterpoint.* Edited and foreword by Leonard Stein (London: Faber & Faber, 1963).
——. *Fundamentals of Musical Composition.* Previously cited.
Interested readers will find the salient discussions from these books excerpted and quoted in Appendix A of this book.

11. Specifically, the passages from *Style and Idea*, p. 201, and *Fundamentals of Musical Composition*, p. 8, para. 2, and p. 9, para. 5, among others.

12. This conclusion has received confirmation from discussions and correspondence with Felix Greissle (formerly editor-in-chief of E.B. Marks Music Company) of New York. Greissle is the son-in-law of Schoenberg and a widely informed musician in his own right, who was close to the composer during the years when these ideas were being formed.

Greissle has stated that "Schoenberg mentioned this term [in his writings] very rarely, but rather only explained it." He derived the idea in large part from studies of Beethoven, particularly from examination of the "head-motive" (*Hauptmotiv*) in Beethoven's music, from which "everything else followed." "Everything," according to Greissle, not only included themes subsequently derived, but also such elements as rhythms, harmonies, harmonic progressions, and key relationships.

13. Louis Rougier, as quoted by Pierre Boulez, *Boulez on Music Today* (London: Faber & Faber, 1971), p. 30. Michael Kassler has suggested a study of Schenker through building a model of Schenker's thought constructs in which a musical work is viewed as a theorem of an axiomatic logical system. Axioms, controlled by rules of inference and decision procedures, lead to theorems of the system. See Michael Kassler, "Toward a Theory That is the Twelve-Note-Class System," *Perspectives* 5, no. 2 (Spring-Summer 1967): 55 fn.

14. Schoenberg, *Structural Functions of Harmony*, p. 194.

15. René Leibowitz, *Schoenberg and His School*, tr. Dika Newlin (New York: Philosophical Library, 1949), pp. 45–49. Leibowitz shows in particular how some of the songs from Op. 1–3 derive their structure almost entirely from particular chord progressions, or elaborate variations and transformations of initial motives. He further points out how *Verklärte Nacht* focuses upon the dissonant ninth chord at the close of a prominent ca-

dential progression early in the work and draws manifold consequences from this chord, using it in all possible inverted positions.

16. Schoenberg, "Brahms the Progressive," *Style and Idea*, pp. 52–101.

17. Quoted by Alan Walker, *A Study in Musical Analysis* (London: Barrie & Rockliff, 1962), p. 133.

18. Hindemith:

We all know the impression of a very heavy flash of lightning in the night. Within a second's time we see a broad landscape, not only in its general outlines but with every detail . . . . We experience a view, immensely comprehensive and at the same time immensely detailed . . . .
  Compositions must be conceived the same way. If we cannot, in the flash of a single moment, see a composition in its absolute entirety, with every pertinent detail in its proper place, we are not genuine creators . . . . Not only will he [the genuine creator] have the gift of seeing—illuminated in his mind's eye as if by a flash of lightning—a complete musical form (though its subsequent realization in a performance may take three hours or more); he will have the energy, persistence, and skill to bring this envisioned form into existence, so that even after months of work not one of its details will be lost or fail to fit into his photo-mental picture . . . . In working out his material he will always have before his mental eye the entire picture. In writing melodies or harmonic progressions he does not have to select them arbitrarily, he merely has to fulfill what the conceived totality demands. This is the true reason for Beethoven's apparently more than philistine bickering with his material: a desire not to improve or to change any *Einfall* but to accommodate it to the unalterable necessities of an envisioned totality . . . .
  Paul Hindemith, *A Composer's World* (New York: Doubleday Anchor Books, 1961), pp. 70–72.

19. Excerpt from a letter of 30 January 1844 by Richard Wagner to Karl Gaillard, from *Letters of Richard Wagner*, selected and edited by Wilhelm Altmann, trans. M.M. Bozman, 2 vols. (London: Dent, 1927). Cited in Gerald Abraham, *A Hundred Years of Music* (London: Duckworth, 1964), p. 121.

20. Roger Sessions, *The Musical Experience*, ch. 2, "The Musical Ear," and ch. 3, "The Composer" (Princeton: Princeton University Press, 1950).

21. Igor Stravinsky, *Poetics of Music* (Cambridge: Harvard University Press, 1947), ch. 3, especially pp. 63–65.

22. "The artist always carries a work of art as a whole within himself. Although aesthetics may insist that literary and musical works, in contradistinction to the plastic arts, are dependent upon time and succession of events, it is nevertheless true that even such works strive at every moment to be present as a whole. Middle and end are alive in the beginning, the past suffuses the present, and even the greatest concentration upon the moment does not obviate concern for the future." Thomas Mann, *The Story of a Novel*, tr. Richard and Clara Winston (New York: Knopf, 1961), p. 220.

23. Babbitt's thinking on durational serialization is set out in a number of articles, among them:
Milton Babbitt. "Some Aspects of Twelve-tone Composition." *The Score*, June 1955, pp. 53–61.
——. "Twelve-tone Invariants as Compositional Determinants." *Musical Quarterly* 46 (April 1960): 246–259.
——. "Set Structure as a Compositional Determinant." *Journal of Music Theory* (April 1961): 72–94.
——. "Twelve-tone Rhythmic Structure and the Electronic Medium." *Perspectives* 1 (Fall 1962): 49–79.
A discussion of Babbitt's application of these principles to his own music (Three Compositions for Piano, 1947) is found in George Perle, *Serial Composition and Atonality* (Berkeley: University of California Press, 1963), pp. 140 ff.

24. Babbitt:

. . . it is precisely in the realm of rhythm that twelve-tone music may conceivably compensate for its loss of tonal functionality. In tonal music, the attendant presence of harmonic weight necessarily reduces rhythm to a resultant secondary role and provides no criteria for the development and structural use of the rhythmic element. With the dissolution of harmonic functionality, however, rhythm is free to emerge as a primary, independent element. Most importantly, twelve-tone principles are capable of giving meaning to this freedom, since the operation of complementation is as meaningful with relation to rhythmic characteristics (duration and order) as to the pitch sequence characteristics of the set. Thus there arises the reality of a rhythmic structuralization totally identical with the tonal structuralization, the two elements integrating with each other without harm to the individuality of either one. In addition, there is made possible the intimate interrelation of durational rhythm, accentual rhythm, textural rhythm, timbral rhythm, and the mutations of all of these.
  —Milton Babbitt, review of René Leibowitz, *Schoenberg and His School*, in *Journal of the American Musicological Society* 3 (1950): 59.

25. Milton Babbitt, "Twelve-tone Invariants," p. 259.

26. Boulez:

When the serial principle was first applied to all the components of sound, we were thrown bodily, or rather headlong, into a cauldron of figures, recklessly mixing mathematics and elementary arithmetic; . . . by dint of 'pre-organisation' and 'precontrol' of the material, total absurdity was let loose; numerous distribution-tables necessitated almost as many correction-tables, and hence a *ballistics* of notes; . . . rhythmic organisation disregarded realisable metric relationships, structures of timbres scorned the registers and dynamics of instruments, dynamic principles paid no heed to balance, groups of pitches were unrelated to harmonic considerations or to the limits of tessitura . . . . The works of this period also show an extreme inflexibility in all their aspects: elements . . . react violently against the foreign and hostile order forced upon them; they get their own revenge: the work does not achieve any conclusively coherent organisation; it sounds bad and its aggressiveness is not always intentional.

—Pierre Boulez, *Boulez on Music Today*, p. 25.

27. Ibid., cf. pp. 37 ff. and 59.

28. Leonard Meyer, *Music, the Arts and Ideas* (Chicago: University of Chicago Press, 1967), p. 285.

29. Ibid., p. 284.

30. Ibid., pp. 286 ff.

31. See Edward T. Cone, "Music: A View from Delft," *The Musical Quarterly* 47, no. 4 (October 1961): 439–453.

32. Boulez, *Boulez on Music Today*, pp. 50 ff.

33. Ibid., pp. 27 ff.

34. Ibid., pp. 83 ff. Other possibilities have been explored by Peter Westergaard in his search for vertical intervallic control between independent parts of a composition, the control effected by row relations, with each part itself representing different row forms. See Peter Westergaard, "Toward a Twelve-Tone Polyphony," *Perspectives* 4, no. 2 (Spring-Summer 1966): 90–112.

35. Babbitt, Leibowitz review, p. 59, n. 24.

36. Peter Westergaard has shown that nonpitch elements also function in the music of Webern in a similar way—not organized separately in their own domains, but serving rather to help articulate and project relations and structure among pitch elements, such as canonic voices and sets. See his article "Webern and Total Organization," *Perspectives* 1, no. 2 (Spring 1963): 107–120.

37. George Perle, *Serial Composition and Atonality* (Berkeley: University of California Press, 1963), pp. 64–65.

38. These concepts of nonnormative events and their connections with a larger sphere of relevance offer a counterview to the notion that such events are either inexplicable or belong to an almost irrational music that arose in the nineteenth century as conventional norms were themselves destroyed. This latter view confuses musical cause and effect. In other words, seen properly, tonal practice broke up as the nineteenth century progressed because compositions carried out possibilities inherent within their premises. In so doing they extended prevalent norms, whether of harmony, tonality, or rhythm. Practice was thus a consequence of premise; premise did not result from practice.

The mode of discussion is important: the structural view is teleological; the historical one descriptive, without insight into cause, viz:

The musical practice of the nineteenth century was characterized by a markedly increased use of the ambiguous chords, the less probable harmonic progressions, and the more unusual melodic and rhythmic inflections possible within the style of tonal music. The distinction between the exceptional and the normal became more and more blurred; and, as a result, there was a concomitant loosening of the syntactical bonds through which tones and harmonies had been related to one another. The connections between harmonies were uncertain even on the lowest—the chord-to-chord—level. On higher levels, long-range harmonic relationships and implications became so tenuous that they hardly functioned at all. At best, the felt probabilities of the style system had become obscure; at worst, they were approaching a uniformity which provided few guides for either composition or listening.

—Leonard Meyer, *Music, the Arts and Ideas*, p. 241.

39. Regarding these procedures, see:
Milton Babbitt. "Twelve-tone Invariants." Previously cited.
———. "Remarks on the Recent Stravinsky." *Perspectives* 2, no. 2 (Spring-Summer 1964): 53 ff.
Ernst Krenek. "Extents and Limits of Serial Techniques." *Musical Quarterly* 46 (April 1960): 211 ff. (concerning his choral work *Lamentatio Jeremiae Prophetae*).
George Perle. *Serial Composition*, pp. 99–100, 139 ff.

40. Analyses of homophonic music in terms of basic shapes have tended to concentrate largely upon pitch, and to a lesser extent upon rhythm, seeing both elements mainly within the context of thematic relationships.

Hans Keller made a study of serialism in Mozart in 1955, in which among other things he sought an explanation in terms of serial thought of the passage that opens the development section in the last movement of the Symphony No. 40. The focus was primarily upon a pitch series, however. (See Hans Keller, "Strict Serial Technique in Classical Music," *Tempo* 46 [1955]: 16–21.) His studies of Mozart ("K. 503—The Unity of Contrasting Themes and Movements," Part I, *Music Review* 17 [1956]: 48–58; Part II: 120–129; "The Chamber Music," chapter in *The Mozart Companion*, ed. H.C. Robbins Landon and Donald Mitchell [London: Faber & Faber, 1965], pp. 90–137) are broader in their concern with rhythm as well as pitch, though both are related largely to theme.

In his book on Alban Berg, Hans Redlich makes reference to Beethoven's serial use of a theme in the A Minor Quartet, Op. 132, but sees the theme essentially in terms of pitch. (See Hans Redlich, *Alban Berg*, [New York: Abelard-Schuman, 1957], pp. 27 ff.) Erwin Stein, writing about Schoenberg's musical principles in 1924 (published in English in 1953), claimed that, "in general, the basic shapes fulfill formative functions similar to those which tonality has exercised hitherto," essentially ascribing to pitch structures the essence of formal organization. (Stein, *Orpheus in New Guises*, p. 75.) Rudolph Reti's book,

The Thematic Process in Music (London: Faber & Faber, 1967), shows a preoccupation with pitch relationships exclusively.

Alan Walker has studied basic shapes in homophonic music in his books *A Study in Musical Analysis* (London: Barrie & Rockliff, 1962) and *An Anatomy of Musical Criticism* (London: Barrie & Rockliff, 1966). Although he has considered basic shapes primarily in their relation to themes, he has given thought to their broader ramifications. In the more recent book he touches upon the possible connection between key schemes and the intervals of the opening theme in the first movement of Brahms's Third Symphony (*Criticism*, pp. 48 ff.). A similar relationship is considered in regard to Tchaikovsky's Fourth Symphony (*Analysis*, pp. 121–126). The earlier book also has some observations concerning rhythmic concordances, for example, between two principal themes in Beethoven's Eighth Symphony, first movement, although it does not go into the matter extensively (ibid., pp. 83–86).

41. Milton Babbitt, review of Salzer, *Structural Hearing*, in *Journal of the American Musicological Society* 5, no. 3 (Fall 1952): 262.

II MUSICAL DOMAINS

PITCH

More often than not, significant features of shape appear early in a work, usually in connection with theme. They reveal not only pitch contours at these moments but other characteristics as well that may have a bearing upon the rest of the piece—rhythmic shapes, articulations, timbres, nuances. If there is an exception to this general rule, it lies mostly with introductions, particularly those introductions to large-scale movements, usually of sonata-form, that are distinguished from the subsequent Allegro by slower tempi and differences in character. Part of the introductory function in these instances seems to involve the disguise of basic ideas, their clear presentation generally following in the Allegro.

Of all the aspects of shape, those involving pitch have been the most studied to date—especially the role of pitch as it concerns thematic shape. In view of the work of Keller, Reti, Rosen, and Walker, it is hardly necessary to elaborate further upon this matter here. What *are* needed are criteria by which pitch shapes can be judged. Failure to develop and to apply such criteria has been perhaps the greatest single cause of questionable studies of this sort in the past, most notably Reti's work and its shortcomings.

The following criteria may serve as general standards for ascertaining structurally significant pitches in thematic shapes.

1. *Points of contour.* Structurally significant pitches usually achieve prominence through their location within thematic contours, for instance, at high points or low points, at beginnings and closings (cadences) of motives or of longer musical ideas.

2. *Rhythm and meter.* Significant notes more often than not lie upon rhythmic and/or metric strong points. This is not to exclude ornamental notes from consideration. Where they are significant, however, ornamental notes will usually lie in some close and prominent relationship to notes that themselves are structurally important. Discerning these relationships is of course a matter of judgment, and not all judgments may be definitive. Ambiguity is the stuff of much musical substance, and ambiguous moments may yield differing yet equally valid perceptions, leading to differing consequences.

3. *Pattern: consistency and recurrence.* These terms effect a partial description of motive itself. This does not obviate their value as a criterion for certain kinds of judgments, such as those posed in item 2 above, concerning ornamental notes. Consistent and recurrent appearance of such notes within a pattern will give them greater musical and structural importance.

A case in point might concern upbeats that serve as antecedents to rhythmically strong and significant pitches. How are we to view these upbeats? Are they themselves significant? For example, throughout Schumann's Fourth Symphony, an upbeat pattern in themes is constant, though of course each theme embodies a different version of this pattern. Clearly these upbeats are significant to the unity of the symphony. Their consistent pattern of recurrence establishes this, despite the rhythmic variety of the upbeats.

4. *Degree position of pitches within a key.* If structurally significant pitches among several different themes correlate, their tonal positions (their positions upon degrees of the key) should generally correlate as well. If they do not, the difference should appear

deliberate, as adjudged by some other criterion (such as contour, pattern recurrence). In these cases, where variance occurs in one aspect of the theme, some consistency or invariance should be perceptible in other aspects.

5. *Harmonic context.* As with degree position, so with harmonic context among differing thematic shapes—there should usually be some similarity in profile. Again, this is a general proposition only. Variances from it should reflect deliberate manipulation, however, not simply chance.[1]

Any statement about the structural role of a basic shape is open to the question whether some simpler and more general context (tonality, harmony, rhythmic convention) might explain the passage at hand as easily and as well as the concept of shape. If it can, then explanation by means of shape may be irrelevant.

The discussion of the opening movement of Beethoven's *Eroica* Symphony in Chapter 6, for example, reveals the thematic ideas constructed of two significant pitch shapes, one of them triadic. It might well be asked whether the sheer prevalence of the triad as the harmonic staple of classical musical language could not account for the triadic themes, making unnecessary the explanation via shape. In such instances, some uniqueness of function or some striking repetition of pattern are reasonable criteria of judgment. With regard to the *Eroica,* it is notable that only some themes share this triadic pattern while others are markedly different, indeed highly chromatic. In addition to the prevalent pitch pattern among the triadic themes, moreover, there are correlated characteristics from other domains—consistent rhythmic and metric patterns; consistent properties of downbeat orientation (as contrasted with upbeat orientation of the chromatic themes); consistent phrasing qualities (elided cadences) in exposition and recapitulation, found only among the triadic themes; and so forth. The weight of this much evidence, correlated solely among these triadic themes, gives true structural status to the triad in this movement; it becomes a significant shape in itself rather than a generalized context.

We should also note the role of compression in the use of pitch shapes, whereby in an initial appearance only the most significant features of a shape may be present, only to appear later in more elaborate versions, fleshed out by embellishment. Keller sees this as a major aspect of creative thinking on the highest level—the pregnant quality, as it were, of an idea and the realization of its potential.[2] Compression can work in reverse as well, the later versions of an idea being condensed from earlier, more florid appearances.[3]

It is illusory to concern oneself primarily with thematic shapes or their pitch aspects alone, as if these are the only or the prime musical forces. They are, if anything, just a beginning stage of the process of musical thought, superficial in their import if divorced from the enriching associations of harmonic structure and rhythmic pulse. It is within these other musical domains that greater and more challenging complexities lie.

HARMONY AND TONALITY

Harmony and tonality are among the more codified and systematized aspects of the so-called common-practice era. The large spate of harmony textbooks, if nothing else, is testimony to this.

Classical Harmony

The concern with harmony in this book is thus not so much one of delineating its system but of understanding its usage in terms of norms—and of understanding those harmonic practices that lie within and beyond these norms. Norms present a question of at least two important dimensions: norms of a period or style, if indeed they can be set out, and norms of an individual work. Ultimately, interest lies with the latter—those standards of regularized behavior established by works themselves.

Musical compositions of the classic-romantic era may operate within the tonal standards of their time, and indeed many do. There seems little question, however, that many works also turn harmonic and tonal usage to their own ends and demands. In effect they establish their own norms. To understand these individual norms, there is need first to understand prevalent stylistic norms. For unique and individual harmonic properties, in extending beyond the usual, are most fruitfully measured by the yardstick of established practice.

There seems little need to go into the features of normative harmony prevalent in classic-romantic music; they are the aspect of this literature perhaps most studied to date.[4] It is well to remember, however, that classical tonal practice was not a static, preordained system. Its usage reflected a continual process of evolution and extension of its resources. At the same time, it exhibited a remarkable degree of systematization over some seven decades of its life, from Mozart, say, through middle-Beethoven or Schubert. This fact alone may have contributed to the unusual degree of unity that is intuitively felt in this music.

Prevalent harmonic norms, as both framework and standard for then-current practice, are sufficient criteria to account for much harmonic activity. What, then, of practice beyond these norms, which almost by definition will be chromatic, or may conceivably involve diatonic syntax by some exceptional set of relations? Are these progressions to be understood in any context beyond that of the unusual?

A more legitimate question is why supernormative progressions can exist at all. Many theorists treat such progressions, chromatic ones in particular, essentially as variants of a stylistic norm—that is, as elaborated versions of an underlying diatonic plan, the chromatic tones in effect constituting atypical, or more elaborate, passing tones. This is frequently valid as description, but prescriptively it does not raise, much less answer, some further legitimate questions. Why the use of such a progression at this point in a work? Can there be structural reasons? If so, from what source would they arise?

The argument returns to the question of individual norms. If unique norms are established within particular works, in this case with regard to harmony, do they provide greater insight, in a teleological sense, into progressions that may deviate from convention? If so, by what standard do these unique norms arise?

The evidence indicates that such unique norms are in fact created and that musical shapes—those underlying musical premises of the most far-reaching formative influence—are the bases from which they arise. Every chord need not be understood within this context, even in exceptional works. Many harmonic events may be adequately explained by the unexceptional syntax of convention. Almost inevitably, however, the major works of this era generate moments at least, and often large segments, in which the uniqueness of shapes inherent in their premises gives rise to unique harmonic events, events otherwise incomprehensible by any integrative standard.

Harmonic Progression

The question of harmonic norms extends to structural levels larger than that of purely local foreground. Schenker convincingly demonstrates that harmonic and tonal activity on middle- and background levels are in essence projections of fundamental progressions extended over wide temporal spans, even to the extreme boundaries of a work. These are structural progressions, rather than prolongations of local chords, providing the principal harmonic points by which a work attains extended form. (Thus we have the underlying *Ursatz*, its I–V–I syntax the basic and ultimate controlling motion, of which all else is elaboration.)

As in local progressions, intermediate harmonies within longer-range progressions also result from line—as the vertical product of confluent outer parts moving from one structural point to another. These passing harmonies are projected upon a larger temporal scale; thus their duration may be considerable. Viewed from a limited perspective of time, they might give the impression of a temporary key center.

One of Schenker's major contributions is his clarification of the meaning of such temporary tonal centers within a large formal design. Through his multilevel graphs he provides a counterview to the misconception of "modulation," showing that tonal centers other than the tonic are not "separate" or autonomous keys—a view existing even nowadays—but rather are tonal points along the path of a fundamental harmonic progression. The fundamental progression, moreover, is of standard syntax; its dimensions, the ultimate ones of the work itself. (The terms "modulation" and "key center," as used in this book, are meant only in this Schenkerian sense.)

Schenker's approach throws further light upon the question of conventional versus individual norms. Since tonal relations in the large are essentially expansions of basic syntax, those long-range sequences that embody conventional harmonies are not problematic. However, what of others that involve unconventional harmonies and key centers? If convention does not account for them, do they emanate from some other structural rationale? Have they, and the lines that produced them, a relation to motivic shape? Further, though Schenker's graphs reveal these moments as "way stations" within long-range structural harmonic articulations, why should these particular way stations exist? Are they unique, intrinsic to the particular piece, or could others serve equally well as points along these long lines of progression? (Why, for example, the E minor section in the *Eroica* first movement [measure 284]? Could F minor have served as well? If not, why not?) What structural principles determine these points, if any?

Guidelines to "normative" progression in the large are necessary for these judgments. Tovey, in his analytical essays, and Schoenberg, in his *Structural Functions of Harmony*, have provided useful ones.[5] Keys characterized as direct relations by these criteria qualify as "normative" by conventional standards. Those one step removed from direct relations enter a hazy area with respect to conventional norms; relations still more distant are hard to equate at all with the norms of the classical system. They require some other criteria for structural integration.

Thus there is little difficulty in understanding vi or V in relation to E♭ major, let us say, in the *Eroica* Symphony. E minor in the same work, however, as mentioned earlier, is hardly normative in conventional terms; it requires some other standard if it is to be understood as tonally integral to the music and not as an aberration.

Norms of convention are obviously inadequate for understanding aberrant relations. Nor do these norms provide a frame of reference consistent with musical premises or resultant process. For these events emanate from sources unique to their particular contexts, their norms created by the works themselves. The consistency with which the music of Haydn, Mozart, Beethoven, and Brahms moves outside of conventional and direct tonal relations gives the lie to aberration as a reasonable view of these relations. (Consistent aberration itself, for that matter, constitutes something of a norm.)

More important, the correlation between the intervallic shape of motive and corresponding pattern in key schemes in the music of these composers is consistent, to such an extent that it strongly indicates a significant connection between these features.

This extension of motivic influence to tonal relations is one of the striking developments of classical practice, as it emerged from the influence of its precedents and as it expanded the possibilities of the tonal system. Baroque music, even within the hands of its greatest and most imaginative master, Bach, employed key schemes that principally explored directly related tonal centers. (This is consistently demonstrated throughout Bach's partitas, concerti, solo sonatas, and so on.) Departure from this practice and exploration of more distant tonal relations are marked features of the music by Bach's most intellectually curious son, C.P.E. Bach, as witness his keyboard sonatas. These key schemes, however, seem not to arise from any internal structural association.[6] They stand largely as experiments, a necessary and perhaps inevitable stage in the process of expanding the usage of tonal materials and beginning the search therein for structural meaning. It was with Haydn and Mozart that experiment gave way to deeper structural import between shape, as local idea, and its correspondence through tonal plan. These relationships are most striking, perhaps, in the music of Haydn, though the idea was adopted and extended by his successors throughout the next hundred years.

It seems obvious that these relationships, if they are musically important, must be established, or "worked in," within the music. If the correlation between motive and key structure is in fact significant, the likelihood is that the music in some fashion highlights and develops this relationship in a way that can be heard and perceived.[7]

Some writers have written on mediant relations, noting the increasing appearance in romantic music of the mediant as the domain in major keys within which second thematic groups appeared. They suggest that the mediant served as a "substitute" dominant. Perhaps so, as a locale for stating subsequent themes. As a substitute tonal function, however, the mediant-as-substitute-dominant theory seems improbable, given the tendencies of tonal behavior. For in major keys the mediant major is twice indirectly removed from the tonic, only three pitches out of seven being common to the two keys. It is hard to see what properties it might have in terms of innate tonal pull that would bind it to the tonic as effectively as the dominant. More likely, the explanation of mediant relations lies elsewhere, either in terms of projection through a large tonal scheme of shape configurations embodied locally within theme and motive; and/or the establishment of tonality through harmonic elaboration of its principal tonal points—tonic, mediant, and dominant.

The in-depth analyses of Mozart, Haydn, Beethoven, Schumann, and Brahms in coming chapters demonstrate in detail both the relation of local harmonic progression to elements of motive and thematic shape and the more far-flung relations of tonal centers to the same source. The *Eroica* Symphony opening movement alone is virtually a thesaurus of such interrelations. By way of extending the scope of this discussion, however, some further examples of both local and large-scale relationships may be helpful.

(1) Few composers of the nineteenth century showed more resourcefulness than Brahms in bending basic shapes to fit widely different compositional demands. It was Brahms's musical thinking in fact that stimulated much in Schoenberg's own compositional procedures.[8]

Brahms's skill in transforming thematic ideas, altering their character, and even disguising their basic features is widely known. Less recognized is the fact that his complex chromatic harmonies often emanate from his basic shapes. These harmonies are contrapuntally conceived, and their chromatic complexity generally lies in embellished part-writing. The sources of these lines lie elsewhere, however. Brahms's subsidiary parts are often derived from formative shapes, giving rise to a harmonic texture in which not only main voices but secondary voices as well are motivic.

Harmony in these instances is neither a matter of melodic accompaniment, nor of contrapuntal texture per se. The total harmonic fabric is generically conceived—a reflection in multiple parts of formative shapes, functioning on greater and lesser levels of prominence. The approach is remarkably akin to serial thinking, despite the limitations upon the behavior of notes that would seem to be imposed by tonality. If anything, it is the harmonic directions dictated or at least suggested by these motivic components that impel the harmonic motion beyond the confines of tonal convention.

Typical of this thinking are harmonies in the first movement of Brahms's First Symphony. The basic motivic shape of the movement is actually twofold, consisting of a series of ascending chromatic steps and an intervallic skip of a third. The thematic prominence of both motives varies throughout the movement.

In introductory passages, both by Brahms and by his classical forebears, motivic shapes tend to appear more as disguised versions of a basic shape than as the original version. This is so here (Ex. 4). The two motives are originally heard as interwoven and interconnected in the ascending line of the strings at the outset of the movement (measures 1–4), a free mirror form lying in the descending winds).

The clearest version of the chromatic sequence is heard in the high winds in the opening measures of the Allegro (measure 38). Note that the middle voice of the counterpoint also expresses the same motive in inversion. The passage thus contains not one statement of the motive, but two statements in contrary motion. The chromatic harmony of the phrase is not an accompaniment to a leading voice, but the result of a dual statement. This passage is characteristic of Brahms's harmonic thinking; its constructive design is consistently borne out by similar harmonic plans throughout the movement.

The three-note chromatic motive is a generating shape for themes of the first movement as well as harmonies. This is seen in measures 42–45 and 130–134, where three of the movement's prominent themes are listed. Note once again how the motive is embedded not only in the thematic lines, but also in the subsidiary accompanying voices, so that the harmony, as before, is determined by the confluence of these formative shapes.

Finally, in Ex. 4, there are a number of phrases from the exposition and development of the same movement—various extensions, transitions, and passages of lesser thematic importance. In all these instances, typically, the three-note chromatic motive without exception is present in multiple versions, not simply as a leading part. As seen before, the harmonies of these passages are the result of multiple thematic statements and are not harmonic "settings" created to accompany themes (measures 60, 84, 121, 161, 261, and 273). Brahms's themes are thus woven into his musical fabric, the harmonies being integral strands of the fabric itself.

Ex. 4. Brahms: *Symphony No. 1 in C Minor,* **first movement**

Pitch

Musical Domains

(2) Schubert's String Quintet in C Major, Op. 163, is a work in which an unusual key relationship emanates from chromatic elements that are intrinsic to the music. The relationship is between keys lying a half step apart, at times juxtaposed against one another abruptly and with dramatic effect.

Chromaticism in both melody and harmony is a prominent shaping element of the opening idea (Ex. 5). It is asserted as early as the second chord, the diminished seventh chord in measure 3, which recurs at the cadence several measures later. It is this chromaticism of ascending or descending half steps to neighbor tones that influences all movements of the work. Chromaticism is continually present as well in small details of part-writing and is a prominent feature of numerous themes, two of which are shown (measures 117, 138). It also generates harmonic progressions throughout the work, of which two typical examples, from the opening Allegro movement, are shown in measures 20 and 53. (Note that the progression at measure 53 finds a close counterpart in the Scherzo.)

The passage at measure 20 is particularly important vis-à-vis key relations; having begun in C major and concluded on the octave B, the passage implies this early in the piece the possibility of juxtaposed key centers a half step apart. (The implication is ambiguous and actually misleading in the passage itself: the tone B would function as V of E minor if a modulation did occur; the augmented sixth by which B was established, moreover, is predictive of such a modulation. It does not occur, however, and B returns to its simpler role as leading tone in C major.)

The idea implanted within this passage is realized through key relations in the following movements. In the second movement, an Adagio in ternary form, the outer sections are in E major and the middle section is in F minor. The modulation from E major to F minor is abrupt and dramatic, using a trill between the notes E and F as a link. The coda encapsulates the modulation as a summary of the harmonic scheme.

In similar fashion the third movement, also in ternary form, establishes the key scheme of C major for the Scherzo and Db major for the Trio. The Scherzo itself, furthermore, has a highly chromatic series of transitory passages built on similar tonal relationships: Ab to G (first strain) and a long passage in B major preceding the return to C (second strain).

The final cadence of the fourth movement consists of a heavily textured chord of the augmented sixth closing into C major in such a way that both outer parts emphasize the half-step relationship (measure 425). The Db–C descending half step of the last measure gives a final confirmation of the relationship.

Ex. 5. Schubert: *String Quintet in C Major*, **Op. 163**

Scherzo:presto

Finale:allegretto

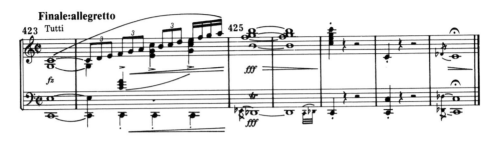

(3) The opening movement of Mozart's Piano Concerto in C Major, K. 503, presents an interesting case of local harmony generated by a motivic unit (a subpremise of the piece) within a harmonic context that is normative even by conventional standards (Ex. 6). As Keller has noted, the opening theme of the concerto (measure 5, harmonic reduction) and a principal theme of its second group (shown here in the key of C, measures 170 and 345) are unified by the same harmonic ground plan, a progression of I–ii$^4_2$–V$^6_5$ in the first phrase of each.[9] The time scale of the progressions is different, extending over eight measures in the first theme and compressed into two measures in the second. Note, however, that the proportions of the harmonic rhythm are the same in each instance:
$$\left(\frac{4:2:2}{1:\frac{1}{2}:\frac{1}{2}} = 2:1:1\right).$$

This harmonic unity extends further into the movement, manifested in many passages of different functions (extensions, transitions, and subthemes). The distinguishing feature of the opening progression noted above, the feature that in fact creates this extensive unity, is the 2–3 suspension found between the bass and a higher part. It is this suspension that generates the $^4_2$ to $^6_5$ positions of the supertonic and dominant harmonies; it is also a prominent element in the harmonic progression of succeeding passages (measures 18, 30, and 63). These passages are extensive, occupying much of the exposition itself and further found in the development and beyond, the music truly responding to the generative influence of a subsidiary compositional premise.

In measures 18 ff., immediately after the statement of the opening theme, the 2–3 suspensions and their harmonic implications—inverted to 7–6 suspensions four measures later as the phrase descends—arise from the thematic imitations in the upper parts. Moreover, the 5–6 voice-leading of outer parts, which distinguishes the opening measures of this early passage in the movement (it is the second large phrase), stems directly from the motive itself and from the suspensions it engenders.

The pattern continues through the broader dimensions of the transition passages to V, shown in harmonic reduction (measure 30). It is further found in themes of the second group, one of which has already been seen in the beginning of this discussion. A second one is shown in measure 63.

Ex. 6. Mozart: *Piano Concerto in C Major*, **K.503, first movement**

Musical Domains

(4) As a final example, consider the Rondo in A Minor for Piano, K. 511, of Mozart (Ex. 7). This is a work filled with chromaticism in its detail and filigree, though little chromatic influence seems to prevail with respect to its large-scale tonal movement, which is generally normative. Local harmonic progressions, however, are frequently chromatic and for the most part emanate from chromatic aspects of the music's opening theme. These chromatic aspects are twofold: the first, the turn motive (bracket *a*) at the opening of the theme; the second, a rising motive (bracket *b*) and its extension (bracket *b'*).

Of the subsequent events emanating from these two chromatic motives, those generated by the turn are perhaps the more interesting, if only because of their less predictable character. These are seen in measures 69 and 180 as Neapolitan progressions, in which the turn motive figures as an upper or a middle line, its contour inverted. These progressions occur just twice in the piece, each time demarcating points of closure in the large phrases. The first progression ends the opening section of the work, prior to the A-major segment (measures 69–70); the second constitutes the coda, the final close (measures 177–183).

By contrast, the directly ascending chromatic line in the opening melody (*b* and *b'*) generates a number of local progressions (measures 13, 46, 71, and 118). Within these local progressions, at least one of the outer lines embodies this same motivic figure, in both ascending and descending (inverted) contours. These progressions fulfill various roles, the first two primarily of local influence; the last two, as with the turn-derived progressions, involved with closure of large sections (the opening A-minor section; the middle section in A major).

Ex. 7. Mozart: *Rondo in A Minor,* **K.511**

These examples of motivically generated harmonic progressions are supplemented by more intensive studies in coming chapters. Further examples lie in Appendix B of this book, itself an outgrowth of the study of the *Eroica* Symphony found in Chapter 6. The *Eroica* abounds in correlations of the kind considered here. This raises the question whether the symphony may be atypical in this regard or whether it represents a general viewpoint of Beethoven's concerning the outgrowth of harmony and tonal relations from contours of shape. In Appendix B this question is applied in analyses of major works from Beethoven's middle period, within his most important genres—the string quartet, piano sonata, and symphony. The correlation found in this study of Beethoven's middle period between "unconventional" harmonic relations and their prototypes in configurations of shape is very high, significant beyond question. Moreover, there are markedly fewer modulations or key relations conforming to this pattern in works whose basic shapes themselves fit more conventional or normative designs—a further indication that the correlation we have noted is a significant one.[10]

NOTES

1. Ernst Oster has shown such a manipulation in the opening of the Scherzo movement of Beethoven's Piano Sonata in A♭ Major, Op. 26. See Ernst Oster, "Register and the Long-Scale Connection," *Journal of Music Theory* 5, no. 1 (1961): pp. 59 ff.

2. Cf. Hans Keller, "K. 503—The Unity of Contrasting Themes and Movements," Part I, *Music Review* 17 (1956): 48–58; Part II: 120–129.

3. Rudolph Reti has shown this in Schubert's "Wanderer Fantasy." See *The Thematic Process in Music* (London: Faber & Faber, 1961), pp. 95 ff. See also the similar discussion regarding Schumann's Piano Concerto in A Minor, p. 96.

4. The system can be characterized in brief by its syntax, which focuses upon the supremacy of the tonic and establishes it through chord progressions primarily of dominant root relations—in effect, I, its primary dominant (V), and those secondary dominants that lie along a diatonic axis. Of lesser importance, though still fundamental, are diatonic chords whose roots are related by thirds. These might be used as temporary substitutes for the primary chords of the system—thus, in major, vi as a substitute for I; ii for IV; iii for V.

This description is skeletal only; a fuller one should discuss the prominence of a two-voice outer framework, whose voice-leading determines both chord position (inversion, root position) and passing harmonies within a phrase. Further, it should explicate Schenker's distinction between local prolongation and truly structural harmony, as well as his concept of structural levels. These concepts are assumed here and accepted as valid, their explication already available in other sources.

5. Both writers characterize direct relations among tonal centers by varying degrees of closeness or distance from the tonic key. Closeness seems measured by two criteria: (1) the relatedness of the secondary key centers (that is, of their root, or tonic note) to the diatonic degrees of the tonic key, and (2) the extent of mutual pitches between both keys.

In regard to (1), those centers that lie upon diatonic degrees of the tonic key are most closely, or directly, related, beginning with the dominant (the mediant, also, in minor keys) and extending outward. (Underlying this plan there seems a further qualifier: namely, the hierarchy of closeness to the tonic inherent in the conventional diatonic syntax of primary and secondary dominants. Thus V is closer to I than ii; and ii closer than iii or vi.)

Diatonic relations altered by changed mode (with some notes mutual to both keys thereby removed) are a step more distantly or indirectly related. (Thus, in major, while vi may be directly related to I, VI is more indirectly related, as its changed mode involves tones chromatic to I.) Still more distant are those tonal centers whose roots themselves lie upon altered, or chromatic, tones of the original tonic (♭VI, to carry the above example one

step further). These become yet farther distant if their mode in turn is altered (♭vi, as altered from ♭VI). Thus one moves to centers like ♭V (tritone) or the Neapolitan as among the most distant of all relations.

It is impossible to designate precisely the qualitative degree of distance beyond some stages of removal; these schemes do not provide airtight contexts for graduated relational systems. They do make major distinctions concerning relatedness, however, that are analytically useful and that conform in large part to common perceptual experience—for example, the close relationship between the tonic in minor and its relative major. The two keys in this case employ fully the same pitches, their distinction lying in the tonal frames placed around these notes and in their tonal definition thereby. Tonic and dominant keys in major, though varying by one pitch not common to both, are still in close and direct relationship, the more so as further judged by their syntactical connection. They are closer, by way of contrast, than I and ♭iii (e.g., C major and E♭ minor), which share only two tones in common and place upon these two completely different tonal perspectives. The "circle of fifths" relationships of secondary dominants to the tonic also have an affective aspect that complements the matter of tonal distance. This has to do with the sense of tension or repose engendered not only by their relationship to the tonic, but by their placement on the sharp or flat side of the tonic axis.

Secondary dominants situated as precedent to I (and based on diatonic tonal degrees) tend to engender harmonic tension (iii, vi, ii, in major). To state them is to establish a syntactical chain whose ultimate resolution upon the tonic, the final point along this chain, is virtually predictable—a built-in expectation in classical music of a deterministic system. The tensions created by tendency and expectation are intensified if chromaticism of mode is introduced at any point along this chain, that is, if vi or ii in a major key become VI or II (the root remaining diatonic).

The circle of fifths carried to the flat side of the tonic pole, particularly through the first two points of this cycle (iv and VII in minor), induce a lack of tension that actually tends toward destruction of the tonic. For IV has the potential of turning I into a dominant (V of IV), and ♭VII (in minor) has the potential of carrying the process of "removal" from I a step further by its tendency to move toward ♭III. While IV may thus create the repose born of resolution, it does so by weakening I, carrying harmonic motion toward remote regions and beyond the point of stability, indeed of identity, that the tonic represents. This tendency may in part account for the care classical composers took to avoid IV as a local center; or to avoid it at least until a substantial amount of music had established the tonic through harmonic syntax expressed on the sharp side of the tonal axis.

6. See Charles Rosen's discussion of this point *The Classical Style* (London: Faber & Faber, 1971) pp. 111 ff.

7. One senses that the unusual in a local event and its larger ramifications may not always have been foreplanned, that these connections may have stemmed from that inspired "moment of recognition" so vital to all creative thinking—the intrusion of chance.

This recalls a discussion of chance by Leonard Meyer in *Emotion and Meaning in Music* (Chicago: University of Chicago Press, Phoenix Books, 1961), pp. 195–196, in which chance, as an inevitable fact permeating all realms of being, is suggested as a corollary element in works of art, an element that adds aesthetic vitality since it mirrors the aspect of uncertainty that we experience elsewhere in life. "The pedants," claims Meyer, "have piously attempted to explain away the inexplicable in order to make their analyses jibe with their mechanistic misconceptions of what constitutes the basis for musical unity, logic, and inevitability. But chance will not be denied . . . . "

Nor would many analysts deny it. Neither would they deny aspects of the musically inexplicable. This thinking, however, may confuse chance and structural logic and their respective roles. The role played by chance in high-level creative work is unquestionable; many artists have themselves commented upon it. Still, chance alone, or the unexpected, are not by themselves sufficient to enhance a work of music. Chance can, after all, lead equally well to the ridiculous or the non sequitur. The true excitement it provokes stems from turning to musical and structural account the odd relationships perhaps revealed in the unforeseen moment and making musical capital of these relationships. This is what is so striking and imaginative in Haydn's use of shapes and of key relations, described by Rosen in *The Classical Style*.

8. See Arnold Schoenberg, "Brahms the Progressive," *Style and Idea* (New York: Philosophical Library, 1950).

9. Keller, "K. 503—The Unity of Contrasting Themes," pp. 120–129.

10. Three other studies on this subject are of interest. One, by Charles Rosen, of Beethoven's *Hammerklavier* Sonata, shows the relationship between the thematic intervals of thirds in the work and the tonal structure of key centers, also interrelated by thirds. See Rosen, *The Classical Style*, pp. 407–434. Rosen makes further correlations of this nature with regard to Haydn and Mozart. See the remarks on Mozart's G Minor Quintet, pp. 88 ff.; his Piano Concerto, K. 503, pp. 254–256; Haydn's Symphony No. 81 (regarding harmonic ambiguity as a subpremise), pp. 157–159.

A second study is found in the article "Analysis Symposium" in the *Journal of Music Theory*, in which Howard Boatwright and Ernst Oster contribute analyses of Mozart's Menuetto, K. 355 (revised by Einstein as 594a), analyses largely concerned with harmonic and tonal relations. See "Analysis Symposium," *Journal of Music Theory* 10 (1966): 20–52.

In a third study, by David Lewin, similar observations are made concerning tonal relations in the music of Liszt. Lewin notes that material in certain of Liszt's works is organized into tonal "areas," often diatonic in nature, the structure of these works being largely determined by the way in which one of these areas is transposed into another. At times these transpositions outline a motive of the piece. At other times they "fill in" an important interval—either diatonically, chromatically, or through a whole-tone scale—the interval so treated having significance as a feature of shape. Elsewhere the transpositions "move through" a whole-tone scale, diminished seventh chord, or augmented triad, structures motivically important as well as something of a norm in the harmonic context of this music. Lewin finds that his observations hold true as generalizations for many of Liszt's works. See David Lewin, "A Study of Hexachord Levels in Schoenberg's Violin Fantasy," *Perspectives* 6, no. 1 (Fall-Winter 1967): 25.

4 DURATION

Duration is seen by writers such as Cone, Komar, Sessions, and Schenker, and I would agree, as the most fundamental and indispensable element of music.[1] In some respects this is readily demonstrable, for musics exist that are built almost entirely temporally—to the extent that they are devoid of tempered or fixed pitch and its derivative structures, using only percussive "noise"—like some African and Pacific music.

Of the three aspects of musical time (tempo, meter, rhythm), tempo seems self-evident, though its implications for structure are subtle. By contrast, rhythm, a primordially physical aspect of music, largely kinesthetic and muscular, is elusive and less understood, less studied in systematic fashion,[2] and the aspect upon which the greatest number of intuitively formed assumptions operate in the practical day-to-day work of musicians.

This elusive quality of rhythm is not a problem confined to music alone. Time itself is so elusive a concept that many fields define and view it in terms useful to their own purview, eschewing what has not yet appeared possible—a universal definition. Thus history frames and segments time, forming periods, eras, epochs, though it is the events, institutions, people within these periods that are of prime interest rather than the segments of time per se. Literature, drama, film, play with time experientially, even altering its physical and sequential nature. The contemporary physical world, which has accepted time as a fourth dimension, still views some events within this world in terms of the three-dimensional cosmology of Newtonian mechanics, where time is an objective measure of rate: for example, studies of terrestrial motion; biological studies of growth, development, aging, decay. Time in this sense is an index for the study of mechanism—*an* index, though not the only one. Other indexes, such as molecular, chemical, electromagnetic, given different perspectives, might be equally valid.

Herein lies one of music's unique aspects. For in music time is primary; it is not a secondary aspect or index. Music *structures* time, incorporates it as one of its fundamental elements. Without time—structured time—music does not exist; no discussion, no experience of music can take place divorced from the phenomenon of time. Rate in music (time) is thus an integral part of musical mechanism, rather than a functional index of that mechanism.

All perspectives of time, regardless of field, must distinguish between time as a differentiated or undifferentiated continuum. Time undifferentiated is a useless concept, for lack of definition or differentiation leaves time incapable of being meaningfully observed or judged. Differentiation, however, requires demarcation, and demarcation invokes two different orders of time: metrical—time unqualified by experience, marked off by mensural means external to a subject or living viewer; or experiential—time qualified by human experience.

Time is further perceived as intrinsically related to motion or flow. It is only through motion or flow that time can be meaningfully apprehended and distinguished from an undifferentiated continuum—perceived, in other words, as change, relative to a constant background. It could be said that the nature of such motion, and the qualities that pertain to and signify motion, are what make temporal frames of reference unique. Moreover, motion need not be a physical entity alone—that is, from point A to point B in space. It may be imaginative, experienced vicariously through physiological and/or emotional correlates. In effect these experiences are internal responses to motion, distillates of the physical qualities instigated by motion. This is an important point with relation to musical affect.

This discussion begins to reveal the uniqueness of music as a temporal experience. For music in fact embraces all the foci of time that have so far been examined. It implants upon a potentially undifferentiated continuum two species of demarcation: the mensural demarcation of beat and, subsequently, meter; and the demarcation of time related to experience, perceived qualitatively through the events of a given musical work. It poses both metrical and experiential frames simultaneously, placing them variously in states of coordination or of opposition and tension. In its articulation of phrase and of larger temporal segments (periods, sections, movements), music further embodies that sense of motion or flow that is the essence of meaningful demarcation of time.

The uniqueness of music as a temporal construct goes still further. For not only does music structure time and incorporate it as a fundamental element; through this structure music controls time in absolute measure and absolute proportion.

A comparison with another time art like drama may make this point more cogent. A dozen actors given Hamlet's soliloquy would probably perform its lines with a dozen variants in terms of pacing, emphasis, delay, inflection, timing, and proportioning of phrases. If "faithful to the text" (and let us avoid that thorny road), none of these hypothetical versions could be declared "wrong."

No such interpretive scope could exist in musical performance without musical distortion. For example, the opening three phrases of Beethoven's *Eroica* Symphony consist of 2 measures of repeated chords and a 12-measure melody followed by a 9-measure melody. A dozen interpreters of this passage, maintaining fidelity to the text, would have to retain these absolute mensural proportions of 2:12:9. Variances might be expected in basic tempo conceptions and in nuances of such elements as articulation and sound. But all such variances would have to reside within the overall phrase proportions and durations, regardless of what tempo might serve as the vehicle for the unfolding of the phrases. The segmenting of time, in other words, is fixed, though the internal shaping of each segment might allow for somewhat varied approaches. No degrees of variance could hold here to the extent that they did with the Hamlet soliloquy, without gross destruction of the musical text.

It is this quality, then, that is special about music among the temporal arts—the absolute structuring of experienced time, in its proportioning and in the control of its unfolding.

MUSICAL TIME

Of the general properties of time, two are particularly important for understanding the way time functions in music. These are, first, the dual aspect of time and, second, its intangible quality.

Duality in time has often been referred to in philosophical writing in terms of objective/subjective time. The terms, in fact the concepts, are inappropriate to music. For all time in music is in some sense experiential—whether the steady beat set up within a musical measure or the expanding and contracting sense of phrase time, uneven in its lengths. Both varieties are intrinsic to a musical work; both are perceived through the ears, the muscles, the body; both are "experienced," in a musical sense.

To speak of objective time, therefore, is confusing, for it implies a time outside of music, somehow not experienced. Meaningful distinctions concerning musical time do not involve objectivity or subjectivity but rather the orders, or varieties, of temporal experience created by music. These, too, are basically dual in nature; useful terms to distinguish between them might be "chronometric time" and "integral time."[3]

Chronometric time refers to that essentially mechanistic, evenly spaced, and in large part evenly articulated time set up within a musical measure (and larger units) in the music of the baroque through romantic eras (extending by and large into our own era as well). Its measurements and demarcations are in the main pragmatic and convenient periodizations.

Integral time, on the other hand, denotes the unique organizations of time intrinsic to an individual piece—time enriched and qualified by the particular experience within which it is framed. The mechanisms by which this integral temporal organization is established are likewise unique to a given work and must be studied anew in each case. Thus while the chronometric "beat" in, let us say, two Mozart piano pieces of similar tempo may be similar, the integral organization of time by phrase, section, motive, "breath" will be different in each piece and cannot be usefully generalized.

The intangibility of time presents yet another musical quandary. Because time is intangible, it constitutes in our perceptual experience a dimension unique from the three-dimensional world of space. The spatial, in music as in all else, is accessible to the senses—it is visible, audible, tangible. Further, it is quantifiable in terms integral to the senses, hence controllable: long, short; high, low; loud, soft.

The temporal by contrast is intangible. It is unavailable to the senses; its perception is in part a trained and intellectual act. Yet any demarcation of temporal periods, however determined, must rely upon tangible phenomena, such as the visual symbols of the clock face; the aural, sonic signals of the clock's tick or hourly bell; the metronome's click. This is a fact of no great importance in studying processes that are functions of time, that is, where time is a qualifier of the processes themselves. The sonic representation of time in music, however, is fundamental, for as we have seen, time is of the very essence of music—a prime element of the language itself, not a qualifier on a secondary level.

Thus time in music poses a contradiction: in a world of physical sound, it is a basic element that is itself nonsonic, yet dependent for its statement and demarcation upon sound. More than any other musical dimension, time in music depends totally upon forces outside its own proper domain—namely, upon sound.

From this contradiction follow a number of consequences, not always clear in their implications. The emphases, for example, by which segments of time are marked off are of varied quality—beat and pulse, rhythmic, metric, agogic. Thus temporal statements are qualitatively different, though not always qualitatively distinct. On the most primitive level, temporal extension depends at the least upon the articulation of time points, articulations which themselves cannot be effected except through noise (percussion) or, more prevalently in our musical system, through sound. Yet sound in musical context is rarely simple; more generally it is sophisticated and qualitatively complex—based upon pitches that are themselves modulated by timbre, register, modes of attack, intonation, and further combined into harmonic structures of various syntactical implications. Only in its more mechanistic aspects (chronometrics, meter, definition of pace) does musical time appear isolated and primarily in temporal terms, though even here autonomy is not complete. For beat or pulse, essential to these more mechanistic aspects, is physically felt and announced at the least via timbre, if not also by means of pitch. More refined aspects of musical time (rhythm, thesis and arsis, anacrusis or upbeat), for their mere definitions within specific musical contexts, invoke harmony, weight, texture, phrase, articulation, cadence—all domains of pitch, nuance, and sound. Thus criteria for both discussing and perceiving temporal structures are neither fully clear nor consistent with the domain of time itself.

TEMPORAL DUALITY IN MUSIC

The dual aspects of musical time—chronometric and integral time—are found in continual and symbiotic relation, at once synchronous and dialectically in conflict.

In its smallest practical dimension, the mechanical, or chronometric, unit of musical time is the beat; in larger dimensions, the unit is meter, with its attendant arrangement of beats. With reference to classic-romantic music, both units were "givens" of a system that existed prior to any act of composition and was established to some extent arbitrarily. Through convention and stylistic evolution, beat and meter were imbued by this era with certain musical characteristics: duple and triple metrical groups; pre-established distinctions between strong and weak beats, up- and downbeats; dance qualities associated with certain meters (and tempi). Emphasis within this domain is metric accent, largely mechanical and virtually automatic, associated mainly with those beats of a measure (or larger dimensional levels) that are strong as determined by these conventions.

Beat and meter—the chronometric aspects of time—were more than purely mechanistic features of classic-romantic music, however. While they were givens of a preexistent system, they at the same time assumed life, indeed were set up anew, through each work. Classical metricality not only established regularity of beat, it also established the expectation of regularity within the ear and the physical system of the perceiver. Thus in hearing a work of Mozart or Haydn, we not only perceive the regular beat inherent in the metrical framework, but we come to anticipate and expect such a prevalent regular beat in the measures to come. Regularity becomes one standard by which the passage of time within the work is understood.

Integral time in music, the other half of the temporal duality, is wholly bound up in the experience of a particular work, arising from the organization of time inherent in that work. This unique temporal organization serves, in fact, as a major premise intrinsic to the work.

The smallest unit of integral time, as contrasted with the chronometric beat, is pulse. The distinction between them is significant. For while we generally experience beat as precise and regular, stated with the blunt, immediate articulation of a click (foot, metronome), pulse is experienced with a far broader range of articulations and is understood, moreover, in intimate relation to bodily experience. Thus pulse may correspond to the gradual rise-emphasis-decay sensation of pulse in the circulatory system; to a similar cycle in breathing, where the tension-repose dimensions take longer to complete; or to the precise, sudden jerk of a muscular spasm.

In all cases, the experience of pulse has both physical and psychological connotations. Its nature and quality are intimately allied with articulation. Think, for example, of a Brahmsian ⎯◁ ▷⎯ or ⌒ · · ⌒ ; a Beethovenian *sf*; a Mozartian series of eighth-note accompaniments, comprised of evenly stated staccato notes. Nor will all these articulations fall into equally spaced time patterns. Some will push time or pull it, stretching or compressing by small degrees the precise, even flow of chronometric time in response to the inner tensions and strains of a musical phrase. Thus a difference, and often a conflict, is experienced between the regularity of metrical beats and the slight deviations from regularity caused at times by the internal demands and articulations of pulse.

Integral time, like chronometric time, is also grouped in larger dimensions than that of pulse, which is its minimal unit. These broader groups are rhythmic in nature (as opposed to metric), distributing and relating, by patterns intrinsic to the work, collections of pulses and longer durations.

Like meter, its mechanical counterpart, rhythm—or at least rhythmic pattern—is to some extent determined by convention, though the constraints on it are fewer. Thus one is not likely to find in Mozart rhythmic patterns common to Bartók or Stravinsky. By the same token, however, within the constraints imposed by style and convention, it is virtually impossible to predict the rhythmic activity of a given Mozart movement without knowing something of the work itself, since this rhythmic life arises basically from premises of the piece. (The same is not true of meter; a prediction of duple or triple meter and their related metric accents will probably describe the metric life of the same Mozart movement in its entirety.) Likewise, where emphasis on the mechanical side of music is predictable and repetitious (metric accent), emphasis in rhythm encompasses a wide variety of types—structural accents, agogics, stresses and other articulations (sf, $>$, $\blacktriangledown$, rf), inflections by contour and harmony, contrasts of the rhythmically more and less prominent—none of these predictable prior to knowledge of the work, all arising from the music itself.[4]

Unlike meter, whose strong beats are in the main implanted precompositionally by means of a system already determined, the strong pulses of rhythmic patterns arise contextually. Because temporal phenomena cannot demarcate themselves, rhythmic strengths and weaknesses (other than stress) are effected by events in other domains, such as harmony (in its progression, tension and relaxation, stability and instability), melodic contour, cadence.

Temporal coordination and/or conflict is a continual state within any work and is found in the relations of the metric to the rhythmic, with their attendant properties, on all levels. Beat and pulse, the minimal units of time, often deviate slightly from each other. On larger structural levels, metric and rhythmic quanta are also at times dissynchronous, the pull and conflict between the two domains creating a continual balance of tensions until the ultimate resolution of final closure. Some specific devices are based upon such conflict: syncopation, hemiola, suspensions, feminine cadences. (Conflict marks suspensions at their two initial phases; the preparation and actual point of suspension; the resolution coordinates a metrically weak beat with a rhythmically weak pulse.) By contrast, the coordination on middle-ground levels of strong metric and rhythmical impulses (as effected through harmonic progression) constitutes what Cone has termed a "structural downbeat," an important point of simultaneous harmonic and rhythmic arrival so powerful that it turns what precedes it into its own upbeat.[5]

Thus the intangible, nonsensory property of time, with its inherent contradiction that time must depend upon physical sound for its articulation, and the dual aspects of time are major determinants of temporal life in music. Prior to a more detailed discussion of tempo, meter, and rhythm, the following chart may provide a convenient summary of the chronometric-integral duality discussed here.

MUSICAL TIME

Chronometric	Integral
Meter	*Rhythm*
Minimal unit: beat	*Minimal unit:* pulse
Emphasis: metric accent	*Emphases:* (1) rhythmic accent (structural) (2) varieties of stress and articulation; agogics; inflections, as in contour (embellishmental)
Determinants: precompositional scheme, established through already evolved conventions and style. These imbue meter with certain musical characteristics: duple-triple pattern, metrically strong-weak and up-down beats, associated dance qualities. Expectation of regularity set up by a work through its metric pattern of evenly distributed beats.	*Determinants:* context, arising from compositional premises of individual piece. Rhythmic strong-weak pulses determined by factors not always within rhythmic domain: harmony (progression, strength-weakness, stability-instability), cadence, melodic contour, etc.

RHYTHM AND METER

Rhythm and meter in classic-romantic music are significant in two fundamentally different aspects: shape and emphasis.

Shape is largely a reflection of thematic shape; it is self-evident as such and poses few problems in its perception or understanding. Some of its implications are studied later in this chapter.

If shape is easy to comprehend, emphasis is another matter indeed. Its features are rarely clear, nor are its criteria. Even its symbols (>, ˢᶠ, dynamic markings) often serve double duty, indicating by the same signs emphases of differing significance, degree, kind, and scope. Through emphasis temporal segments are delineated and marked, and their level of importance imparted to the listener. It is by emphasis, then, that rhythm and meter function in the unfolding of music in time. To understand these functions requires that temporal factors be ordered in some sort of theoretical framework.

TOWARD A THEORY OF TONAL RHYTHM

Any theory of rhythm concerning tonal classic-romantic music must encompass at least four basic aspects of musical time. They are (1) the intangibility of time; (2) the dual nature of time (chronometric versus integral time); (3) levels of temporal structure; and (4) emphasis, as it pertains to time.

Our earlier discussion of time has already established its intangible aspect and its dual nature, and the manifestation of both these properties in musical time. To these concepts can now be added that of levels of temporal structure, a view that projects the musical organization of time onto layers of differing dimension and scope—from limited ones of foreground prolongation to more extended middle- and deep-structure layers. This concept has been established through the rhythmic studies of Cooper and Meyer (*The Rhythmic Structure of Music*), Cone (*Musical Form and Musical Performance*), and Komar (*Theory of Suspensions*), all cited earlier—Cooper and Meyer being among the earliest to extend to the temporal domain the concept of structural levels that Schenker so effectively developed in his studies of line, harmony, and tonality.

Musical time, as it operates on broader structural levels, extends its metric-rhythmic duality to wider periods. This duality was just studied in its smallest practical dimensions of beat-pulse. On more extended levels, meter is successively structured from beat to measure to what Cone has called "hypermeasure," a grouping of measures in which the measure itself serves as a beat. Rhythmic periodizations extend successively from pulse to motive (or motive-group) to phrase.

The earlier table of musical time in its duality can now be extended to several successively higher complementary levels:

MUSICAL TIME

Chronometric (Metric)	Integral (Rhythmic)
Beat	Pulse
Measure	Motive (or motive-group)
Hypermeasure	Phrase
Macroperiodizations of hypermeasure groups	Macroperiodizations of phrase groups

On all these levels, properties earlier associated with metric or rhythmic domains generally hold. Metric levels of periodization are mechanistically related to an individual work. Essentially they provide temporal ground plans within which musical activity takes place. In this sense meter is like a temporal yardstick, extending into time, segmenting and quantizing time by units (beats, measures) that are "neutral" chronometric modules. All rhythmic periodizations, by contrast, arise from properties intrinsic to musical ideas of an individual work. They are neither uniform nor predictable.

The coordination-conflict relationship between the metric and rhythmic operates on all levels. This has been studied in detail on the level of beat-pulse. On the measure-motive level, motives or motive-groups generally lie within the confines of measure. The two domains are generally coordinate at this level: strong and weak pulses within motive usually agree with metrically strong-weak beats of measure, though the beginnings (upbeats) and endings of motives may extend slightly beyond the measure or measures that frame them metrically.

Coordination-conflict relationships on the broader levels of hypermeasure-phrase are more complex. As with measure and motive, hypermeasures and phrases may or may not be congruent in their extreme limits; it is not unusual to find phrases with an anacrusis of almost measure length, thus creating different boundaries between phrase limits and those of the underlying hypermeasure.

These boundaries, whether congruent or otherwise, are not difficult to determine. More problematic is the determination of accentual properties between phrase and hypermeasure—in brief, whether they are downbeat or upbeat oriented, and whether the emphasis patterns of the two domains are or are not similar. Before this can be discussed, it is necessary to determine how strong and weak beats and pulses are established on all levels, i.e. to study emphasis itself.

"Emphasis" is used here as a generic term, encompassing all manner of intensification by which one particular point in musical time is distinguished from another and given greater prominence. Within this all-inclusive category there are three significant distinctions to be made. First, it is important to distinguish between structural and nonstructural emphasis. Second, it is important to recognize that both kinds of emphases operate within the dual domains of musical time. Third, we must delineate emphases, particularly structural emphases, on the various levels of temporal structure just discussed.

Structural and Nonstructural Emphasis	The designation of structural emphasis as "accent" has already been established. However, the designation of nonstructural emphasis as "stress," which some writers have suggested, seems inadequate as the antonym to "accent." For in fact there are a variety

of nonstructural emphases, of which stress—the dynamic intensification of a beat or pulse—is just one. Other types would include agogic emphases,[6] emphases of contour and inflection,[7] of articulation (· , > , ▼ , – , ±) and dynamics, of register (especially registral extremes), of texture, and of weight. To some extent these designations intersect, which causes no problem in comprehension as they all fulfill similar nonstructural roles.

Nonstructural emphases are ornamental in their purview. They add foreground interest to a musical context, for example, articulations (staccato, marcato) and stresses (*sforzandi*). However, they could hypothetically be removed from this context without changing the music in any deep-structure sense. The passage would be less lively or exciting, perhaps, but in its overall significance it would remain unaltered in fundamental or functional terms.

By contrast, structural emphasis (accent) cannot simply be stated. A sudden loud noise, for example, could not create such an emphasis. While a noise of this sort might make a successful stress, it would be unconvincing as an accent. For accents, being structural, must be established—that is, worked or built into the musical fabric. It suffices to recognize the many possible ornamental, nonstructural emphases without amplifying them. The interesting problems concern structural emphases, their nature and variety, and how they are articulated.

Duality of Structural Emphases

Metric time and rhythmic time each have their own variety of accent. In classic-romantic music, metric accents are largely determined by convention and style on the level of measure—the next higher level after beat itself. Essentially these are the familiar and long-established patterns of strong-weak beats found in duple and triple meter, implanted by usage over a long period of time, though set up anew with each piece. Their properties have already been discussed. They constitute metric accent—the structural emphasis of chronometry.

Hypermeasures also have conventionally determined strong-weak patterns. These are generally duple in nature, with an alternation between strong and weak measures, or a four-measure pattern in which the initial measure is primary, the third measure of secondary strength—a correspondence in effect with duple pattern in $\frac{4}{4}$ measure, projected onto the next larger plane. The four-measure hypermeasure is a staple module of classical music. Hypermeasures are not always duple, however; often their asymmetric dimensions result from metric-rhythmic conflicts that force their alteration from the duple. These conflicts generate powerful musical processes that will be discussed shortly.

Levels of Structural Emphases

The same criteria that determine accents on the level of measure are also operative with motive, the rhythmic aspect of this level. The strong-weak patterns of a motive are usually congruent with those of measure and in fact are determined by these metric accents, though a motive may overlap—particularly in its upbeat—the measure that frames it.

The principles that determine strong-weak pulses on the broader rhythmic level of phrase—the level complementary to hypermeasure—are more complex. While hypermeasures generally have a symmetrical ground plan of duple character that also determines their strong measures, phrases operate under no such restriction. Since phrases emanate from qualities integral to a work, they may be of varying lengths and varying strong-weak pulse schemes.

The criteria for judging these strong pulses are neither singular nor always clear. Basically they lie either with metric principles of accent or with those principles integral to rhythmic pulsation, which generally involve the scale of relative stability-instability inherent in harmonic progression. Further, phrase pattern—in both its rhythmic and metric shape—may be relevant.

Common problematic spots in determining emphases are found in the antecedent and consequent phrases of opening musical statements. These often involve a I–V progression in the antecedent phrase and a reverse V–I answer in the consequent. (The beginnings of Beethoven's *Pathétique* Sonata, the Allegro of Mozart's Symphony No. 39, and Mozart's *Jupiter* Symphony are cases in point.) It is not hard to determine that the opening phrase in these cases, by virtue of its stable tonic harmony and attendant weight, is downbeat-oriented. However the following phrase reverses the harmonic and hence the stability pattern, yet it too feels downbeat-oriented. In these cases the metric pattern of strong-weak prevalent in the underlying hypermeasures—and the repetition of rhythmic patterns in the two phrases, where the initial statement has strong-weak emphases—seems more powerful influences than harmony. They reinforce the downbeat orientation of both phrases.

Frequently hypermeasure and phrase, or groups of hypermeasures and phrases— their next higher temporal periodization—are coordinate with one another in terms of their strong-weak patterns, if not always with regard to their temporal limits.[8] This is particularly true of initial statements of themes, as we have just seen. Sequences are further examples, operating under conditions of accent similar to those just discussed.

With the extension of musical ideas onto still greater macroperiodic levels, conflicts usually develop between the rhythmic and the metric. Phrases vary in length, coming into opposition with the tendency of hypermeasures to continue their prevalent pattern. Cross-accents are felt between the noncoordinate strong beats of hypermeasure and strong pulses of phrase, creating ambiguous patterns that can be heard in terms of strong points within one temporal domain or the other or in terms of both.

In these moments the power of the rhythmic surpasses that of mechanistic metrical scheme. Phrase, with its strength of rhythmic accent, predominates. The two domains may remain in conflict until some further asymmetry in phrase brings them back into phase. At other times, hypermeasure may be forced by the superiority of rhythmic strength to change and to extend its recurrent and symmetrical plan. This process and its conflicts of accents generate powerful and incremental rhythmic tensions of upbeat character—large-scale structural tensions that are not resolved until the following structural downbeat, where once again metric and rhythmic strong points, together with harmony and line, coordinate to establish and initiate a new musical period. These upbeat events are here termed "structural upbeats," a useful complement to Cone's characterization of their following downbeats.

Conflict between the metric and the rhythmic is a pervasive and powerful impellant to forward motion. Specific devices utilizing this conflict on local levels were mentioned earlier—syncopation, hemiola, feminine cadence, suspension (which can also be projected onto larger structural levels, a central point in Komar's study). To this list should be added phrase elision. By forcing one temporal point to serve double duty, as both cadence and initial impulse of the following hypermeasure-phrase, elision effects a structural realignment. The previous phrase is foreshortened, its strong-weak pattern (and that of its hypermeasure) altered, thus adding to the force of the succeeding structural downbeat. The false cadence effects conflicts similar to those of elision, blunting by incomplete resolution the downbeat force inherent in closure and thus realigning degrees of tension and repose.[9]

This discussion has moved in scope to large periodizations that span the greatest temporal lengths—beyond the successive levels of hypermeasure-phrase and groups of hypermeasure-phrases. It seems evident that on these macrolevels the primary features of interest are the articulations of structural downbeats and their attendant preceding structural upbeats. The rhythmic, in other words, is the supreme focus here. The metric, by contrast, is of little consequence, subsidiary to the more powerful integral elements dictated by rhythm. Cone has suggested that an entire movement can be seen as a succession of structural downbeats, each turning the preceding passage into its own upbeat, this transformation occurring continually to the extent that the movement is experienced as one huge upbeat and resolution at some final cadence.[10] On these extended levels the distinction between the metric and rhythmic is less rewarding, analytically, than the study of such large-scale structural up- and downbeat articulations and the means by which they are effected.

Rhythmic Definition by Harmonic Progression

While on lower levels articulations are integrated and to some extent determined by metric features, this is not the case on macrolevels. On these broad planes periodic definition of strong and weak—upbeat and downbeat—is determined by harmony or, more precisely, by harmonic progression. Thus the temporal—in this case, the rhythmic—is determined and delineated by features not of its own domain.

Structural downbeats on these macrolevels effect a powerful coordination of line and harmony. Of the two elements, harmony seems the definitive one. It would be impossible to effect cadence, closure, downbeat, without the working of harmony, whereas line—for example, phrase endings—may extend beyond these downbeat points. Line could, conceivably, even be extracted from the compositional mix without destroying the sense of resolution, stability, emphasis—in short, of downbeat—that harmony creates.

Further coordinated with harmonic articulation at structural downbeats is weight—weight effected through dynamics, texture, timbre, and nuance. These are secondary features, however; from a structural point of view, they are ornamental features of emphasis. While they add to the power of articulation provided by harmonic syntax, they are at the same time expendable; hypothetically they could be removed without destroying the sense of downbeat. Often, in fact, structural downbeats occur without the aid of such embellishments—articulations gentle in character, soft in dynamic, untouched by agogic emphasis, yet with no loss in clarity or force as downbeats.[11]

If harmonic progression defines large-scale rhythm, what harmonic principle determines rhythmic strong-weak pulses on these broad levels? It is the principle of instability-stability, which might otherwise be characterized as tension-repose, or tension-resolution. Harmonic stability, in other words, is downbeat-oriented; instability, upbeat-oriented. Put more fully, those exact points where harmonic stability is established also articulate rhythmic downbeats.

Downbeats, however, are not necessarily points in time only. On these large levels they endure beyond their point of articulation until giving way—via the same principle of stability-instability—to upbeats. Upbeats likewise extend beyond temporal points alone. They embody essentially a crescendo of musical energy, whose length and degree of intensity depend upon context, but whose prime determinant is harmonic instability—from its inception until that moment of its downbeat resolution.

The principle of instability-stability and structural rhythm correlates with physical tension and resolution as an experienced, bodily response to music. Rhythm is if anything a physical sensation—kinesthetically and muscularly felt, in some cases even viscerally experienced. Large-scale rhythmic articulation is often sensed and understood intuitively, even by those who lack the sophistication for more subtle musical perceptions. It reaches beyond the aural to evoke a fundamental and largely physical knowledge.

Such a response is not necessarily simple. We can perceive complex structural articulations simultaneously, even articulations that may be different in nature. These may evoke responses of differing intensity, even of contradictory nature. The arrival at measure 83 in the first movement of the *Eroica* Symphony is a case in point. This is the moment when the transition to the dominant key has been completed, establishing the scene for the second thematic group. The downbeat of measure 83 is the point of resolution of the long preceding V of V progression, the B♭ harmony established here effecting a powerful structural downbeat on the first beat of the measure.

This is a downbeat of some enduring stability: B♭ prevails as a local harmony for several measures and remains as a tonal region for a substantial time. Within measure 83, however, the initial theme of the second group begins, an upbeat-oriented phrase whose own downbeat does not occur until its fourth measure. Thus measures 83 ff. are perceived on two contradictory levels.

Rhythmic stability and instability are relative values. Their definition by means of harmonic context places them in continually different perspectives. Thus, while tonic harmony is obviously the most stable of possibilities, I_6 is less stable than I_3^5, and I_4^6 is dominant-oriented and relatively unstable. I is more stable than V and secondary dominants, yet on some levels V—as secondary key center within large-scale harmonic schemes—serves as a point of stability (or relative stability) for harmonies focused around it.

Some musical examples can illustrate these principles.

(1) Consider Mozart's C Major Piano Sonata, K. 545, first movement. Viewed from a middle-ground level, a structural downbeat beyond the opening measure does not occur until measure 11, where V is reached (Ex. 8). Moreover, the first structural upbeat on this level is not initiated until measure 9, the transition toward V, where ii_6 introduces rhythmic-harmonic instability. The first eight measures are downbeat-oriented; their harmonic activity is local and does not disturb the primacy of the downbeat initially established by I.

Note that although a downbeat is established at the cadence (measure 11), the chromatic accompaniment figure in measure 13 leads to a less stable local downbeat (V_6) in measure 14, which launches the second group. (Also note, on a local level, that measures 5–8, for all their surface activity, are essentially a rhythmic and harmonic expansion of measures 3–4, and are thus structurally stable.)

(2) The opening theme of the *Eroica* Symphony, first movement, covers a 12-measure period (really 13 measures, though the cadence at measure 13 is an elision, see Ex. 36). Of this period, the first four measures constitute a prolonged structural downbeat; the following measures, until the final one, a long upbeat.

Harmony delineates this distinction. The opening four measures are stable—a prolongation of the tonic triad. The fifth measure of the theme introduces the C♯, a pitch

Ex. 8. Mozart: *Piano Sonata in C Major,* **K.545, first movement**

measure: 1   3   4   5   8   9   11   13   14

                                                                      ii₆   V   V₆

↓   Point of establishment of structural downbeat

↱   Point of initiation of structural upbeat

with implications for the entire movement. The dissonant, unstable C♯ turns the rest of the phrase into a long upbeat that lasts until the tonic resolution at the cadence. (The D at the end of measure 4 can be viewed as part of this upbeat; or it can be heard—prior to the C♯ that ensues—as a passing tone of limited harmonic implication.)

(3) Brahms's Second Symphony, first movement, plays upon rhythmic ambiguity as a major structural premise. Ambiguity arises in the opening two measures, where it is unclear which measure is upbeat and which downbeat. The question recurs throughout the opening phrases of the work and is not resolved therein. The only true resolution is found by viewing the music on a broader level—that beyond hypermeasure. It then becomes clear that the first 43 measures of the movement constitute a great structural upbeat, resolving to the first true structural downbeat at measure 44.

The criterion for this view is the unstable harmonic quality of these 43 measures, as defined by the bass line (Ex. 9 diagram). Harmony and bass are dominant-focused from the beginning of the movement. Thus the D of the opening measure is a local tonic only. Structurally it is an upbeat to the establishment of the dominant bass in measure 2. The four measures on a bass of D (measures 5–8) present D not as a stable tonic, but as a passing phase of a dominant-oriented A–D–E–A bass progression (the bass notes are also chord roots), the last A continuing as a dominant pedal until measure 44.

As the first structural downbeat in the piece, measure 44 is thus the first moment of structural accent as well. Several musical forces combine to intensify this event: (a) the heavier orchestral texture at this point; (b) the greater dynamic weight created by this texture (*p* at measure 44 is greater than *p* in measure 1 in terms of decibels, or absolute—as well as psychological—loud-soft); (c) the two-measure local upbeat before measure 44, an expansion of the opening motive; (d) the expanded phrasing of the original horn motive, now in the tonic, at measure 44. (The relation of this violin 1 passage to the horn motive—and to the opening motive of the piece—is explicit in the recapitulation, where the two themes are played together [measure 302]).

Ex. 9. Brahms: *Symphony No. 2 in D Major,* **first movement**

(4) The opening 22 measures of Mozart's Symphony No. 40, first movement, illustrate virtually all that has been established in the foregoing discussion of rhythm: hypermeasure-phrase, their coordination and conflict; structural up- and downbeat; stress; feminine harmonic progression. These features are in fact critical for shaping these measures properly in performance.

Consider the following, in connection with Ex. 10. Hypermeasures and their metrical strong-weak accents follow the normal duple pattern for the opening eight measures, as indicated by the solid-line brackets. Phrases (indicated by large slurs above the music) coordinate with hypermeasures (indicated by brackets below the music) in the opening measures. The strong-weak accents of both fall together, though the phrase beginnings and endings do not match those of hypermeasures. Conflicts between phrase and metric accents develop by measure 9, to be discussed shortly.

Ex. 10. Mozart: *Symphony No. 40 in G Minor,* **K.550, first movement**

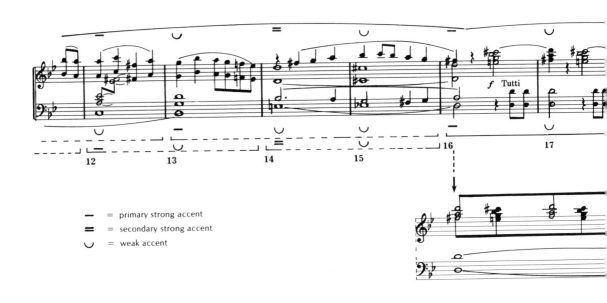

— = primary strong accent
= = secondary strong accent
∪ = weak accent

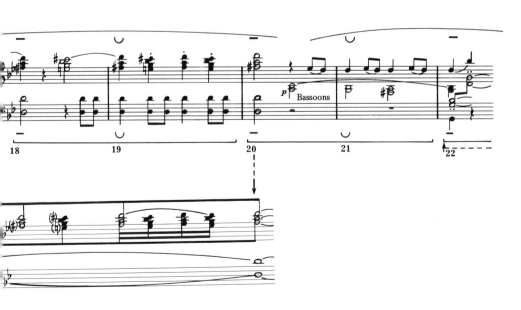

The two-measure hypermeasure pattern is established from the outset since the first two measures act as an upbeat. Thus the first downbeat, structurally, falls upon the third measure. On the face of it there is nothing to establish this point, as the music begins on a root-position tonic chord—in other words, upon ultimate stability. Why, then, should the third measure be strong (downbeat) and the first two upbeat?

The answer lies not in these first four measures, but in the subsequent statements of this opening theme, as in measures 20, 103, 114, 164 (the recapitulation), 183, and 285 (coda). In all these cases the opening section of the motive (♪♪|♪ ♪♪ ♪ ♪♪) is harmonized on the dominant, the following ♪ ♪ 𝄽 falling on the tonic and thereby receiving a downbeat accent.

Accentual weight, therefore, must be different between the downbeats of measures 1 and 3. Measure 3 needs the emphasis of a structural downbeat. Measure 1, a metric accent only, poses a difficult nuance to effect: it needs sufficient weight to propel the music into motion; yet as it also initiates the phrase upbeat, it must be lighter than the downbeat pulse that follows in measure 3.

On the level of hypermeasure and phrase, conflicts begin by measure 9 with cross-accents between the metric and rhythmic domains. The third phrase, which begins with a downbeat (measure 10), is feminine, its dominant harmony falling upon the strong pulse. The prevalent phrasing pattern of ◡ — accents is thus altered by adjacent strong measures 9 and 10. Several things mark measure 10 as strong: the change of rhythm, texture, and timbre in the bass from the preceding measures; the more extended rhythm of the new melody itself.

The metric and rhythmic conflict engendered in measures 9–10 persists through the following measures. The extension of the new motive of measure 10 generates the first harmonic instability great enough to create a structural upbeat, one that persists until the downbeat on V at measure 16. This instability begins in measure 11, with i being replaced by less stable i_6; it grows progressively, the upbeat tension maximized by measures 14–15. So powerful are these tensions of phrase that they force the extension of hypermeasure periods beyond their duple pattern and lessen the weight of metric accents in measures 9–15.

Weight and texture contribute to the downbeat force of measure 16. The two countermelodies introduced in measure 14 not only add textural weight (the upper one is scored over three octaves) but enter on highly unstable harmony, their resolution at measure 16 intensifying the power of the downbeat.

Measures 16–20 provide the only *forte* in the music so far. Their dynamic is not a structural one, however; nor is the emphasis they give to the diminished chord—the first tutti of the piece—structural. All emphases in these measures are stresses. Likewise the syncopation effect created by these chords is a surface event and in a structural sense is actually illusory. For the passage is no more than a four-measure establishment of the newly arrived dominant; the V chords on each downbeat are rhythmically stronger than the more dissonant and more prominent chords that precede them. This is shown in the reduction of this phrase as seen below measures 16–20.

Finally, if viewed on an *Ursatz* level, the entire 22 measures of the opening constitute no more than a local prolongation of the tonic; the initial downbeat of measure 3 prevails. In long-range terms, the first change to a structural upbeat occurs in measure 24, when the harmony truly begins its inflection away from the tonic.

The theoretical framework so far developed for tonal rhythm can be summarized as follows:

1. Time has been seen as an intangible continuum that depends upon tangible (sonic) factors for its demarcation. Within this basically contradictory condition music must function.

2. The experience of time is dual in aspect (chronometric/integral), the features of each aspect being complementary, for example, beat-pulse, measure-motive. The two poles are continually in coordinate or conflicting relationship.

3. Time in music is structured upon levels of differing span, fulfilling foreground-to-background roles similar to Schenker's concepts of line and harmony.

4. Emphasis, by which time is demarcated, falls into two classes—structural and ornamental. Structural emphasis is accent, operative in both metric and rhythmic domains. Ornamental emphasis encompasses a variety of types, such as stress, agogics, articulations.

The criteria by which accent (structural emphasis) can be determined vary, dependent upon the level on which accent functions: (a) On the level of measure-motive, metric accent is the prime factor in both metric and rhythmic realms. (b) Criteria for the level of hypermeasure-phrase lie within a mix of such elements as harmonic progression, metric accent, and accents prevalent in repeated patterns. Individual contexts determine which of these may be paramount. Where phrases extend in length beyond normative periods, rhythmic factors are prime. (c) On the broader levels of periodization, harmonic progression, with its effect of stability-instability, is the major determinant of structural down- and upbeats. Metric accent is of little consequence on these levels.

As just mentioned, accent constitutes structural emphasis, while stress and other ornamental emphases are surface matters. Within the framework of structural accents, ornamental emphases are projected in numerous ways. Many are inflected, emanating from features of theme, such as:

Contour (registral extremes of linear shapes)
Pattern (emphases created by prominent features such as contour extremes, rhythmic groupings)
Articulation and stress (features such as sfz , rf , sfp , $\cdot$, $>$, $\blacktriangledown$. These may underline or may emanate from properties of phrase, or they may be implanted upon phrase details.)
Dynamics, texture

Ornamental emphases may or may not coordinate with rhythmic/metric accents. In either case they are heard as local events that do not affect large-scale structure. To say that an emphasis is ornamental is not to diminish its musical importance but to classify its function. Nonstructural emphases are obviously vital to musical foreground, as is the continual crossplay between them and structural accents.

RHYTHMIC SHAPE

Rhythmic-metric shape contributes to musical unity in various ways, depending upon the level of structure considered. On large-scale levels, greatest interest lies in the articulation of periods through structural up- and downbeat patterns, and in the control of tension and resolution that generates these patterns. On lesser levels rhythmic shape as embodied in motive, as well as in rhythmic up- and downbeat patterns of phrase, is relevant.

Frequently, different themes within a work embody not only similar pitch shapes, but similar rhythmic shapes. This is clear in the first-movement studies of Haydn's Symphony No. 104, Beethoven's *Eroica* Symphony, and Brahms's Second Symphony, which follow. Beethoven's Eighth Symphony, first movement (Ex. 11), is another example, the themes reflecting variation and transformation of rhythmic patterns basic to the original motive, at times altered by metric shift (see measures 12, 37, 41, 52).[12] The pattern treated this way, a segment of the opening theme, is exploited by further metric shift in the development section (see measure 168).[13]

One of the most extensive uses of reiterative rhythmic pattern in Mozart lies in the slow movement of the C Major Piano Sonata, K. 330, shown in Ex. 12. In virtually every measure of this movement the rhythmic figure ♪♪♪ | ♩· serves as a background, underlying the shapes of all motives. The three-note upbeat pattern (indicated by ⌢) in the example) is usually heard undisguised, or in the slightest of variants. The ♩· downbeat, on the other hand (indicated ⌐), is only heard as such in the middle section of the movement and in the coda. In its other appearances it is disguised by embellishments. All of these, as in the opening phrase, clearly fit within the underlying downbeat pattern.

The background is omnipresent, absent only at the cadences, where the demands of closure result in a different pattern (see double brackets). Here, too, the music is subtly unified. The rhythmic pattern of the cadences themselves—in melodic lines and in harmonic rhythm—is similar, though different from the ground rhythm that controls the rest of the piece:

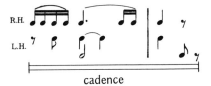

cadence

Mozart's D Major Quintet has a further subtlety (Ex. 13). In rhythm and meter the opening motives of the introductory Larghetto and of the Allegro are virtually identical, even to the extent of the turn and trill figures. The different tempi, of course, make the second motive in effect a diminution of the first. More interesting, however, is the shift in pitch between the two figures by one scale degree. This creates inverse harmonic contexts and inflected accents for the two figures and disguises the fact that they are virtually identical in rhythmic shape.

Ex. 11. Beethoven: *Symphony No. 8 in F Major,* **first movement**

Ex. 12. Mozart: *Piano Sonata in C Major,* **K.330, second movement**

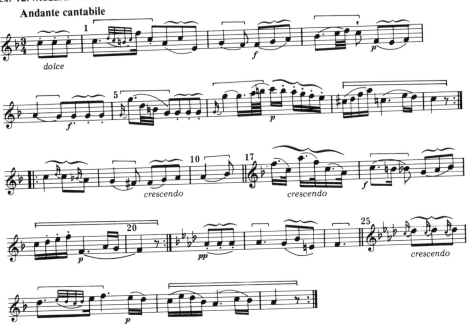

Ex. 13. Mozart: *String Quintet in D Major,* **K.593, first movement**

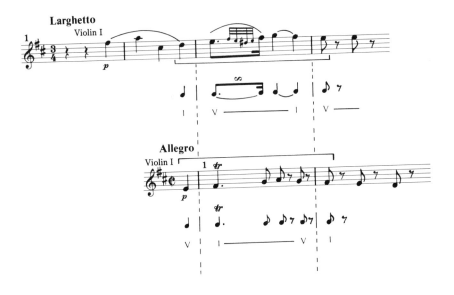

This last example raises the question whether rhythmic shape as an element of theme is autonomous to any significant extent. Can it be perceived as motive in itself, divorced from the contours and harmonies of pitch with which rhythm is usually heard?

Our perception of music seems strongly if not prevalently influenced by pitch and the structures of pitch, such as line and harmony, and less oriented toward purely rhythmic structures. It is not clear whether this is an inborn aspect of perception or a result of conditioned modes of perception and their reinforcement through Western musical training.

Certainly rhythm is a prime factor of shape, indeed of our perception of shape. The same pitch contours, in fact, altered greatly in rhythmic shape may not even register as related in pitch. Moreover, in many works an important motive will appear in guises in which pitch contour and harmonic context are different from the original, where in fact rhythm is the only constant element of the shape. Perhaps the most famous example of this occurs in the first movement of Beethoven's Fifth Symphony, where the statement of its motive

is later heard all upon one note

—the rhythm alone retained.

It was established earlier that pattern correlation and repetition are factors for unity and coherence. These relationships are found among rhythmic shapes of themes, as just shown, as well as pitch shapes. They make a case for rhythmic autonomy, or semiautonomy, perhaps, as a fact of cognition.

TEMPO

In the smallest practical dimensions—pulse or beat—by which the passage of time is paced and controlled, the integral and the chronometric aspects of time in music are intrinsically in conflict. The terms "pulse" and "beat" themselves are indicative of this. Pulse is indigenous to the inner tensions of musical articulation, at times implied, more often explicitly stated. It is strikingly akin, as mentioned earlier, to pulse as we experience it within the human body—in heartbeat, pant, sigh, laugh, hiccup, erotic surge, muscular contraction—all actions capable of degrees of tension. Beat, on the other hand, is mechanical—the given tap of foot, baton, metronome—a precise, exact indication of temporal passage, little qualified by musical implications and thus capable of infinite extension. While temporal pace (tempo) can be precisely and mechanically measured, it is rarely felt within musical experience or context with this metronomic precision.[14]

Pulse in music is intimately related to articulation and is subject to the slight chronometric distortions associated with phrasing. These contractions and expansions are miniscule, expressible in small fractions of a beat, yet sensed. Good performance demands a control of these subtle temporal conflicts so that deviations in pulse are confined within broader groups of chronometric beats, the two domains maintaining constancy over large musical spans.

Articulation greatly affects the perception of pulse in its relation to beat. Pulse and beat may exist in congruence, devoid of conflict, in music such as a march, where the articulation is precise, accented, and quickly attacked. On the other hand, notes with characteristics like the following will imply or suggest pulse more by inflection than by direct articulation (Ex. 14–16). In such cases the exact moment when the beat is announced may be late or even uncertain. Yet the psychological sense of pulse remains, communicated by subtle, secondary musical elements such as timbre and intensity, operating within the overall dynamic "corona" of a note.

Ex. 14. Haydn: *Symphony No. 100 in G Major,* **first movement**

Ex. 15. Mahler: *Symphony No. 5,* **II, 3., Scherzo**

Ex. 16. Weber: Overture to *Der Freischütz*

The opening measure of Webers' Overture to *Der Freischütz* is an extreme example of this. It is a measure rhythmically undifferentiated (one sustained note), yet inflected in pulse by the steady crescendo from **pp** to **f** at the next measure, when the second note is announced. Well-executed, the phrase implies accurately the coming statement of the C in the second measure, its anticipation gauged through the inflection of the crescendo.

This continual conflict and pull between the poles of pulse and beat, between integral, psychological time as embodied in phrase and mechanistic chronometric time, is in itself generative of musical motion. It is one of the most direct and accessible sources of excitement in performance—most evident in jazz, in fact a source of its "swing," and in numerous subtle ways present in the performance of classic-romantic music. *Tempo rubato,* which Chopin and later romantic composers made a major feature of their music, is, if anything, an extension or exaggeration of this principle carried out over a longer time span than single beats or pulses.

Tempo, speed of pulse, is not the absolute quantity that chronometric designation would make it appear. In practice it exists within a narrow range of oscillation, a property that, again, has roots in the psychological quality of musical time. Likewise, an "ideal tempo" is rarely absolute. With the same individual it will vary at different times, dependent upon bodily and/or psychological states, or even upon external physical conditions such as hall acoustics, not to mention the considerable physical and psychological discrepancies created by the tuning frequency (pitch) of instruments. (A at 440 c.p.s. is a different musical phenomenon from A=444 or A=436.)

Thus a tempo designated as M.M. 80 may more truly function over the course of a movement within a range of 80–84, or perhaps even 80–88. Such an oscillation from slower to faster speed in the first case represents an increase of 4/84 (1/21) of a beat, or approximately 1/28 of a second; in the latter case, 8/88 (1/11) of a beat, or approximately 1/15 of a second. Similarly, a tempo at M.M. 60, ranging in performance from 60–64 or 60–66, would represent an increase from the slower limit of 1/16 to that of 1/11 of a beat.

These discrete differences in speed are within perceptible limits. Their musical significance, however, depends upon stylistic and contextual determinants. Within some styles of contemporary music, particularly electronic music, the differences could be important.[15] Within classic-romantic style, they represent virtually no change of tempo. One has only to "solfege out" the slice of time represented by this oscillation to recognize how small a deduction of beat lengths these represent.

Quantities of time as small as these seem not to have been within the temporal conception of the classic-romantic era, as witness the fact that whenever notation like the above (64th or 32nd notes) appears in this literature, it is in slow tempos in which the unit of beat is the eighth note, not the quarter note. Such minute oscillations, particularly over the long course of complete movements or entire works, do not disturb the psychological integrity of a prevalent tempo. If there are discrepancies between the extremes of these ranges, they lie only in the domain of absolute, mechanical time. This would seem to be the point of Beethoven's remark, reported by Schindler, that his music demanded changes of tempo, but "mainly perceptible only to the sensitive ear."[16]

The domains of mechanical and psychological time are easily confused in discussing tempo since designations, if given as metronomic and especially if indicated by the composer himself, have about them an authority that would seem to embrace all aspects of pace. Yet a welter of questions lies behind such designations. How did the composer determine the marking? Did he sing through the entire movement or scan the opening phrases alone? Does the marking represent a mean tempo, settling between any oscillations? Did the tempo please when restudied over many different days (and mental and physical states)? Was the marking tested so?

These points are germane to an understanding of the wider role played by tempo in providing unity in classic-romantic music. The most notable property of tempo in this wider role is the maintenance of a constant pulse speed, both within movements bearing sections of differing tempos (such as the overture or classical introduction and subsequent Allegro in sonata form) and within movements of single tempo; and further, among the different movements of a multimovement work. By this means, the process of compositional unfolding is regulated under an overall temporal umbrella, all else in the music serving in a sense as functions of a steady forward motion.

Continuity of pulse and proportional notation, by which that continuity is expressed, were subjects much discussed in classical and preclassical times. Arthur Mendel has indicated in several articles their role in the performance of Bach and earlier music;[17]

Neal Zaslaw gives an extensive picture of this interest in the eighteenth and nineteenth centuries, regarding both tempo and its manner of notation.[18] Johann Quantz, in his treatise on playing the flute, implies that continuity of a singular pulse was a prevalent belief. He states that basic tempo was "the pulse beat at the hand of a healthy person," which would seem in the neighborhood of 80 beats per minute. He then tells us that basic tempos were:

Allegro assai (♩)

Allegretto (♪)

Adagio cantabile (♫)

Adagio assai (♫)

If each of these observed a pulse of about M.M. 80, the relationship of tempos is implicit.[19]

Relatively less attention in print was paid to this subject in the nineteenth century vis-à-vis the music of its own time, though one gets the impression from indirect evidence that awareness of this sense of continuity was something of an unspoken tradition among better musicians of the time. How far into the music of the nineteenth century the practice continued is debatable. Cone feels it became less and less a factor with romantic composers, and was virtually nonexistent with Tchaikovsky.[20] Yet it is demonstrable with Brahms; I would suggest even with some of Tchaikovsky (witness the Fourth Symphony); with Mahler; also with Moussorgsky and Debussy. Reinhold Brinkmann indicates that Schoenberg was aware of it (this is confirmed by informal remarks to me by members of Schoenberg's Viennese and Berlin circles) and that Mahler, in his musical direction of Mozart operas, sought unity through this means.[21] The subject is very much alive today.

Organic unity through continuous pulse is a psychological aspect of musical time—relevant only in the most superficial way, in terms of beat measurement, to mechanical time. Within the course of a movement, lasting perhaps 5 to 8 minutes, or a work, lasting 20 to 30 minutes, minute oscillations within a small tempo range are not of musical consequence. What *is* of consequence is the psychological projection of temporal continuity and identity, especially as it relates movements to one another. Differing musical character, articulation, gesture, local focus of pulse—all functioning under the same temporal concept—by their foreground differences tend to disguise or obscure this larger background control. Yet just as within the domains of pitch and rhythm a variety of ideas has been seen to emanate from one controlling concept, so within tempo the same process is manifest.

Continuity of pulse within a movement of single prevailing tempo is a commonly used means of developing forward drive, cumulative intensity, and other coordinative features of growth. Within the overall temporal umbrella provided by a steady pulse, the inner units of subpulses felt as foreground grow proportionately smaller, usually by ratios of 2:1, as the music progresses.[22]

Continuous relations of tempo also unite classic-romantic movements of slow introductions followed by an allegro section. This is true of both the overture and the large movement, which may be part of a greater, multimovement work. Illustrations will be found in Examples 17–21, together with suggested metronome markings. (Note: In the final Maestoso of the Academic Festival Overture, Brahms indicates ⟵ ♩ = ♪ ⟶. The equivalent here is ⟵ ♩ = ♩ ⟶. The other tempo relationships are implicit in the score.)

Ex. 17. Mozart: Overture to *The Magic Flute*

Ex. 18. Rossini: Overture to *An Italian Girl in Algiers*

Ex. 19. Haydn: *Symphony No. 100 in G Major,* **first movement**

Ex. 20. Beethoven: Overture to *Prometheus*

Ex. 21. Brahms: *Academic Festival Overture*

An example of unified tempo among different movements of a multimovement work is found in Ex. 22, Mozart's Piano Sonata in C Major, K. 309.

Ex. 22. Mozart: *Piano Sonata in C Major,* **K.309**

A word about ratio is relevant at this point. Tempo relationships that can be characterized by ratios of 1:2:4:8 are fundamentally under a 1:1 ratio. A "master pulse" is operative, essentially unchanged among all movements, though the metric structure and/or practical performance problems of individual movements may require a foreground pulse smaller or larger than the master pulse.

Not all intermovement tempo correlations exist in simple 1:1 (or 1:2) ratios, however. Ratios of 2:3, or their inverse 3:2, are common, particularly where minuet movements are involved. Triple meter with its asymmetry easily generates such phenomena as syncopation and hemiola. The minuet, with its combination of triple meter, moderate tempo, and often *galant* style, seemed to stimulate these metrical interplays in the classical ear. What is more, to a striking degree the increase or decrease of pulse by means of 2:3 or 3:2 ratio, especially to or from a minuet, emanates from some rhythmic feature of motive in the various movements involved, and often serves to highlight this motivic feature. Frequently, too, a change in pulse speed will in later movements return to the original tempo by means of the inverse ratio, creating a symmetry of tempo design.

Ratios of 3:4 seem to have been less common, though they are found, often arising, as in 2:3 ratios, from motivic associations, as in the *Haydn Variations* of Brahms, discussed in Ex. 27.

Ex. 23–26 show several cases in Mozart and Haydn where the pulse in minuet movements increases by ratio of 2:3 from preceding movements. In all cases rhythmic aspects of the motives play a prominent role in these proportions. In Mozart's Symphony No. 40, the syncopation in the first measure of the minuet, so important to the rhythmic life of this theme, falls on the beat where the prevalent pulse from the previous movement would be felt. The cross-rhythm here functions not only in terms of motive structure internal to the movement, but across movements as well. Likewise in the Mozart String Quartet, K. 428 (Ex. 24), the "thrown" figure on the third beat of the minuet falls where the prevalent beat of the previous movement is felt.[23] The minuet in the Haydn Symphony No. 104 (Ex. 25) with its *sforzandi* fits the same description. (Note also that the Haydn movements do not correlate in tempo as precisely as those of Mozart; they require a broader range of oscillation—48–56, or 15 percent of a beat—to fit together. This is characteristic of Haydn, whose tempi are not as unified as Mozart's.)

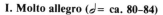

Ex. 23. Mozart: *Symphony No. 40 in G Minor,* **K.550**

Ex. 24. Mozart: *String Quartet in E flat Major,* **K.428**

Ex. 25. Haydn: *Symphony No. 104 in D Major*

Ex. 26. Mozart: *Violin Concerto in G Major,* **K.216**

The Mozart Violin Concerto in G Major, K. 216, in Ex. 26 bases its tempo inter-relations upon accompaniment rhythms rather than foreground melodies. These rhythms are shown below the staff in the example. As they indicate, the 2:3 increment in pulse from the first to the second movement stems from the constant subpulse in the eighth and triplet figures in inner voices. By this same rhythmic figure, the second and third movements maintain a constant 1:1 ratio. This work, particularly in its first two movements, is a striking example of the way musical character, phrasing, articulation, gesture—as foreground qualities of each movement—mask the metrical continuity of the background pulse.

A test of the validity of the continuous-pulse lies in the following question: By establishing a range of tempo oscillation rather than a fixed absolute tempo, and by further suggesting 2:3 and 3:4 tempo ratios as well as simple 1:1 or 1:2 ratios, is a system established where any tempo can be related to any other tempo by these ratios, since the extremes of each range approach closely to each other? For example, is the faster end of the 60–66 range close enough to the slower end of the 80–88 range (4:3 ratio) to fit into this scheme any tempo lying in between? Is this a kind of tempo "fudging," making these ratios meaningless because they are all-inclusive?

The argument does not convince, as seen below, where its elements are shown graphically. Allowing a range of oscillation of approximately 5–9 percent of a second (1/21 to 1/11 of a beat), and setting up a scale from 60–66 through 80–88 to 120–132 (4:3 and 3:2 accelerations in tempo, effecting an overall increment of 60–66:120–132, or 2:1), the difference between the adjacent extremes of range in 4:3 ratio are seen to be 17.5 percent of the preceding beat; in 3:2 ratio, 26.7 percent of the preceding beat. These are significant and easily perceptible differences. Thus, many tempi lying within these interstices would be heard as different—they would not fit into the ranges of proportionate relations.[24]

Tempo range of oscillation ca. 5–9% (1/21–1/11 of beat)
Beat in all instances represented by metronomic indication

Ratio	4	:	3	:	2
Tempo range	60–66		80–88		120–132
Minimum difference in speed between adjacent extremes of proportional tempo ranges		(66–80) 14		(88–120) 32	
Minimum speed difference as proportion of preceding beat		$\dfrac{14}{80} =$ 17.5% of 66		$\dfrac{32}{120} =$ 26.7% of 88	

These percentages of time differences between proportional tempi hold, of course, regardless of the speed of a given initial tempo. It is the ratio, in other words, that is fixed. Obviously the real-time difference in speeds will decrease as these ratios are applied to faster tempos. Indeed a point-of-no-return can be reached where tempi are so fast that the differences between them are hard to perceive. This does not happen in classic-romantic repertoire, however. It is rare to find an operative pulse much greater than about M.M. 160 in this music. Beyond this point the phrase is felt by the larger pulse (80+, instead of 160+), where the rule of proportional tempi is once again significant.

The *Haydn Variations* of Brahms is an example of symmetrical use of proportional tempi whereby a change in speed and a return to the original tempo is achieved by means of a ratio and its inverse. Both 4:3 and 3:2 ratios are used in this manner. In all cases these ratios emanate from rhythmic properties of motives in the adjacent variations involved. The bases for these ratios, in other words, are intrinsic to the music, and are thus heard and felt.

The ratios are also used to create large-scale symmetrical designs of tempo, as the temporal ground plan of the *Haydn* Variations in Ex. 27 reveals. Several sets of tempo symmetries span different segments of the music, extending to its extreme dimensions so that the tempo of the opening theme equals that of the concluding Finale.

Brahms reveals tempo, pulse, and the qualitative feel and flow of musical motion upon different levels and perspectives in this work, particularly in the transitions between variations. Perhaps the most subtle and complex example of this is the transition between variations VI–VII. The Grazioso character of variation VII flows naturally if the pulse is felt by the dotted quarter note—a slow tempo of M.M. 33–36. This pulse is most easily established if the preceding Vivace variation (VI) is felt at its close by the full measure, rather than by the quarter note that is its foreground pulse. This is so because it is the measure that is extended by half its length through the 2:3 ratio to create the leisurely motion of the dotted quarter that governs the Grazioso. To feel the measure in variation VI, however, is to experience a conflict of character, since the quarter-note pulse, strongly marked, is the dominant quality of motion.

The opening of variation I, by its reiterated quarter notes, also imposes a sense of differing perspectives of pulse, tempo, and motion. The repeated notes make clear the 2:1 diminution of the chords that close the preceding theme. To feel this, the variation must be perceived by its foreground pulse of quarter notes. If variation I is felt by the half note,—in other words by the pulse of the previous section, which is here a background pulse—the long line of the violin theme with its flowing character is established virtually automatically.

Proportion plays a critical role in the transition between variations II–III. The 4:3 ratio operative here is found in the ♩. ♩ ♪ ⁷ motive of variation II on two levels (see bottom line of Ex. 27). The full motive of variation II occupies three-fourths of the measure, establishing by this proportion the quarter-note pulse of the theme, with its long and flowing line, in the following variation. In a smaller perspective, the inner proportions of the dotted motive ♩. ♩ ♪ ⁷ as indicated by brackets, occupy three-fourths of the foreground quarter-note beat and serve thereby to set up the eighth-note subpulse of the bass line in the opening of variation III.

The inverse ratio of 3:4 returns the music to the original tempo at variation VI. The means here are simpler and easily perceived: namely, a constant subpulse, retained

Ex. 27. Brahms: *Variations on a Theme by Joseph Haydn*

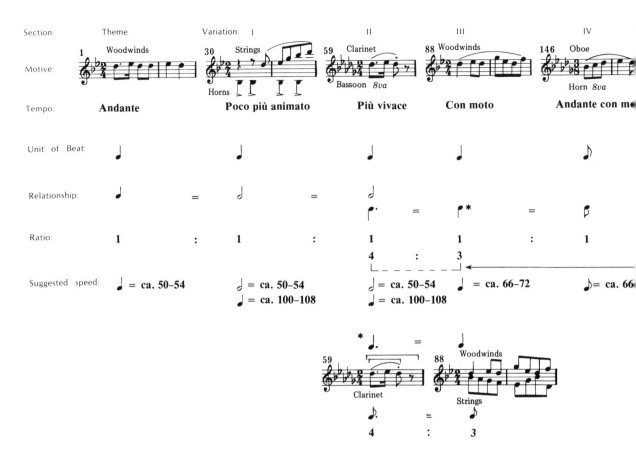

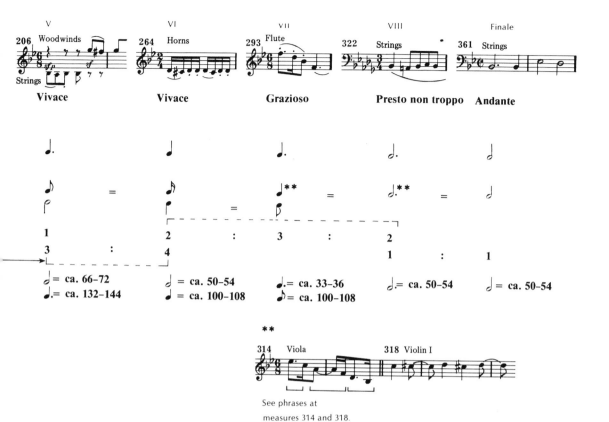

See phrases at
measures 314 and 318.

Duration

in both variations V and VI. And as shown on the bottom of Ex. 27, the tempo of variation VIII (a reduction via 3:2) is set up by the syncopated figures that close variation VII. The rhythms of these figures occupy two-thirds of the prevalent dotted quarter-note beat in the Grazioso.[25]

The influence of continuous pulse is not uniform among various composers of this period. It is striking how closely integrated in tempo the works of Mozart, Brahms, and Schumann seem to be. With Haydn, the tempi are less closely aligned, though there is a definite sense of relationship.

Beethoven presents yet another problem, with his tempi in general and with the question of continuous pulse as well. The debates about Beethoven's tempi and metronome markings are not ended yet. Nor are his works as unified by continuous pulse as those of other composers of his time. Yet his metronome markings often indicate his perception that certain movements within a work were indeed so correlated. At times the markings suggest two such tempi operating throughout a piece, certain movements corresponding to each.

While the principle of continuous pulse gives no solution to Beethoven tempi, it can be useful in working out problematic tempo questions. The First Symphony and Second Symphony, considered in Ex. 28 and 29, are cases in point. Some of Beethoven's metronome markings here indicate tempi that appear too fast either for practicality or for projection of what seems the music's proper sense of gesture—a frequent problem with these markings.

Actually these are general questions, applicable to all matters of uncertain tempo. They divide into four issues: (1) Are the markings in fact those of the composer? (2) Assuming they are, was the composer's metronome accurate? (3) Assuming it was, must we accept these tempi for performance, if they seem too fast for: (a) proper musical projection of character and gesture; (b) overcoming practical performance problems, such as articulations and hall acoustics? (4) Assuming a "no" decision to (3), can we then turn to other general tempo ranges that have evolved in the performance tradition of the particular work?

There are rarely satisfactory bases for answering any of these questions. The first two demand musicological evidence that may or may not be at hand, accurate, or reliable. The third is conjectural. As for tradition and question (4), there is much to respect in those aspects of tradition that can be substantiated through credible evidence. Rules for the execution of ornaments; articulation, as it was affected by physical characteristics of older instruments—concerns like these come under such a category. The performance traditions of particular works are another matter. One famous musician's dictum that "tradition is *Schlamperei*" may have seemed a bit harsh, but his colleague's modification that "tradition is the last bad performance" has behind it, unfortunately, too much truth to be ignored.

At best, tradition in these matters is a shaky criterion. Internal evidence ultimately forms the most solid basis for judging these problems, particularly where the judgments must stand up under practical performance situations and must establish conceptual perspectives as well. The concept of temporal continuity (continuous pulse) offers at the least a systematic handle on the problem.

Ex. 28 poses the tempo problems of the Beethoven First Symphony in two ways. Beethoven's tempo and metronome markings are given on one line, together with comments upon tempi that seem too fast. On the line below, a different solution is worked out based upon continuous pulse.

The diagrams (Ex. 28) point out disparities built into the tempo markings. For one, Beethoven's *Adagio molto* in the first movement is faster (88) than his plain *Adagio* in the fourth movement (63). Another is that the two *Allegro molto e vivace* markings common to the third and fourth movements are curiously divergent in speed by a wide margin (108 and 88—ca. 23 percent). Third, tempi in three of the four movements, taken at the given M.M. speeds, seem too fast, for the reasons indicated.

The suggested solution alleviates some of the problems. The similar tempo markings of the third and fourth movements (*Allegro molto e vivace*) achieve congruity. (Nothing, of course, can reconcile the contradictions between the two *Adagio* markings.) Movements which in the original seem too fast may work better in the unified-pulse tempo. Note also that the suggested tempo range of 80–88 embraces Beethoven's initial pace. Further, the 2:3 ratio for the Andante achieves Beethoven's tempo for this movement also, and serves as well, by its quarter-note relationship with the prevailing pulse, to highlight the motivic fourth, important as a shape to the entire work.

The third movement is problematic, possibly not capable of a fully satisfying solution. One question is whether the tempo derived by continuous pulse is too slow. It feels slightly so. On the other hand the tempo marking is Menuetto, not Scherzo. Presumably the terms still had different connotations for Beethoven, though one was evolving toward the other in his hands around the time the First Symphony was written.

Ex. 28. Beethoven: *Symphony No. 1 in C Major*
1) Beethoven's tempi:

I. Adagio molto: Allegro con brio	II. Andante cantabile con moto	III. Menuetto: allegro molto e vivace	IV. Adagio: Allegro molto e vivace
C ♪= 88 **₵** ♩= 112	**3/8** ♪= 120	**3/4** ♩= 108	**2/4** ♪= 63 **2/4** ♩= 88
fast? (especially for melody in mes. 4?)		too fast (breathless?)	too fast (breathless?)

2) Suggested solution

I. ♪ = 80–88	II.	III.	IV.
♪ = ♩ = ♩	=	♩. =	♪ = ♩
	♪= 120–132	♩.= 80–88	♪= 40–44
[2 :	3 :	2]	
		too slow?	

I.   II.   III.   IV.

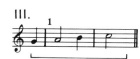

Finally, the unified pulse highlights in each movement the intervallic and rhythmic properties of the head-motive (see bottom line of Ex. 28), in all cases the rhythmic shape—anacrusis-to-downbeat—outlining a perfect fourth.

Beethoven's Second Symphony (considered in Ex. 29) does not present the incongruities of tempo indication found in the First Symphony. The given tempo markings, however, do present performance problems, as suggested, for the first and second movements. The first is rather fast for clear articulation of its rapid notes, and both seem a bit too pressed to allow the musical character and gesture of these movements to be projected. The solution suggested in the example addresses these problems. It also achieves several tempi that are virtually those indicated by Beethoven.[26]

Schumann's Third Symphony, studied in Ex. 30, has some particularly interesting problems connected with its tempi. The given tempo markings bear little significant relationship to one another, with the exception of the first and second movements, and furthermore seem too fast. This appears particularly glaring in the third movement, in character basically a *Lied*, suggesting the more pensive as well as romantic side of Schumann's personality as it is reflected in many of his songs. This character, its reflection in the movement marking *Nicht schnell*, and the pace indicated by ♪ =116 do not fit together. (Even "tradition" has ignored the metronome marking, but this is having both sides of the argument too much one's own way.)

The exact ratio of 3:2 for the first two movements, indicated by Schumann's markings of 66 and 100, is a significant tempo relationship, however. It provides a clue to important structural relations within the work as they affect both temporal and motivic domains.

As the suggested solution to the tempi problems shows, a mean tempo can be found that is not distant from Schumann's opening marking (56–60 instead of 66). The modified overall speed of pulse brings the middle three movements into relationship with one another, retaining Schumann's desired 3:2 ratio between the opening movements,

Ex. 29. Beethoven: *Symphony No. 2 in D Major*

1) Beethoven's tempi:

I. Adagio molto: Allegro con brio	II. Larghetto	III. Scherzo:allegro	IV. Allegro molto
$\frac{3}{4}$ ♪= 84 C ♩= 100	$\frac{3}{8}$ ♪= 92	$\frac{3}{4}$ ♩= 100	¢ ♩= 152
too fast? too fast?	too fast?		

2) **Suggested solution**

I. ♪= 76–84   II.   III.   IV.

♪ = ♩   =   ♪   =   ♩   =   o

[4 : 3]   [3 : 4]

Ratios achieve Beethoven's tempo range   ♩.= 101–112   o= 76–84

♩= 152–168

1) Schumann's tempi:

I. Lebhaft	II. Scherzo sehr mässig	III. Nicht Schnell	IV. Feierlich	V. Lebhaft: Schneller

$\frac{3}{4}$ 𝅗𝅥. = 66 $\frac{3}{4}$ 𝅗𝅥 = 100   **C** ♪ = 116   **C** 𝅗𝅥 = 54   **C** 𝅗𝅥 = 120

too fast?   too fast?   too fast?   too fast?

2) Suggested solution:

I. 𝅗𝅥. = **56–60**   II. 𝅗𝅥 = **84–90**   III. ♪ = **84–90**   IV. ♪= **84–90**

Lebhaft
V. 𝅗𝅥 = **84–90**

𝅘𝅥 = **42–45**

Schneller
𝅗𝅥 = **126–135**

3 : 2   3 : 2

3) Motivic and rhythmic relationships:

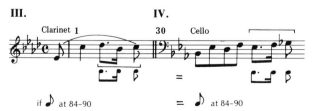

and also provides a tempo for the third movement that is more consistent with its character. The entire symphony achieves a further unity through tempo under this scheme, as the 3:2 ratio by which tempo increased from the opening movement also serves as the means for determining the final pulse in the coda (*Schneller*).

Schumann indicates simply "faster" (*Schneller*) for this coda without providing a precise indication—common practice at the time for such small proportions as a coda. Herein enters one of the more fascinating aspects of the whole temporal ground plan of the work. It involves in its early origins what in the twentieth century has become a widely developed technique of tempo control: metrical modulation. For while the change in tempo at this coda is not precisely indicated by words or explicit mathematical ratios, *heard* features of the structure do in fact constitute built-in determinants (ratio) for the transition.

The 3:2 ratio for accelerated pulse seen earlier in the symphony would seem the logical criterion to use in establishing the last tempo in relation to its predecessor. Schumann in fact incorporates this relationship into the score. The horns at the close of the last movement play, almost as a closing motto, a variant of the symphony's opening theme (note measure 295 and its indicated derivation from measures 1–4), in the process introducing what to this point are the only triplets found in the last movement. The triplets, moreover, themselves emphasize the main points of contour from the original theme through their duple slurs, and it is this proportion of 2/3 of the beat that sets up the new and faster tempo of the coda.

The symphony is thus unified in tempo as well as in motive (shape), the two aspects of the music working in conjunction with each other. The 3:2 ratio of pulse that relates the first and second movements, as well as subsequent movements, is in fact manifested immediately in the first movement. Indeed, Schumann's two metronome markings of 66 and 100 for the movements are but an indicator of this relationship, not its structural embodiment. The relationship inheres motivically in the opening measures of the first movement (measures 1–6), centering about the syncopation on the second note of the melody. The phrase is rhythmically and metrically ambiguous, as it implies both a ♩. pulse in $\frac{3}{4}$ meter and a ♩ pulse in $\frac{3}{2}$. The syncopation focuses upon this ambiguity while also serving to point up the half-note prominence in rhythm which, as 2/3 of the measure-pulse, establishes the 3:2 ratio functional in later movements.

The artistically interesting property of ambiguity is not so much its lack of clarity as the manifold directions in which latent tendencies within its premises may be resolved. Schumann plays upon this property throughout the first movement of the Third Symphony, rarely making clear which metrical conception is the "proper" one (if either, in fact, is), and implying both at different points. Thus by measure 7 the notation reveals the beat as clearly ♩. ($\frac{3}{4}$ with one pulse to the measure); eight measures before letter *A* (Breitkopf & Härtel, original edition) the notation implies $\frac{3}{2}$; while at measure 281 (and many other places in the movement) it implies both possibilities within the same phrase.

Details in the score further confirm the 3:2 ratio between the opening two movements. Note how the rhythmic submotive ♩. ♪ ♩, often heard throughout the first movement, is related to and metrically congruent with a similar submotive within the subsequent movements. The relationship of the two motives is heard in its clearest perspective because of the 3:2 tempo ratio; by means of this ratio both motives are played at the same speed.

Brahms's First Symphony incorporates subtle and sophisticated uses of tempo, particularly of metrical modulation, all based upon a continuous pulse. Ex. 31 shows the temporal ground plan of the four movements, all of which are related by direct 1:1 (or 1:2) ratios. The same relationship holds among several intramovement sections, notably in the first movement between the introduction (*Un poco sostenuto*) and *Allegro*, and in the fourth movement from the *Allegro non troppo* onward. The overall temporal plan, therefore, is essentially conventional in terms of pulse relationships.

What is most interesting is the controlled metrical means by which transitions in tempo (metrical modulation) are effected in other sections of the work. Most notable in this light are the transition (1) from the end of the first movement (end of coda to codetta) to the beginning of the second movement; and (2) similarly, from the end of the third movement (*poco a poco* to coda) to the beginning of the fourth movement to *Allegro non troppo* (Ex. 31).

In these instances (except for the *Adagio–più andante* of the fourth movement, discussed later) Brahms creates, in effect, a built-in ritard of an overall 1:2 ratio by means of the successive ratios 2:3:4. These ratios are achieved by maintaining a constantly steady subpulse within the beat and increasing the duration of the beat by units of 2 to 3 to 4 subpulses in the successively slower sections. (Note that the *unit* of subpulse is changed in its notation as the ritard takes place, going in the second to third movement change from $\flat^2$ to $\flat$ to $\flat$. However its *durational value*—the amount of time this subpulse receives—remains constant.)

An ultimate subtlety concerns the indication *poco a poco*, moving toward *Più tranquillo* in the coda of the third movement. The passage is two measures long, its first measure containing four sixteenth notes to the pulse. By the third measure (the arrival at *Più tranquillo*) the pulse, by means of the 2:3 tempo ratio, contains six sixteenth notes. The *poco a poco* transition thus implies a designed metrical control whereby the pulse of the second measure (and its rhythmic figure) is elongated so that it is played in the space of five sixteenth notes (Ex. 31).

In similar fashion the final tempo transition, the eight-measure *stringendo* leading to the coda of the fourth movement, indicates a metrically controlled modulation of tempo, though the indicators are not as apparent as in the third movement *rallentando* just discussed.

The final *stringendo* (measure 383) effects an ultimate transition of 2:1 ratio (the coda is twice as fast as the preceding *Allegro non troppo*, further confirmed by the ¢ marking). In only the first measure and a half and the last two measures of the *stringendo* are the quarter- and/or half-note pulses clearly defined. The passage in between obscures the pulse through syncopated figures in the violins. From the start of the passage until the two measures before the final tempo, there are in fact four groups of three half notes each, the first of these providing eight subpulses to the half note through the second violin figures. This suggests that the conductor should keep constant the speed of these subpulses and reduce the duration of the subsequent three-half-note groups from 8 to 7, 6, 5, and finally 4 subpulses. The result is a graduated and controlled accelerando of 2:1 overall ratio. Brahms's syncopated figures in these measures reinforce this view; they seem to serve a structural as well as embellishmental role. By reducing the clarity of any internal subpulse, they make more flowing and natural-sounding the reduction of subpulses over this passage. At the same time their rhythmic properties assist forward propulsion of the phrase.

Ex. 31. Brahms: *Symphony No. 1 in C Minor*

Movement and section:	**I. Introduction**		**Codetta**	**II.**	**III.**
Tempo:	**Un poco sostenuto**	**Allegro**	**Meno allegro**	**Andante sostenuto**	**Un poco allegretto e grazioso**

Pulse:

Unit; relation: $\frac{6}{8}$ ♪ = $\frac{6}{8}$ ♩. = $\frac{3}{4}$ ♪ = $\frac{2}{4}$ ♩

Suggested speed: ♪ = 96–104   ♩. = 96–104   ♩ = 48–52   ♩ = 96–1[...]

Large-scale ratios: 1 : 1 : 2 : 1

Tempo transitions:

Ratios: 2 : 3 : 4

Thematic motives: Cello ... Horns / Tympani ... Strings

Constant sub-pulse:
The controlled metrical means: ♩ = ♪ = ♪

Number of sub-pulses per beat: 2   3   4

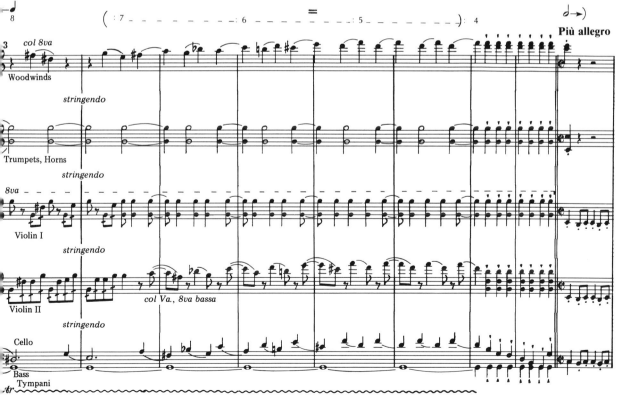

The increase in tempo in the last movement from *Adagio* to *Più andante,* by a ratio of 4:3, (Ex. 31) emanates from rhythmic properties of 4:3 ratio that are prominent among the ideas of the *Adagio.* The increment in speed is actually set by the figures two measures before the change at measure 30. Thus ♪ in the *Adagio* becomes ♩ in the *Più andante.* The timpani roll at this 4:3 change shows what care Brahms gave to small detail in effecting this plan of metrical modulation (see measure 28). Though the strokes across the double-bar line go from 12 to 6, this does not indicate a tempo twice as fast, as a first view might suggest.

Following as it does the abrupt tutti chords, the roll creates the effect of a *rallentando* without the pulse actually changing in duration. This is done by having the timpani play consecutively fewer strokes per beat, reducing the measured strokes by a ratio of 4:3:2 (unmeasured: 16: 12: [8]). Were there no change of tempo to the right of the barline, the strokes at that point would be eight to the beat. However with the tempo increase here (*Più andante*) via a 4:3 ratio, the beat beyond the double bar is three-fourths the duration of the previous beat. Thus what would be eight strokes reduces to $\frac{3}{4}$ X 8, or six strokes.

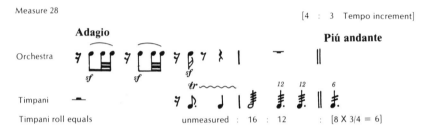

It seems clear that tempo changes by means of metrical modulation were a deliberate aspect of Brahms's musical designs. Further confirmation of this is found in the Second Piano Concerto at the final coda. Here again an increase in pace occurs via a 4:3 ratio, these proportions inhering within rhythms of many themes found in the movement, as well as in figurations of the solo piano part at places like measures 1 and 165 (Ex. 32).

Rhythmic preparation for the tempo reduction is set up in the solo piano 12 measures prior to the coda by grouping the sixteenths in threes (measure 365). The triplet figures that follow in the coda equal the preceding groups of three sixteenths.

The metronome markings (104:138) between these sections further confirm the 4:3 ratio. This is the more interesting since metronome markings are not common in Brahms. Hans Gál, in his editor's remarks on this score in the complete edition of Brahms's works, notes that the metronome markings appear as blue-pencil additions to the original manuscript, apparently added by Brahms after the work was completed and later struck out.[27]

The transition to the coda of the last movement of Brahms's Violin Concerto in D Major involves a 4:3 tempo reduction virtually parallel to that in the Second Piano Concerto. The tempo proportions arise in similar fashion from the principal motive of the movement, in this case: . At the transition,

Allegro giocoso... effecting the 4:3 reduction:

ma ben marcato

Ex. 32. Brahms: *Piano Concerto No. 2 in B flat Major,* **fourth movement**

NOTES

1. Schenker is a curious case in this regard. Rhythm plays at most a minor explicit role in his theory. Yet the concept of musical composing-out or unfolding (*Auskomponierung*), although it is effected through spatial (tonal) structure, is intrinsically a temporal phenomenon.

2. Arthur Komar discusses some of this small and not fully satisfactory literature on pp. 4–6 of his study, *Theory of Suspensions* (Princeton University Press, 1971).

3. It is important to distinguish between the terms "dual" and "duality," which are used here to denote two different varieties of temporal experience, and the term "dualism," which implies a structural division of time. Dualism is not used here, nor is it implied.

Much contemporary thinking about time sees it as a unified phenomenon, rather than a dualism. Time as a unified phenomenon, however, is distinguished by different orders or varieties in our experience of it. These varieties are themselves hierarchic. Chronometric time subsumes several temporalities within a noetic category, while integral time, a different category, corresponds to the unique individual experiences of time. On a higher level, the integral subsumes the chronometric by virtue of its greater interest and richness as temporal experience. These views hold for music, as they do for other areas of experience.

4. The distinction made by Cooper and Meyer between accent and stress is a useful one, incorporated in part here, though these writers do not make the distinction between beat and pulse that is basic to this discussion of rhythm and meter. They note that strong beats are distinguished from weaker ones as a result of *accent*, which is seen as the architectonic designation of a pulse as outstanding in contrast to the pulses that surround it. An accented pulse thus becomes a focal point in relation to which unaccented or less accented pulses are grouped and heard. Accent is further distinguished from *stress*, which is defined as the dynamic intensification of a pulse, whether accented or unaccented.

Accent is thus strong by virtue of structural designation. Stress, on the other hand, is not structural; it is in effect dynamic embellishment of a phrase, a surface phenomenon, contributing to the character of a musical line, and not necessarily in intrinsic relationship with structural accent. See Grosvenor Cooper and Leonard Meyer, *The Rhythmic Structure of Music* (Chicago: University of Chicago Press, 1960), pp. 7–8.

5. Edward T. Cone, *Musical Form and Musical Performance* (New York: Norton, 1968), p. 24.

6. Inflection may be a useful focus in exploring the relationships between music and language, a subject that has interested both musicians and linguists. In their presentation through sound—music by means of performance, language through speech—both media are inflected structures, communicated through graduated intensities of sound. Inflection serves to underscore, to emphasize, to shape some aspects of meaning.

Furthermore, both media are temporal—periodized and rhythmic—their periodic rhythmic structure (as well as other meanings) also imparted through inflection. This inflectional aspect of their communication may be one of the deeper levels of mutuality between the two media.

7. The meaning of agogics has been modified in contemporary usage. It originally pertained to emphases created by prominence of duration within rhythmic pattern. It has also been applied to the heavy-light patterns of poetic feet. In its contemporary usage it refers to the many subtle emphases that may accrue to a musical line by way of contour, articulation, etc.

8. They are not always coordinate, however. Some of the exceptions have become famous places in the literature, as witness the spot in the first movement of Mozart's G Minor Piano Quartet (measures 57 ff.) about which Schoenberg (cf. *Style and Idea* [New York: Philosophical Library, 1950]) and Cone (Communications to the Editor, *Perspectives* 1, no. 2 [Spring 1963]: 206–210), among others, have written.

Cone explains the metrical placement of downbeat in the "wrong" part of the measure as the result of phrase extensions or elisions that shift the "true" measure, though the composer may not have felt the need to change the metric notation (nor might convention allow it). Thus the rhythmic—the articulation of phrase at its point of inception—supersedes the metric in strength.

Chapters 2 and 3 of Cone's *Musical Form* are concerned with problems similar to those discussed here (as is Schoenberg's chapter "Brahms the Progressive," in *Style and Idea*).

9. Cooper and Meyer find a similarity between the patterns of alternating strong and weak pulses in musical rhythm and strong-weak syllabic accents in poetry ($-\cup$, $\cup\cup-$). Cone has amplified and refined this concept. He suggests an initial downbeat (/) going through a weaker period of motion ($\cup$) to a cadential downbeat (\ ), thus extending patterns like $-\cup$ or $\cup-$ to ones of $/\cup\backslash$. Different kinds of downbeats, varied upbeats , feminine cadences (\/) , and elisions further refine patterns into ones like $\wedge/\cup\backslash\backslash/$.

The refinement can continue infinitely; every work presents a qualitatively unique version of these properties. If we can understand the nature of these emphases and evolve criteria for characterizing them structurally and their points of demarcation, we should be able to encounter individual cases. Very likely it is large-scale articulations that will be most valuable to study, for it is on these broad levels that rhythmic structure exerts perhaps the most basic compositional control.

10. Cf. Cone, *Musical Form*, pp. 24 ff. Komar has mapped the slow movement of Beethoven's *Pathetique* Sonata on successive levels of temporal structure. See the Appendix of his *Theory of Suspensions*, pp. 151–161.

11. See, for example, the recapitulation of Mozart's Piano Sonata in F Major, K. 332, first movement.

12. See Alan Walker, *A Study in Musical Analysis* (London: Barrie & Rockliff, 1962), pp. 83–86, for another view of the metric shift with respect to the second theme.

13. Hans Keller, in his studies of Mozart, has found similar rhythmic relationships. See his observations concerning the Piano Concerto in C Major, K. 503 ("K. 503—The Unity of Contrasting Themes and Movements, Part I, *Music Review* 17 [1956]: 48–58); the D Major Quintet, K. 593 ("The Chamber Music," chapter in *The Mozart Companion*, ed. H.C. Robbins Landon and Donald Mitchell [London: Faber & Faber, 1965], p. 133); and the Eb Clarinet Trio, K. 498 (ibid., pp. 135 ff.). See also Keller's article, "Functional Analysis: Its Pure Application," *Music Review* 18 (August 1957): 202–206, in which he discusses the A Major Quartet, K. 464, first movement, finding that the second subject accompaniment is a rhythmic diminution of the first subject accompaniment.

14. The experience of the "click track" in Hollywood movie studio supports this point. At one time in the history of film scoring, music was written to coordinate with screen action in segments timed to fractions of a second. Composers would design phrases to fit so many beats at a certain metronomic tempo in order to attain the required length. The music would then be recorded by using a click track, with conductor and each player wearing an earphone over one ear through which a continual click-beat would be heard at the designated metronomic speed.

The procedure turned out to be musical torture. Players could not play naturally or "musically" in this fashion, though some, to preserve a livelihood, trained themselves in the technique, which essentially meant repressing a natural feel for phrase and rhythmic shape.

15. Babbitt, a leading composer in the electronic medium, has warned against the danger of constructing, via this medium, temporal events that in their speed and complexity exceed the "present discriminative capacity of the auditory apparatus under the most generous temporal conditions." See "Twelve-tone Rhythmic Structure and the Electronic Medium," *Perspectives* 1 (Fall 1962): 49–79.

16. Anton Schindler, *Biographie von Ludwig van Beethoven*, 4th ed. (Münster: Aschendorff, 1971), 2: 243.

17. See Arthur Mendel. "A Note on Proportional Relationships in Bach Tempi." *The Musical Times*, December 1959, pp. 683–684.

——. "A Brief Note on Triple Proportion in Schuetz." *Musical Quarterly* 46, no. 1 (January 1960): 67–70.

——. "Some Ambiguities of the Mensural System." *Studies in Music History*. Ed. Harold Powers (Princeton: Princeton University Press, 1968), pp. 137–160.

18. Neal Zaslaw, "Mozart's Tempo Conventions," *Report of the International Musicological Society, Copenhagen*, 1972 (Copenhagen: Wilhelm Hansen, 1973). On this same subject, see also Curt Sachs, *Rhythm and Tempo* (New York: Norton, 1953), and Irmgard Herrmann-Begen, *Tempobezeichnungen* (Tutzing: Schneider, 1959).

19. See Johann Joachim Quantz, *On Playing the Flute*, ed. and tr. Edward R. Reilly (New York: Free Press, 1966), pp. 286 ff.

20. Cone, *Musical Form*, p. 78.

21. Reinhold Brinkmann, *Arnold Schönberg: Drei Klavierstücke, Op. 11—Studien zur frühen Atonalität bei Schönberg* (Wiesbaden: Franz Steiner, 1969), pp. 11–12.

22. Charles Rosen has noted this phenomenon in several works. Cf. Rosen, *The Classical Style* (London: Faber & Faber, 1971), p. 64 (Beethoven's Fourth Piano Concerto); pp. 228 ff. (Mozart's D Minor Piano Concerto, K. 466); pp. 59–60 (Mozart's Piano Concerto in Eb Major, K. 271); pp. 251 ff. (Mozart's C Major Piano Concerto, K. 503). Cone has also studied it in Bach's D Minor Clavier Concerto. See *Musical Form*, pp. 59 ff. Also see pp. 73 ff. for discussions of Haydn and Beethoven sonatas in this same light.

23. The autograph copy of the K. 428 quartet had a time signature of ¢ for the first movement. The original published edition carried the changed marking of ₵ The tempo marking for the third movement was *Allegro* in the autograph and appeared as *Allegretto* in the original published edition. Alfred Einstein, in his "Critical Report" in the edition of *The Ten Celebrated String Quartets*, comments that the change from *Allegro* to *Allegretto* can only have been made by Mozart. Obviously these re-markings have a bearing upon the relationships of pulse among the movements.

Apparently Mozart's tempi were not always easily arrived at, nor were his indications of tempo always sure in his own mind. A perusal of Einstein's "Critical Report" on the quartets makes this clear, as it is a comparative study of the autographs and first or other early published editions. In a number of quartets among the celebrated ten, tempo markings were either changed from original indications or were modified by added words (*poco, molto, allegretto* in place of *allegro*). Time signatures in some cases were altered from ₵ to ¢ . Whether these changes indicate different fundamental conceptions of tempi, or whether they were efforts by Mozart to make as clear as possible a conception which he felt was inadequately conveyed by the original wording (or whether they were in part editor's alterations) is not certain and possibly cannot be answered. See W.A. Mozart, *The Ten Celebrated String Quartets*, ed. Alfred Einstein (London: Novello, n.d.), "Critical Report," pp. xvii–xxvii. The information concerning the K. 428 quartet is found on pp. xx–xxi.

24. A further word to clarify proportional relations:

(1) A distinction is important between continuous pulse, which is a background time frame, and foreground pulse, by which motion in individual movements is felt. Continuous pulse is constant and unchanging; foreground pulse may or may not be.

(2) The notated unit of pulse in itself has no inherent tempo. Moreover this unit is often different from movement to movement (e.g., first movement: ♩ ; second movement:♪); third movement:♩). No metrical relation exists among these units unless indicated by ratio or equivalence. The notated unit should be read simply as "pulse" or "beat."

(3) As continuous pulse is constant, so are equal units of subpulse. In performance, transitions between proportional tempos can easily be made by grouping the constant subpulses according to indicated relationships; for example, in transition from ♩ to♩., where♪ is constant: ♫ to ♫♪ = 2 : 3

This also holds if the notated units of pulse are different; for example,

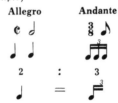

If subpulse is constant and ratio is 2:3, think:

Allegro   **Andante**

25. Readers may find it interesting to consult Allen Forte's article, "Exact Tempi in the Brahms-Haydn Variations," *Music Review* 18 (1957): 138–149. Forte shares a number of premises stated here: that the tempo relationships are proportional and integrated as part of the basic plan of the work; that the given verbal indications of tempo are mainly suggestive, the precise specifications residing in structural aspects of the music; and that the temporal proportions arise from motivic properties of the variations. He sees the nature of these motivic and rhythmic properties, however, in terms partly different from this analysis, leading to some conclusions about tempi divergent from those given here.

26. Rudolf Kolisch's article, "Tempo and Character in Beethoven's Music" (*The Musical Quarterly* 29 [1943]: 169–187, 291–312) offers a different approach to this problem. The premises of Kolisch's argument are in many ways common to those underlying the discussion here: namely, that tempo is intrinsic to a work's conception, rather than "added" after the act of creation; that tempo inheres within properties of motivic structure, shape, and thematic character; and that verbal tempo indications are approximate only, the true indices of "right" tempo lying within deeper elements of the music.

Kolisch's conclusions, however, vary considerably from those here. He finds Beethoven's metronome markings fully correct. Also, he finds that movements among Beethoven's total *oeuvre* which bear the same tempo indications (particularly with respect to their qualifying adjectives) generally fit into "families" of similar musical character, as well as similar metronome markings, meter, and motivic shapes. In other words, Beethoven had a system of musical typology defined by character, motivic shape, meter, tempo description, and metronome markings.

Absent from Kolisch's conclusions are considerations of the internal relations of tempo or pulse among the different movements of an individual work. By his scheme two Beethoven movements from different works and idioms (a symphony and a quartet, for example) might have closer affinities of tempo than they would with the other movements of their respective pieces.

27. Cf, Hans Gál, "Revisionsbericht," *Johannes Brahms Sämtliche Werke* (Leipzig: Breitkopf & Hartel, 1926–28; reprinted Ann Arbor, Michigan: J.W. Edwards, 1949), Vol. 6, p. iv. (Why the deletion one can only conjecture.)

5 PHRASING AND NUANCE

Pitch and duration, the primary elements of musical constructs, are integrative and interdependent. Pitch cannot exist independent of duration; nor can duration be manifested without pitch (or sound) as its demarcator.

The elements of phrasing and nuance, by contrast, are secondary, their functions coordinative with constructs of pitch and duration. Works are not built of timbre, dynamics, and articulation[1] (certainly not classic-romantic works). Though these secondary elements are associated with musical events, they could hypothetically be withdrawn from the scene and leave the music recognizable, albeit less interesting. This is not true of primary elements; withdraw (or, more realistically, distort) pitch or durational elements from a phrase and the phrase itself may disappear.

The term "domain" applies to these secondary elements in a loose sense only. It draws a convenient circle around an assorted group of characteristics—such as register, timbre, texture, modes of articulation, stress, dynamics—that are not intrinsically related. It is possible to construct true parameters for some of these elements—register, for example, or dynamics. Contemporary total serialism has done so, forming the elements into spectra of strictly controlled units of structure, their structural role a step closer to a primary one. This was not the function of these elements in classic-romantic music, where they served in assisting capacities, helping to define and project features of phrase and section.

At times, however, these secondary elements achieved intrinsic significance in classic-romantic music. By their frequency of appearance and their independence—that is, through no consistent association with any one particular motive or idea—they assumed a greater degree of autonomy and, because of this, greater importance as structural elements in their own right.

Igor Stravinsky has noted this in studying the Great Fugue of Beethoven:

The importance of design . . . is apparent in the *Overtura*, a thematic index identifying the different versions of the subject as well as prognosticating and priming the larger components of the form. Each thematic version is endowed with distinctive secondary attributes (counting pitch and rhythm as primary): a trill and appoggiatura, for instance, in the version destined for the most complex treatment, and a slow tempo and soft dynamic in the version predicting an episode in the same speed and volume. *These secondary characteristics constitute a set of referents with which to identify thematic material in remote transformations, as well as to construct alternative views: silhouettes, for example, on the analogy that the full-face is revealed only in the pitches; and fragmentary contrapuntal refractions, as in the double mirror, rhythmically speaking, with which the A-flat Fugue begins.* (Emphasis added.)[2]

In such a capacity these characteristics engage in a limited dialogue as integral entities. A limited and subsidiary dialogue, certainly—not, however, an insignificant one. The following examples may be illustrative.

(1) The first movement of Schubert's *Unfinished* Symphony contains a nuance of unusual autonomy. This nuance—of phrasing, dynamics, and articulation—consists of a loud and accented attack, variously indicated as *ff, fz, fp,* followed by a diminuendo extending from one to four measures.[3]

The nuance occurs throughout the movement, as shown in Ex. 33, to such an extent that in itself it assumes aspects of an integral motive. Its appearances are associated with a variety of different themes, allied with no particular one (save for similarities of exposition, recapitulation, and coda). The closest correlation with any recurrent pattern is that of an unchanging harmonic background which is sustained during each statement of the nuance. The harmonic contexts are not the same for each statement, however, nor are they as a group sufficiently similar to constitute an independent harmonic motive. The nuance thus seems an independent idea, though a secondary one in the hierarchy of musical ideas.

Ex. 33. Schubert: *Unfinished Symphony*, **first movement**

(2) Throughout the orchestration of Brahms's Variations on a Theme of Haydn, two species of nuance maintain notable consistency and stability of character. Each involves manner of articulation, lengths of phrasing, timbre, and dynamics.

Both species are illustrated in Ex. 34. In Nuance A the prevalent (though not exclusive) qualities are string timbres (muted in variation VIII) heard in long legato phrases of prevailing *piano* character, often *dolce* and generally (though not specifically indicated) *cantando.* These qualities are prominent in variations I, III, IV, and VIII.

The qualities are later shared by winds as well as strings; the long-line legato and *dolce* character is retained, despite changes in timbre. The qualities thus acquire something of a special, quasi-autonomous character, forming a qualitative "submotive" of timbre and nuance.[4]

The second species of nuance, Nuance B contrasts with Nuance A by articulation that is consistently marked, detached, and of largely staccato character (occasionally *poco tenuto* as well). The predominant timbre is of woodwinds and horns. When this is complemented by strings, it is with their most closely allied timbral and articulative qualities, such as spiccato, marcato, pizzicato. Dynamics are varied.

These nuances are employed in a fashion different from those of Nuance A. Although they constitute the predominant character of the opening chorale, they are predominant in only two variations, V and VI. Elsewhere, as in variations I and II, they are heard either in contrast to other properties (the bell-like pedals in variation I versus the long string lines) or as a subelement (the "punctuation" motive of variation II).

Variation VII alters the character of Nuance B, the articulations modified toward the opposing *dolce* quality and the phrases lengthened. It is perhaps not accidental, in light of this, that variation VII involves the most integrated use of the two nuance groups.[5]

(3) Schumann's Symphonic Etudes for Piano are similar to Brahms's *Haydn Variations* in their "orchestrated" development of secondary elements as quasi-autonomous, independent of a particular motivic association.

Three secondary elements in particular stand out in the Symphonic Etudes as significant structural features. All are shown in Ex. 35. One is the full, sonorous texture found in the chords of the opening theme (Nuance A) subsequently found, retaining this same character, throughout the variations. Second is a contrasting element of staccato attack, generally *secco* (though they are not always so indicated, it is difficult to play these phrases otherwise), and frequently marcato (Nuance B). Both these elements are further found in combination.

Finally, there is a third element of still greater contrast, which might be described as quasi-impressionistic: music of diffuse texture, generally legato and often *p,* in which clarity of harmony and articulation are subservient to a broader "wash" of color and sound as background accompaniment (Nuance C).[6]

Ex. 34. Brahms: *Variations on a Theme by Joseph Haydn*

Nuance A

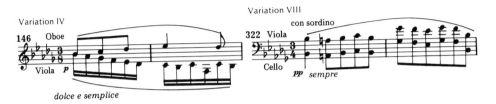

Musical Domains

Nuance B

Chorale

Variation II

Variation V

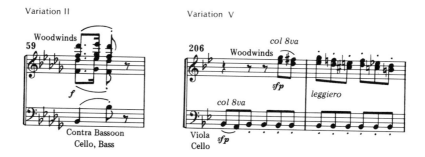

Variation VI

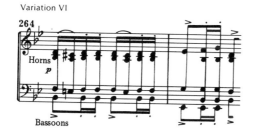

Variation VII

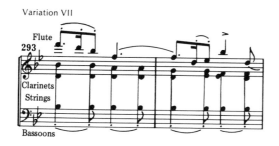

Ex. 35. Schumann: *Symphonic Etudes for Piano*

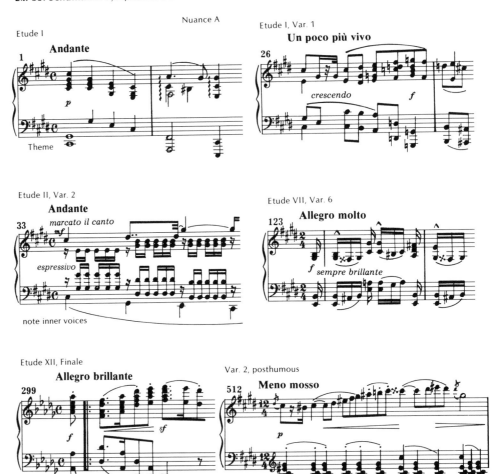

Etude XII, Finale

Allegro brillante

Nuance C

Etude XI, Var. 9

Andante espressivo

Var. 1, posthumous

Andante, tempo del tema

Var. 2, posthumous

Var. 5, posthumous

Moderato

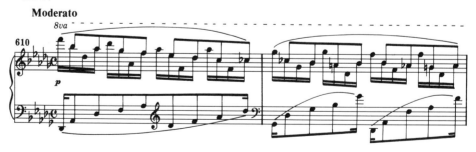

Two existing studies augment these examples.

(1) Ernst Oster's article "Register and the Long-Scale Connection" shows a subsidiary prominence attained by register in making large-scale sectional divisions.[7] Works by Beethoven, Schubert, and Mozart are studied by Oster, as is Schenker's concept of *obligate Lage,* or obligatory register.[8] By this was meant a single and primary register, maintained throughout a composition by the fundamental line and fundamental bass. It is by means of this primary register that large-scale connections are effected. While registrations such as these often project motives, they also establish for register itself a significant degree of autonomy in the hierarchy of musical events and values created by a given work.

(2) In a study of Mozart's Menuetto, K. 355 (Einstein revision, K. 594a), Howard Boatwright finds that the augmented triad, as a sonority, functions as a compositional element in much the same way as a motive. He examines the contexts of this harmony from many points of view to see whether some conventional reasoning can explain its existence and continual use. He finds that no context—such as conventional syntax, passing harmonies resulting from voice-leading—provides satisfactory answers, and concludes:

The number of augmented chords in this little piece, as well as their prominence, can only suggest that Mozart simply wanted those sounds, and that he was so much a master of the harmonic system of this time that he could bend it to his subjective musical desires. At the same time, in that remarkable fusion of aurally and intellectually motivated procedures characteristic of the greatest composers, there is present with the augmented chords in bars 5–9 the element of motivic development.[9]

In the music examined so far, elements of phrasing and nuance achieve some degree of autonomy by virtue of their independence, that is, by their lack of exclusive association with a particular thematic idea. Analyses in the following chapters contain examples of coordinative relations, where in fact these elements do unite with particular ideas. In these analyses the nuances emerge as prominent aspects of the music, despite their secondary association.

The first case is found in the triadic shapes of Beethoven's *Eroica* Symphony, first movement. In their presentation—in both exposition and recapitulation—the orchestral textures in which these themes are clothed are consistently heavy and the articulation of the themes is generally accented. (The exception is the opening phrase of the movement, which introduces both triadic and chromatic shapes significant later in the work.) The chromatic shapes largely contrast with the triadic shapes in their musical character.

A similar case is found in the opening movement of Mozart's Symphony No. 40 in G Minor, the associations here concerning the up- and downbeat properties of themes. Downbeat themes are heavy in texture, *forte,* and generally marked in articulation, while upbeat themes are diametrically opposite in character.

None of the information in these analyses is powerful enough in its implications to suggest that secondary elements are significant features of structure in and of themselves. The information does suggest, however, a structural role for phrasing and nuance that is deeper than that of foreground musical character alone.

NOTES

1. Though Schoenberg in "Farben," from *Five Pieces for Orchestra* (Op. 16), made of timbre a central (but not exclusive) structural feature. Webern and Berg used elements like timbre, dynamics, and register as referential elements to assist the delineation of phrase and larger sections or to emphasize particular musical associations. Cf. George Perle, *Serial Composition and Atonality* (Berkeley: University of California Press, 1963), pp. 18 ff. and 23 ff.

2. Igor Stravinsky, review of Joseph Kerman, "The Beethoven Quartets", *New York Review of Books* (26 September 1968), p. 4.

3. Schubert's manuscripts make poor distinctions between accents (>) and short decrescendo markings ($\Longrightarrow$). He apparently intends $\textit{fp}$ markings to mean $\textit{f} \Longrightarrow \textit{p}$. See Martin Chusid's discussion of these problems in his edition of the *Unfinished* Symphony, Norton Critical Scores (New York: Norton, 1968), p. 46 ff.

4. The qualities are also associated with the theme as variants; so, however, are the quite different sonorities found in the other variations. Thus, thematic association is not the source of their uniqueness as secondary elements.

A further point: if the work is played maintaining a continuous pulse (see Chapter 4), then variation III $\quad\rlap{\,\bullet}{} = \quad\rlap{\,\uparrow}{}$ variation IV. This results in the flowing eighths of variation III moving at the same speed as the flowing sixteenths of variation IV, further underlining the connections in timbre and nuance that link these contiguous variations.

5. A further detail regarding tempo: if performance maintains a continuous pulse, the relation between variations V–VI is in ratio of 3:4. This means that V $\quad\rlap{\,\uparrow}{} = \quad\rlap{\,\uparrow}{}$ VI, with the result that once again, as with variations III–IV, the connection in timbre and nuance is emphasized by pulse.

6. The confused numbering system for these variations presents a dilemma initiated by Schumann himself and continued by his father-in-law Friedrich Wieck and others. Feeling that the third and ninth variations were too diffuse in character to warrant the title "variation," Schumann called each of them an étude. For the 1837 edition (a theme and twelve variations) he used the title "Symphonic Etudes," but later revised it for republication in 1852 as "Etudes in the Form of Variations."

Finally, in the 1920s, Alfred Cortot researched a Schumann manuscript at the Mariemont Library in Belgium, uncovering a set of ten études (variations) on the same theme—apparently an early version of the composition. Cortot's edition offers a set of twelve études (variations) with an appendix of five "posthumous" variations, which Schumann had drawn from this manuscript into the 1837 edition.

Obviously there is an opportunity here to bring out a critical edition explaining the confusion in musicological terms and then putting away this Laocoön once and for all through a unified numbering system.

7. Ernst Oster, "Register and the Long-Scale Connection," *Journal of Music Theory* 5, no. 1 (1961): 54–71.

8. Cf. Heinrich Schenker, "Organic Structure in Sonata Form," tr. Orin Grossman, *Journal of Music Theory* 12 (1968): 164–183. See also *Der Freie Satz* (Vienna: Universal, 1935 and 1956), sections 268–270.

9. Howard Boatwright, "Analysis Symposium," *Journal of Music Theory* 10 (1966). See section III, pp. 27–30.

THE CONCEPT OF UNITY: ANALYSES

6

The first-movement studies presented in Chapters 6 and 7—Beethoven's *Eroica* Symphony, Mozart's Symphony No. 40, Haydn's Symphony No. 104—and the broader studies of relationships among the movements in Schumann's Third Symphony are mainly concerned with unity, inquiring into the many dimensions wherein a basic musical conception may be manifest. They are essentially an exploration along the lines of Schoenberg's *Grundgestalt* concept. Fundamental concepts of Schenker are assumed in many of the analyses that follow. The analyses present views complementary to those of Schenker, distinguished mainly by difference of perspective and focus.

The *Eroica's* first movement is prototypical of much that has been discussed earlier. The musical shapes and concepts from which its unity springs are multidimensional and complex, lying within intersecting domains, at times enigmatic in context. The discussion that follows mirrors this complexity. While musical events are isolated here into separate parameters for the sake of clarity, these are artificial distinctions. In the music pitch, rhythm, harmony, nuance are interrelated. It is not possible, or desirable, to view them separately beyond a certain point, even for analytical purposes.

The properties of shape that exert an organizing force upon the materials of the entire movement are found in the opening theme of the work, seen in Ex. 36 (measures 3–15). As indicated, the formative elements of the basic shape divide essentially into two segments. The predominant feature of the first segment (the cello melody) is its triadic structure. By contrast the second segment, whose beginning overlaps the final Eb of segment one (measure 4 of the theme), is striking for the series of half steps upon which it is built. Its chromatic C#—dissonant and harmonically ambiguous—and the motive Eb–D–C# (measures 4–5 of the melody) are the outstanding features of the entire theme. The half step functions in some motives as a single interval, while elsewhere, as indicated, it forms a series of two unidirectional intervals. In its local, simple, chromatic form of D–C#–D at the outset (the first nontriadic notes heard), it is reflected in the G–Ab–G of the first violins.

The triad-derived and half-step-derived segments of the first theme are the predominant shapes underlying this theme and all subsequent themes. They are also the shaping factors for virtually all subsidiary motives and lesser melodic ideas in the movement, whether their functions be thematic, transitional, extending, or cadential.[1] These shape segments also determine significant harmonic events, modulations, key relations, rhythmic structures, and in many instances elements of phrasing, dynamics, and articulation. In short, the shape segments exert a far-reaching influence in virtually all domains of the movement's structure. They are the central germ of the music. This influence is examined on the following pages, isolated into separate parameters (theme, harmony, tonality, key relations, modulations, duration, secondary elements) for analytical purposes.

DOMAINS (1): THEME

The basic shape of the opening theme is seminal for the entire movement. Ex. 36 lists subsequent themes—of all degrees of importance—in two columns, indicating those that are triad-derived and those that are half-step-derived. As the chart shows, these themes reflect features of one or the other shape segments, some sharing characteristics of both.

Ex. 36. Beethoven: *Symphony No. 3 in E flat Major,* **first movement**

Triad-derived themes

Half-step derived themes and subsidiary motives

The Concept of Unity: Analyses

The pitch relationships contained in these two segments function on two broad structural levels: they determine features of themes proper, as demonstrated; they exist as subsidiary motives.

The second structural level is itself diverse, as these subsidiary motives fulfill different roles, such as (1) thematic foreground roles, as subsidiary motives proper or as various melodic embellishments; and (2) middle- or background roles, in which shapes serve motivically to articulate larger-scale melodic lines and phrases and to establish intermediate tonal levels.

The carrying out of motives on local levels provides the least interesting perspective. The relationships are easy enough to perceive, and this kind of development has received enough attention from other writers to need no elaboration here. It suffices to provide a few samples, involving triad-derived (measure 135, lower strings) and half-step-derived motives (measures 75, 606, and 620) respectively.[2]

There follow several instances in which the three-note, half-step-derived motive functions contrapuntally on the middle-ground level, doing so over extensive periods (measures 83 and 248–284). Structure on this level is very much an amalgam of intersecting domains. While these lines constitute an extension of motive, they are at the same time the primary determinant not only of harmonic progression over these same periods, but also of modulations to transitory key centers. Moreover, because these progressions by their gradations of harmonic tension control the establishment of structural downbeats, the lines further effect large-scale rhythmic articulations.[3]

The Concept of Unity: Analyses

The three-note chromatic motive E♭–D–C♯ and its inversion, E♭–E♮–F, are found on local and more extended levels throughout the movement. The two forms of the motive provide a symmetrical pattern revolving around E♭ which, as tonic, serves as the axis of this symmetry. These manipulations of shape, by their focus around E♭, reinforce the tonic—an interesting mode of development. In this regard note: (1) the original motive and its melodic extension (inverted) on E♭–E♮–F and subsequent pitches (measure 17); (2) the presence of the motive in the main theme of the second

group (measure 83). In this case the original pitches, in permuted order, determine the changes of major-minor modality in the theme. (3) the subsequent use of this motive as the long middle-ground line (D♯–E–F) that generates the most extensive and extreme modulation of the movement—to E minor (measures 248-284) in the development. In this perspective E minor is not only an extension of the chromatic motive, relating the key centers of E♭ major and E minor; equally important, the new center is *established*—that is, worked, or built into the music—by means of this motive.[4]

Unity in Beethoven's *Eroica* Symphony

To return to thematic matters, the E minor theme, which comes in the development as a seemingly new idea (measure 284), actually arises from the triadic segment of the opening motive.[5] The origin does not lie in the oboe melody but in the lower lines (cellos, basses), to which the oboe is a counterpoint. The *sfp* dynamic marks the thematic outline of the cello line (the first note, E, being emphasized through the harmonic resolution to E minor, just concluded). Schema a shows the motivic outline indicated by the *sfp*. The pizzicato bass notes are part of this complex, however. Heard in conjunction with the E–G in the cellos (the F♯ is simply a passing tone), the amalgamated line of cellos and basses embodies the opening motive, metrically displaced (Schema b)—a mosaic-like construction of the melody.

The three-note chromatic motive is also present, though as a decorative foreground element. It occurs in the third measure of the phrase, the only nondiatonic segment of the cello line, in the passing tones D♯–D♮–C♯ (Schema c). Thus the same chromatic motive is again focused around the E♭ tonic, in this case heard as an enharmonic (and quasi-chromatic) D♯.[6]

The relevance of this passage to the total form is clarified in the following measures where the disguised form of the triadic idea sensed in the E minor theme breaks forth in C major (measures 300 ff.).

The Concept of Unity: Analyses

DOMAINS (2):
HARMONY,
TONALITY,
KEY RELATIONS,
AND
MODULATIONS

Many of the harmonic progressions and modulations in the *Eroica* are understandable in terms of the prevailing conventions and harmonic syntax of the common-practice era. There are a considerable number of these harmonic events that do not lie within these conventions, however, their chromaticisms pushing to, if not beyond, the boundaries of then-extant tonal practice.

These events, in the *Eroica* and elsewhere, raise the question of how they are to be understood. Are they to be accepted at face value as "unusual," enigmatic, idiosyncratic? (The question of norms returns again.) Or are they to be accepted as absolute compositional decisions, beyond explanation? (Schoenberg himself spoke this way about one set of modulations in this movement, as will be seen.)

Certainly not all aspects of creativity are rational or accessible to the clarification of analysis. The kinds of events under consideration here, however, are so basic to the music, and so frequent, as to leave one little convinced or satisfied by the "enigma" argument.

The question is clouded by a traditional view of harmonic and tonal relations, which sees these matters as a syntax that is largely predetermined. As a result harmony is often regarded as an accompaniment to ideas, rather than as a plausible embodiment of idea itself; tonality is seen as a frame of reference within which musical ideas are worked out, rather than as a manifestation of idea.

Schenker's view of harmony as a result of linear forces is an antidote to this traditional perspective. Schoenberg's sense of idea as imbuing all aspects of music complements Schenker's view, the two differing more than anything else in focus or emphasis. Both views are relevant to the question of chromaticism in the *Eroica*, as well as to the relationship of chromatic shape to chromatic harmonic schema. The evidence that follows indicates that the relationship is indeed causal—a result of the interpenetration, within differing perspectives, of formative shape.

HALF-STEP-
DERIVED
INFLUENCES

Local Levels:
Chord of the
Augmented Sixth

The augmented sixth chord appears in numerous places in the first movement, always resulting from half-step melodic motion in contrary directions in outer voices, melodic motion which often embodies the full three-note chromatic motive. The chord captures attention not only by its striking dissonance, but also by its prominent and often climactic position in harmonic progressions, serving in several of these progressions as the focal point of modulation. Its constant chromatic-motivic origins and its consistent use in these contexts elevate its stature in the hierarchies of the movement beyond the incidental—that is, beyond the result of local counterpoint. The chord is itself an extension of a structural idea.

The most striking early use of the augmented sixth chord occurs in measure 44, (see arrow), where it is the focal point of the first activity in the movement that is

truly destructive of E♭ major as the prevalent tonality—the modulation from tonic to V of V prior to the establishment of the dominant key and second thematic group. This chord is a reappearance, with greater tonal consequence, of its initial prototype heard in measure 22, the earlier harmonic context a local one of embellishment. The potential importance of the chord is suggested in this early appearance by the crescendo to *fp*, an emphasis more than coincidental, it would seem, in view of the future significance of this harmony.

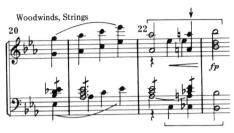

The chord returns again in striking fashion as the focal point of a closing-group motive in measure 133 (also measure 535 in the recapitulation), its dissonance once more highlighted by a *sfp*. It confirms the destination of a modulatory passage in measure 219, in the development. Similar chords appear as passing harmonies in numerous progressions, three of which are given in measures 76, 119, and 122.

In measures 22, 119, and elsewhere, the melodic lines of bass and soprano that give rise to the augmented sixth chord are themselves versions of the Eb–D–C# basic-shape motive. In measure 44, the first focal point of modulation, this motive is in the upper part, while the bass is a different motive. This is not incidental; the bass motive, derived from the original shape, plays a particular role at such points of large-scale structural demarcation—a role to be studied shortly.

Structurally Derived Local Dissonances

Works of art shift the balances among their elements, bringing to the fore what elsewhere appears incidental. The *Eroica* reflects this in certain chordal dissonances, whose clashes of pitch reflect the elevation into a structural hierarchy of an event seemingly innocuous in origin.

This origin lies within the shapes of the opening theme—the major premise of the movement—specifically, the passing tone D in its fourth measure. The note is the first dissonance, in fact the first nonmember of the Eb triad to be heard in the movement, an event that in itself should signal its potential import. Its context as a simple passing tone is ordinary enough; it is only in retrospect, when heard in the more complex association with C#, that its potential ramifications are perceived.

Yet even on the simpler level of passing tone it has implications, for it places the leading tone in juxtaposition with the octave. As the movement unfolds, certain transformations give the latent dissonance new prominence. It is placed in new contexts, giving it a musical importance which it lacks initially; its rhythmic position, orchestral weight, articulation are strengthened; its linear pattern is made vertical.

The new contexts take two forms. One is the harmonic juxtaposition of dominant harmony (often a diminished seventh chord) versus tonic pedal, the result embodying the aural clash of leading tone against tonic. The second involves a more subtle transformation: the verticalization of the total harmonic context in which the D originally appears and its reorientation into a different chord position.

The following passages give some instances of the first form of new context, associated in two cases with prominent themes, the second case (measure 144) exploiting the dissonance cadentially. The same dissonance is the essence of the "wrong key"

Unity in Beethoven's *Eroica* Symphony

horn call just before the recapitulation (measure 394), the tonic orientation of the call with its E♭ causing one of the more curious clashes with the D of the dominant, since the latter note is absent from the scene. (Beethoven two measures later leaves no doubt about its "real" presence; the resounding "correction" is a stunning moment, which says something about the hearing of well-intentioned editors who once presumed to put this situation to rights by transposing the horn call to a "proper" dominant position.)[7]

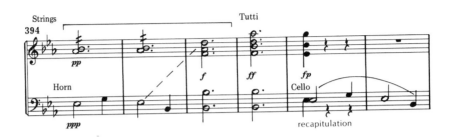

The second form of this dissonance is found in measures 276–283, the powerful chords with their E versus F pitches, that precede the arrival in E minor. These chords place in still further intersecting planes the chromatic relations between E♭ major and E minor and the means by which the relations are effected. For the chord in measure 276 is also linear in the sense that it partakes of the F–E♮–D♯ line that structures the whole passage. At the same time it is a variant of the parent shape referred to in the opening theme (measures 5–6). Thus key, chord, pitch, line—all are placed in new contexts. The resolution of the chord to the minor ninth harmony on B (measure 280) reduces one tension of large-scale purview while exploiting the half-step dissonance on a local level by means of the C versus B within the chord itself.

The Concept of Unity: Analyses

Middle-Ground Levels: Harmonic Progressions, Modulations, Key Relations[8]

Local harmonic events emanating from tonally unusual shapes like the chromaticisms under study have an immediacy about them, a special character of sound and dissonance, that easily commands attention. This is less evident with progressions lying upon deeper levels, distributed as they are over greater musical dimensions. These deeper progressions are significant indexes, however, of the resources and capacities of tonality as a system of structure.

These observations are applicable to the *Eroica* first movement. Two of its chromatic modulations in particular are directly allied with the three-note half-step-derived motive, and in fact manifest this motive upon the larger field of tonal movement. They are (1) the passage at measures 178–186 and (2) the bass line of the entire development section, a line in which some pitches serve as temporary tonal centers, others as passing or neighbor tones in the course of modulatory motion in the large.

Both result in temporary tonicization of keys related by varying remote degrees to the tonic. Not only are these relationships unusual for the period; the sequences of key centers themselves and the means by which they are effected are likewise beyond then-prevalent conventions.

Key scheme

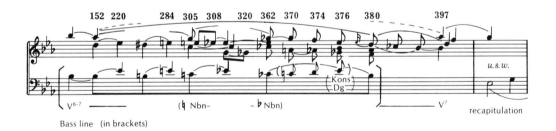

Bass line (in brackets)

Even Schoenberg considered the passage in measures 178–186 as somewhat excessive[9] and seems to have overlooked the fact that it fits within a systematic key scheme suggested by his own theories. The passage is perhaps the most extreme modulation in the movement, temporarily establishing the consecutive minor key centers C–C#–D. These centers, however, clearly constitute an inverted version of the Eb–D–C# basic shape first heard in the opening theme.

Schenker, in his analysis of the *Eroica* cited earlier, reveals a broader projection of the three-note motivic shape, which in fact serves as the bass for the entire development section. His example reveals a bass line progressing through the pitches Bb–B♮–C–Cb– Bb. The line is the controlling factor, harmonically and tonally, of the section; Bb, the dominant, is the prevalent harmonic influence, the other tones in effect chromatic neighbor tones over a span of some 245 measures.

Other harmonic relationships hinge upon this chromatic shape. One is the relationship of the tonic key of E♭ major to the E minor tonality in which the "new" theme in the development enters at measure 284. It is this passage and its tonal relations that Schoenberg described as "one of the most extravagant ventures" in the movement.[10] Yet the juxtaposition of these keys as a motivic projection is emphasized by the return of the same "new" theme in E♭ minor shortly afterwards, at measure 322. Moreover, the motivic means by which E minor is reached—the D♯–E–F line sustained over 36 measures prior to measure 284—and the recontextualization of chords, pitches, line already discussed further intensify this relationship. A second passage involves the famous "wrong key" statement of the theme by the horn—the moment of tonic-versus-dominant harmony immediately before the recapitulation.

The chromatic shape E♭–D–C♯ heard at the outset of the movement gives rise by implication to yet another motive, one used sparingly, whose appearances for the most part serve to demarcate large-scale sections of the movement. The implication lies with the C♯ and its harmonic ambiguity. From a purely aural standpoint—with matters of note spelling aside—it is unclear whether this pitch is indeed C♯, the chromatic lower neighbor of D, or D♭, whose harmonic tendency would lead it to resolve downward on C. In its initial appearance the pitch functions as a true C♯, resolving upward (measures 6–8). Its other possibility is exploited at the parallel place in the recapitulation (measures 407–411), where its resolution downward to C creates a local secondary dominant, temporarily deflecting the music to the key of F.

This C, though "unspoken" at the outset, is nonetheless present by implication—nor is its influence withheld until this explicit realization at the recapitulation. It is the generator of a further shape, E♭–D♭ (or C♯)–C, a line at times embellished with neighbor tones, including the intermediary pitch D, and at times not. See schema below (measures 407–411).

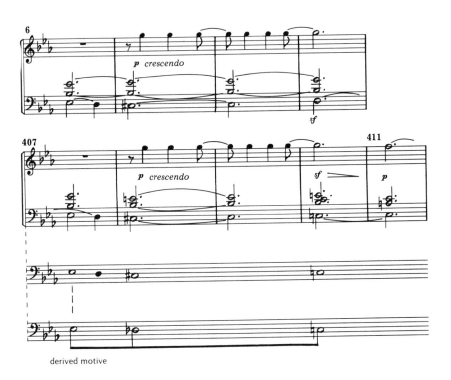

derived motive

The line functions almost exclusively as a bass, and as such motivates a series of significant modulations. It is notable that these appear in what might be called parallel places with regard to the sections of the movement, namely the beginnings of the development, recapitulation, and coda. All emanate, moreover, from the motive stated also in a parallel place—the beginning of the exposition. The bass line thus initiates the first striking harmonic activity in each of these large sections—sections that are themselves the foremost temporal articulations of the movement.

In the opening of the development, as can be seen (measures 152–160), the modulation from the key of B♭ major to C major rests upon a chromatically embellished version of this bass, descending from B♭ to G (V of C major). In the recapitulation, the melodic motive E♭–D–C♯ extends further to C♮ (measure 404), realizing the alternate solution of the ambiguous C♯.

The most striking modulation founded upon this bass line occurs at the start of the coda, from measure 551 to 561. This is the much-discussed passage in which the key centers seem almost bodily lifted from their foundations and unceremoniously set down on new levels. The passage, like others in different contexts before it, alters previous perspectives: the derived bass-line motive is here heard in its "pure" form, unembellished—the first time it is so stated on this major structural level (though earlier it appears this way locally, as will be shown). Yet the harmonies built over it are in large part analogous to those of the parallel passage at the start of the development though transposed to the tonic. Here at the coda they are again "pure," unembellished— their stark purity the source of their unorthodoxy (E♭ major followed by D♭ major) and their startling effect. Variant, it would seem, comments upon variant in this passage. For the passage initiates the coda, which in this movement is as much a further development section as it is a postscript.

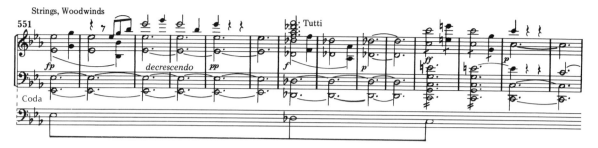

Thus the derived bass-line motive appears as a major demarcator. In each case its appearance is in some way carefully garbed to bring it to perceptual attention: in the harmonic ambiguity of the exposition and recapitulation; in the spare texture and soft dynamics at the beginning of the development, in strong contrast to the preceding measures; in the harmonic shock that initiates the coda.

The motive appears elsewhere on levels nearer the surface; correlations like the foregoing are not so notable in these instances, for they are lesser moments. There are four of these local instances, the first (measure 312) a brief moment in the development, itself a variant of an earlier and similar passage (measure 180).

The second instance lies beyond the opening of the recapitulation where the motivic extension of the bass from C♯ down to C deflects the music to F major (measure 408 of large schema). Harmony here is clearly generated by the derived bass-line motive. The return from F major to E♭ major (II to I) could easily be effected through a simple secondary dominant chain (II–V–I). It is not, however; the modulation to D♭ major intervenes, projecting the derived bass-line motive on three tonal levels, as indicated in measures 408–440.

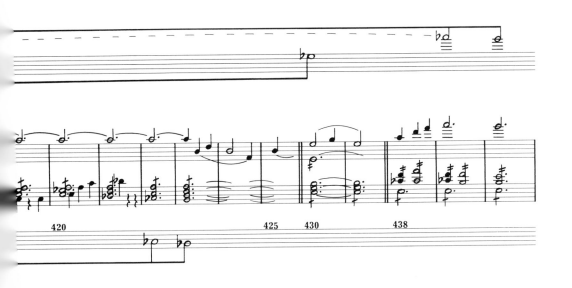

Third, in measures 43–45, shown below, the bass line has a demarcation role of tonal importance, involved with the first harmonic activity truly destructive of Eb major as prevalent tonality—the moment initiating the transition to V. This moment has been studied earlier, when the augmented sixth chord was seen as a local matter, a result of the half-step-derived motive in the soprano. It now becomes clear that the bass in the progression belongs to a different hierarchical order.[11]

The last local instance is the passage at measure 27. Functionally this passage is purely local in purview—a prolongation of the dominant in a I–V–I progression. The dissonance engendered by the V_2^4 inversions, however, stems from a different source—the derived bass-line motive (here: Bb–Ab–G) as bass.

A final point: in studying earlier the varied roles of the omnipresent half-step-derived motive (Eb–D–C♯, Eb–E♮–F, D♯–E–F), the motive was focused around Eb in the majority of cases. Thus in its variant guises and recontextualized roles it had the further effect of intensifying Eb as the pitch central to the movement (as tonic). A similar role seems to be fulfilled by the derived bass-line motive. For, again, the majority of its statements lie upon the pitches C–Db–Eb, focusing still further upon the tonic as centerpoint.

The foregoing discussion indicates that in the *Eroica*'s first movement the relationships between certain temporary key centers and the tonic Eb, and the modulatory processes that establish these temporary centers express, in the large, similar pitch relationships found in the opening theme—that is, in the basic shape of the movement. This raises the question whether such relationships between thematic motives (chromatic ones in particular), key centers, and modulations are unique to the *Eroica*—and are, in effect, a curiosity—or whether such structural interrelationships were a basic part of Beethoven's musical thought.

The Concept of Unity: Analyses

The question is investigated as a subordinate part of this study with details presented in Appendix B. In it are examined sonata-form first movements from middle-period Beethoven works (the same period that produced the *Eroica*) in three major areas of his output: the symphonies (Second through Eighth), string quartets (Op. 59 through 127), and piano sonatas (Op. 14 through 81a). The point of inquiry in each case is whether, in movements that contain chromatic elements as part of their basic pitch shape, this chromaticism is subsequently reflected in modulatory patterns and key relations. Conversely, in movements whose basic shapes do not contain such chromatic elements, are there no, or significantly fewer, such relationships.[12]

The evidence in both cases strongly suggests a positive conclusion and strengthens the impression that, for Beethoven at least, the purview of basic shapes was multi-dimensional. In virtually every instance where initial themes contain a striking chromatic element, this shape is manifested in the large as described above. In many of these cases Beethoven highlights the initial thematic chromaticism dynamically by such means as as a crescendo, diminuendo, *sf* (as in the *Eroica*), as if to denote the significance of the basic shape at the outset. In contrast, those movements whose thematic shapes are fundamentally diatonic have markedly fewer modulations or key relations that conform to this anomalous pattern.

The modulations in these chromatically influenced works are basically of two types. In one, the key centers reflect the chromaticism of the thematic motive in a manner similar to the minor tonal centers C–C♯–D in measures 178–187 of the *Eroica*. In the other, the pitches of the chromatic motive (sometimes transposed, inverted, or occasionally permuted) are found as an upper or bass line distributed over a wide expanse of musical time—a characteristic Schenkerian middle-ground voice-leading line. Certain of these pitches determine the harmony (or temporary key center) by serving as chord roots. Others serve simply as other notes of the temporary key (such as third, fifth). In all cases, the prevalent harmonic-tonal complex results from the influence of these pitches. (An equivalent instance in the *Eroica* is the bass line of the development, outlining the basses and/or major key centers B♭–B♮–C–C♭–B♭.)

The harmonic progressions in Beethoven's development sections also confirm the accuracy of Schoenberg's view of tonality, outlined in *Structural Functions of Harmony*, that within a tonal work there is only one tonality—the original key. All other keys of the work are not "separate" keys but are in effect chord centers, related to the tonic either closely or by varying degrees of remoteness. Seen in the perspective of the entire work, these temporary centers are chords within a large-scale progression, initially emanating from and returning to the tonic.[13] This is an exact description of Beethoven's procedures, particularly in his developments, whether temporary centers are those of conventional progressions, such as secondary dominant chains, or the chromatic progressions so consistently generated by his chromatic motivic shapes.

HARMONIC INFLUENCE OF THE TRIAD-DERIVED BASIC SHAPE

A study of the influence of triadic shape upon the harmonic activity of the *Eroica* is difficult, because in the triad one is dealing with the most common terms of the tonal system, the most basic of its harmonic vocabulary. Determining a unique harmonic influence of triadic shape is more complex yet, for to apply the criterion of the triad-as-motive to the realm of harmony is virtually to pose a tautology.

Is the *Eroica*'s triad-derived motivic shape of any harmonic consequence, as its less usual chromatic shape has clearly been shown to be? Possibly. If so, some unusual properties or characteristics of triadic events are required to establish their motivic

Unity in Beethoven's *Eroica* Symphony

aspects as significant beyond the norm. Two such cases do appear in the first movement: the first is that of the opening chords; the second is the chordal aspect of the second theme at measures 83 ff.

The repeated opening chords, as rhythmic and phrase studies in future pages will show, constitute more than just an introductory phrase. They are in effect a submotive—one of rhythmic, textural, dynamic, and registral aspects. Like the derived bass-line motive, this phrase also serves to demarcate large sections of the movement. (The two submotives, in fact—bass line and repeated chords—work in tandem fashion, as discussed later.)

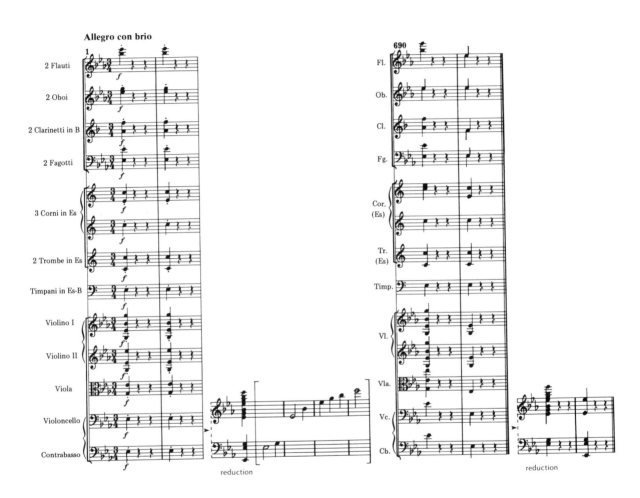

Integrated into the formal scheme of the movement, as these repeated chords are shown to be, it should not be surprising to find them integrated as well into the ideational, or motive-shape, conception. The clue to this integration lies in the deliberate spacing of the E♭ major chords. The opening chord, spelled from the bass upwards, yields literally the pitch sequence of the opening motive, with the exception of the second clarinet's intermediary G. The closing two measures share in large part the same detail, [14] the intermediary G being played by horn and clarinet this time. (N.B. The low E♭ of the basses is simply an orchestral doubling.)

This first case is suggestive, rather than proof positive; the one fact not fitting the pattern is the G of the second clarinet. What is further striking about the opening chord, and supportive of the motivic pattern, is the unusual close spacing of E♭–G in the lower register, a spacing strongly doubled in brass and strings (as the G of the second clarinet is not). More normal for an "ordinary" chord would be an octave interval in this register, either unfilled or, at most, filled with an intervening fifth. So many thirds make overly heavy acoustical doublings, particularly in this register—a basic convention of which Beethoven could hardly have been unaware. The opening chord and its rationale must remain one of the enigmas of the *Eroica*. It seems supportive, however, of Schoenberg's musical view that verticalization of a motive is but one of its many potential guises.

The second theme, occurring at measure 83, was previously shown to contain both triad-derived and half-step-derived properties. The influence of the latter is evident in the motion of the inner parts. (Further affinities with the chromatic motive are discussed in coming pages in terms of the long upbeat character of the theme and its texture and dynamics, both familial characteristics.) This theme is the second case in which the triad-derived motive appears of harmonic consequence. Showing triadic influence here are the sound and the presence of the individual chords themselves. As in the first case, this instance presents a somewhat special concept. It would not be surprising to find any theme in this work supported by triadic harmony. This theme, however, in its initial measures is not so much *supported* by triadic harmony; it *is* triadic harmony— the major triad, repeated seven times, is an event in isolation, so to speak, unsupported by any other pitch event. Thus its "triadicity" is a germinal concept, emphasized by repetition alone, a characteristic device of Beethoven's style.

DOMAINS (3): DURATION, SECONDARY ELEMENTS

The thematic ideas of the movement are unified in rhythmic respects, both in their rhythmic shapes and in their patterns of upbeat and downbeat orientation. The rhythmic features fit into generic groupings, based upon their triadic or chromatic nature.

The groupings are illustrated below. The opening theme of the movement is again presented, divided into its two basic-shape segments, together with subsequent themes as they share these patterns of shape. The patterns are rarely clear-cut or absolute; as the chart indicates, many themes share both triadic and chromatic properties, though some incline more one way or the other. Three themes, however, two of them in the closing group of the exposition, are notably triad derived, as indicated (see left-hand column).

Several things about these themes and their rhythmic properties are clear from this chart. First, the two segments of the opening theme have fundamentally different rhythmic accents in their large-scale articulation. The triad-derived segment has its strong rhythmic impulse on the first note of the phrase. It has, in other words, a *downbeat* character, or strong-weak pattern (— ◡), the remaining notes receiving less emphasis or weight.

The half-step-derived segment, on the other hand, has a contrasting character in terms of rhythmic accent. The series of syncopated Gs in the first violins give this phrase an *upbeat* quality, the ensuing downbeat, or point of rhythmic accent, occurring toward the end of the phrase (◡ —).[15]

Triad derived segment   Half-step derived segment

Triad derived themes

Half-step derived themes
and subsidiary motives

Themes derived from elements of both basic shape segments

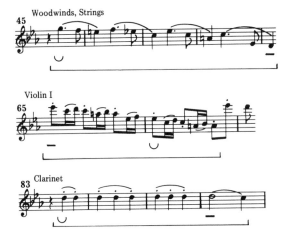

The upbeat and downbeat qualities encompass the segments in their largest rhythmic dimensions. The patterns of accent, in other words, are underlying or background rhythmic inflections.

Grouped below the opening theme are other themes and motives of the movement that are either triad derived, half-step derived, or derived from elements of both basic-shape segments. The most significant aspect of rhythmic unity among these themes lies in their underlying patterns of rhythmic accent, or inflection, which are the same as the parent segments.

The families of themes derived from these segments also share mutual rhythmic shapes. Thus the triad-derived themes are mostly composed of rhythms such as (1) ♩ ♩ and (2) ♩ ♩ ♩.

Many of these rhythmic motives are obvious variants of one another, particularly among those with chromatic generic roots. The process of variation is carried further, becoming one of transformation, effected by displacement of rhythmic pattern (a device of Beethoven's seen earlier in this study). The formal functions fulfilled by various rhythmic motives are also changed in this process.

For example, the latter segment of the opening theme and the theme that opens the second group (measure 83) are related. Both share the long upbeat inflection, as well as the reiteration of a single note upon a long crescendo, leading to downbeat resolution that involves a *sf* ═══ . Also, as indicated by the superposition of both themes, the contours of each theme are mirror images of each other, each theme lying basically on the same third degree of the scale. Moreover, the quarter-note repetitions of the second theme derive from the syncopated Gs of the opening theme segment, the syncopations "straightened out" by displacement onto, instead of off, the beat.

Other instances are shown here. All center around these same rhythms in new contexts. In the first instance, the syncopated rhythm of the opening theme is reused as an accompanying pedal point to the E minor theme at measure 284 (violin 1); it is used

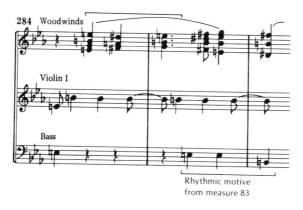

Rhythmic motive
from measure 83

in a similar way as pedal against the contrapuntal development of two themes at measure 186 (violin 2, then violin 1; see also measures 322, 581, 647). In the E minor theme

of measure 284, the contrabass voice, with its upbeat character and rhythmic pattern, is derived from measure 83; so also is the upper line. Finally, the rhythm of the fugato motive at measure 236 and that of the first-violin line in the long dissonant transition to E minor in measure 248 stem from the preceding transitional motive under development (measures 224 ff.). The ♪ ♩ motive in this passage is rooted in an earlier triad-derived motive found in measure 25.

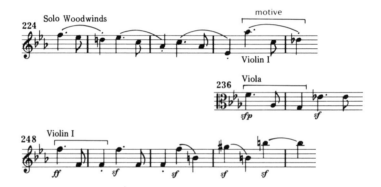

The generic properties of these themes extend beyond shapes of rhythm and contour, and beyond harmonic implications, to encompass secondary elements. With respect to orchestral texture and weight, for example, it is striking that the three triad-derived themes that emanate from the opening segment are all full and heavy. By contrast, virtually all the half-step-derived themes, with the exception of the passing phrase of measure 123, are of thinner texture and weight.

A significant correlation is further maintained with respect to dynamics and to aspects of phrasing and articulation. If the half-step-derived opening theme segment is studied in terms of these features, the following are notable: (1) the segment has a pronounced crescendo character (and to a lesser extent that of a diminuendo), the crescendo serving to emphasize the long upbeat inflection of the opening notes; (2) the segment is essentially legato in its articulation; and (3) the prevailing dynamic level is soft (*p* or *pp*) though, as noted above, with crescendo-diminuendo dynamic curves within this level.

A number of themes and lesser motives derived from this segment share these characteristics. The majority of them are legato in quality. Several have a crescendo or diminuendo character as well, some embodying ◁▷ variations in intensity.[16]

The triad-derived segment of the basic shape and the themes derived from it are also correlated in their contrasting qualities. For example, (1) both derived themes and the parent shape have no crescendo, diminuendo, nor ◁▷ character. Their prevailing dynamic level is steady. (2) In contrast to the ◁▷ qualities of the chromatic motives, all of the triadic themes are marked by sudden accents (sf or fp). (3) With the exception of measure 23 the derived triadic themes are notably nonlegato, as well as forte, in their prevailing dynamic level.[17]

The two-measure tutti chords that initiate the movement were seen earlier as a verticalization, in effect a compression, of the triad-derived segment of the opening theme. They also serve a rhythmic function concerned with the broadest proportions of the movement, that is, demarcation of the large-scale structural downbeats that open each main section. The resources of such secondary elements as dynamics, articulation, register, orchestral texture, and weight are marshaled to define these moments. The schema illustrates these places. As can be seen, the chords precede the structural downbeats (indicated with arrows). While their rhythmic foreground varies, their basic metric-rhythmic contour remains. Their character as a two-measure unit is also preserved, in some cases extending to three measures through an elision into the downbeat.[18]

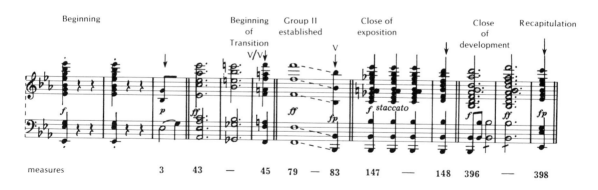

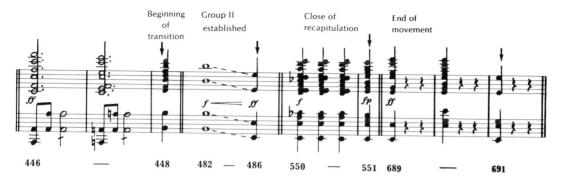

By virtue of their placement, these chords are always upbeat oriented—antecedents to the structural downbeats they initiate, posing a curious contradiction to the usual light-heavy, weak-strong nature of up- and downbeats in this movement. For in their orchestral texture, dynamics, articulation, extreme registral extensions, and other secondary properties, these upbeat chords are strong—heavy, marcato in character, forte in dynamic. Moreover in virtually all cases the downbeats that follow them are in stark contrast—soft, legato, lyrical in nature, the textures more transparent, the registers reduced from extreme spans.

Register among these chords, in both upper and lower extremes, is carefully maintained at each sectional point. Large-scale melodic lines, in other words, tie together these sections and their mottos by means of these registral pitches—a point of Schenker's discussed in Chapter 5. Thus register is in itself a compositional element, shaped to project and to articulate major junctures. The junctures are further marked by the paired presences of these chords and by the derived bass-line motive (E♭–D♭–C), which appears early in each new section.

The large-scale rhythmic dimensions of the first movement are further unified by the numerous phrase elisions that occur throughout. Elisions were, to be sure, part of the prevalent musical vocabulary. Their use was generally restricted, however, in order to maximize the cumulative effect of forward motion caused by the cadential foreshortening of a phrase. What is unusual in the *Eroica* is not the presence of elisions but their preponderance. The illustration provides an overview of these elisions within the exposition alone. Similar moments are found throughout the movement.

The Concept of Unity: Analyses

These elisions unify on more important grounds than that of their frequency alone, though their continual presence turns this kind of event into something of a compositional premise. Their generic sources can be seen to lie within the opening theme itself in two respects. (See measures 3–15.) One is the obvious presence there of two elisions: the first effecting the link between measures 4–5 of the theme (the connection between the triadic and the chromatic so important to the movement); the second elision appearing at the end of the phrase itself (the downbeat note that elides with the following phrase).

The second respect in which the sources of elisions inhere in the opening theme involves the up- and downbeat orientations of the theme segments. In the opening measures, the weaker end of the triadic segment closes (elides) into the weaker (upbeat) opening of the chromatic segment; likewise the downbeat close of the chromatic segment elides with the downbeat opening of the following motive. A glance through the subsequent themes will show a number of them with similar inherent tendencies and orientations.

A final point concerns the unifying effect of tempo. The opening measures of the first movement, with their singular chords, establish a time frame that sets up the pulse for the movement itself. The four movements are related to this initial pulse.

The problematical aspects of Beethoven tempi and metronome markings have been discussed earlier. The *Eroica* is not entirely free of these problems, though they are less knotty than some in his other works. The following seems a likely set of tempo relations:

I	II	III	IV
Allegro con brio	**Adagio** assai	**Allegro** Vivace	**Allegro** molto

Beethoven's metronome markings first appeared over a decade after the *Eroica* was completed, in the now-famous issue of the *Allgemeine Musikalische Zeitung* (Leipzig) of December 17, 1817. They are:

I	II	III	IV
♩. = 60	♪ = 80	♩. = 116	♩ = 76

It is clear from this that at least part of the premise offered here agrees with that of the composer. By his own markings, movements one-three two-four share virtually the same pulse. The tempo problems are more extensive, however, for Beethoven's markings for the sections of the last movement read as follows:

Allegro molto	**Poco andante**	**Presto**
♩ = 76	♪ = 108	♩ = 116

There is surely an error or a publication misprint here, since the concluding *Presto* ♩ = 116 , ♩ = 58 by this scheme would be slower than the opening *Allegro molto*. Note that the *Presto* marking indicates a kinship with movements one and three. Does the error lie with the *Allegro molto* marking of the fourth movement?

It is something of a puzzle. What is clear is that Beethoven himself sensed a steady pulse relationship among some movements of the work. Whether one can find a mean tempo range that will unite all movements satisfactorily (focused around ±60) remains an inviting question. It is interesting that, rightly or wrongly, many conductors have taken the second movement at a slower tempo than marked, one that in fact approaches 60 (they have taken the last movement more slowly as well).

What should be done with the tempo indications of the last movement? Is it reasonable to interpret the verbal indications as descriptive, connoting character as much as speed? Is it more sensible to reverse the *Allegro molto–Presto* metronome indications, which gives:

Allegro molto	**Poco Andante**	**Presto**
♩ = 116	♪ = 108	♩ = 76
(♩ = 58)		

Could this have been the original meaning, marred by a misprint in the published article? The reversal provides for an acceleration from *Allegro molto* to *Presto*. Coincidentally it also relates the fourth movement to the third movement in terms of a common pulse. Absolute solutions to this question are unlikely. Continuous pulse relations, however, hover in the background.

Certainly the situation is anomalous. It is hard to believe that in a work integrated to such an extraordinary degree the factor of tempo—that ultimate durational control over all other aspects of structure and unity—would not itself be unified. It is plausible to seek the key to this question within evidence that is deeper and more internal to structure than surface indications alone.

1. How well this fits Schoenberg's statement that all ideas in a work, regardless of formal function (such as transition, elaboration, codetta), must have an intrinsic structure and not be "mere trash." See Arnold Schoenberg, "Brahms the Progressive," *Style and Idea* (New York: Philosophical Library, 1950), pp. 63-64.

2. One must be cautious in ascribing thematic significance to triadic motives, since the triad is such a common convention of classical harmony. While triadically derived *themes* seem important in this work, one cannot extend the influence of these shapes to lesser material without evidence of significance, such as recurrent pattern, rhythmic features, correlation of texture, and dynamics. In this regard the excerpt at measure 136 is interesting, as the imitational byplay of motive in the strings does appear significant by virtue of contour, articulation, rhythm, and similar qualities.

3. The chromatic line in either or both outer parts, extended over large periods, was a prime determinant of chromatic harmony during this era. Chromaticism on these levels was structurally integral, rather than a decorative elaboration of diatonic syntax. These questions are pursued in other analyses that follow and in Appendix B.

4. See also Schenker's analysis of the *Eroica* with regard to these motivic lines. Heinrich Schenker, *Das Meisterwerk in der Musik*, vol. 3 (Munich: Drei Masken Verlag, 1930), especially the graphs with their voice-leading indications.

5. See also Charles Rosen, *The Classical Style* (London: Faber & Faber, 1971), p. 393, on this theme; and Schenker, *Das Meisterwerk*, graphs.

6. This theme poses another problem regarding both motive structure and phrasing. The shape of the theme extends from the initial note *through* the first beat of the third measure; the second phrase is a reiteration of this shape, likewise with an upbeat orientation. The phrasing slurs contradict the structure, embracing the metric units of two measures and the rhythms created by harmonic change, but not the rhythmic placement of the motive within these measures:

(indicated phrasing)

(motivic structure of phrase)

The first notes in measures 3 and 5 might well be included under the preceding slurs, lending better agogics to the four-measure phrase articulations.

7. In the same passage further half-step tension exists between the G of the horn and the A♭ of the accompaniment, reminiscent of the similar relationship found in the first violins in measures 7-11 of the opening theme.

Schenker seems to have sensed the relationship of the events in this passage to an elemental formative shape when he stated in *Harmony* that "the phenomenon, which in reality should be understood as a passing note or a suspension, seems to be unfolded here in the symphony's main motif itself." Heinrich Schenker, *Harmony*, ed. Oswald Jonas, tr. Elizabeth Mann Borgese (Chicago: University of Chicago Press, 1954), p. 163.

8. These terms are subject to some confusion in meaning. Conventional theory regarded modulation as a transfer of locus to a new key or key center. In this sense a piece could move to a number of different keys in the course of its *Durchführung*, or working out.

Schenker has demonstrated that this is a shortsighted view of harmonic motion which gives a distorted perspective. He shows that in tonal music of this period there is only *one* tonality of a work, its true tonic, which harmony on all levels serves to establish and to "unfold." Thus the move to the dominant in sonata-form expositions is not a move to a new key, but the temporary establishment of a dominant harmonic region within the prevailing tonality, as part of a longer, tonic-oriented structural progression.

The discussion of harmonic activity here embraces the Schenkerian concept. In the absence of an adequate terminology, however, conventional terms are inevitable. "Harmonic progression," "modulation," "key relations," and related terms should be understood here in the above sense.

9. "Beethoven's *Durchführungen*, with their dramatic inclinations, often aim for even greater contrasts than structural considerations require. In the Eroica this can best be seen in [measures 178-186]." Arnold Schoenberg, *Structural Functions of Harmony* (New York: Norton, 1954), p. 153.

10. Ibid.

11. The ordered association of motive to function in this movement is carried out to a remarkable degree. For example, in the recapitulation, in the passage parallel to the one just studied (measures 445-450), the music does not destroy E♭ as a tonality, for the conventional reason that the transition will further reestablish the tonic as locus for the second thematic group. The moment is thus a lesser one in the hierarchy of tonal activity. As a corollary, the bass does not embody the derived bass-line motive. In its place is the half-step-derived motive (present also in the alto), effecting a simple progression of ii-V. There is in fact no chord of the augmented sixth, though its constituent elements remain, reordered:

12. Chromatic rather than diatonic cases are examined since they tend further to deviate from conventional norms of the period and of

the tonal system itself. If they are found to relate in this fashion, several conclusions appear convincing, with respect to Beethoven at least: namely (1) that individual works establish and follow their own norms, and (2) that shape as a formative premise is manifest in diverse musical domains.

13. This view of tonality is shared by Schenker as well.

14. I am indebted to Professors Milton Babbitt and Edward T. Cone of Princeton University for this insight.

15. Precisely where in the phrase this downbeat accent occurs might be open to question. It can be heard at measure 15, the elided cadence with the next phrase—the sf⟹p in measures 10–11, being embellishmental stresses rather than structural accents. Some listeners may hear the downbeat before this point. There is no doubt, however, that the downbeat accent occurs late in the phrase, the preceding notes forming a long upbeat. It is this point that is of concern here.

16. Although the themes at measures 45 and 152 do not have explicit crescendo or ⟨=== ===⟩ markings, they have acquired these nuances, rightly or wrongly, in the performance tradition of the *Eroica*. There may be a valid musical basis for this practice: in their final measures, both themes resolve either dissonant neighbor tones or other suspended notes through a change of chord. ⟨=== ===⟩ nuances before these final measures emphasize the fluctuations of tension that are intrinsic to the harmonic structure. Similar examples of the same nuances with the same structural correlation are found at measures 164 ff. and 403 ff.

17. In these last two characteristics (nonlegato, *forte*) the derived themes differ from the parent shape (the opening theme of the work). The derived themes as a generic group, however, share these characteristics consistently among themselves—characteristics, furthermore, that are markedly dissimilar from those of the other shape-generated group.

18. In two places (measures 79–83 and 482–486), parallel spots in exposition and recapitulation, the rhythmic motto is extended by two more measures.

7

UNITY IN OTHER WORKS

The relevance of "idea" (Schoenberg's basic shape) to the totality of a musical work is not limited to the *Eroica* nor to Beethoven. The studies that follow illustrate the relationship in music of Mozart, Haydn, and Schumann. In each case the sense of compositional premise gives insight into enigmatic moments in these works, whether of tonal relations, rhythmic-metric structures, or matters of tempo.

MOZART'S SYMPHONY NO. 40

The first movement of Mozart's Symphony No. 40 offers a case in point, as the opening of the development moves to the remote region of F♯ minor. How does one reconcile the tonic key, G minor, to F♯ minor, a region Schoenberg described as so distant as to be almost unrelated?[1]

The modulation, which juxtaposes the two key centers a half step apart, and the manner of progression into F♯ minor, emanate from features prominent in the movement's basic shape, found in the opening theme. They are (1) the half-step interval repeatedly expressed in the E♭–D motive and (2) the underlying line of the theme itself, a descending diatonic stepwise sequence through a perfect fifth (D–G), to which the upper E♭ serves as neighbor tone (Ex. 37).

Ex. 37. Mozart: *Symphony No. 40 in G Minor,* **first movement**

This descending line of a fifth is fundamental as a background shape to many of the themes, as illustrated.[2] The half-step interval, on the other hand, is explicit thematically as foreground, and motivates chromatic, often dissonant progressions in the exposition (see score, measures 14–20, 48–50, 56–70).

These two features of the basic shape have been sufficiently integrated into the music by the close of the exposition to provide a basis for the modulation to F♯ minor that follows. Their foreground-background roles reverse at this moment; the abrupt tonal transition, effected by the four-measure phrase in the winds (measure 102), makes explicit the underlying background shape—the descending line implicit in the opening and subsequent themes. The D on which the transition begins becomes an ambiguous note, turned from its former position as the upper limit of the descending fifth into the neighbor tone lying above that fifth. It serves as the basis for recontextualizing this line and placing it on a tonal level a half step lower.[3] Thus the transition from G minor to F♯ minor, which projects the neighbor tone of the basic shape and the most evident motive in the movement, is made by means of the other component of that shape—the descending-fifth line.

The byplay of foreground-background recasts perspectives to a further extent, for the descending line in the winds, revealing as it does the underlying conceptual shape of the movement, serves almost as a summary of the movement itself. Its placement in this respect is apt; it initiates the development, the section that by function explores the implications of musical ideas.

Recontextualization of this descending fifth goes a step further as the development begins. The interval from D to G is heard here with a transient and very different harmonic underpinning, and in a chromaticized version (see measures 105–115). This chromaticization of the motive seems to serve a further function as demarcator of large sectional segments in the movement. For the fifth is chromaticized only at particular places: the beginning of the second group and closing group, in exposition and recapitulation (measures 48, 65—shown here; also 231, 254); the opening phrases of the development, just discussed; and the passages that immediately precede the recapitulation (measure 160) and coda (measure 281).

melodic over line

102

harmonic reduction

Strings

Cello, Bass

Bassoons

109

110

115

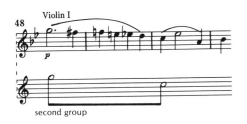

48 Violin I

p

second group

65 Violins

f *sf*

closing group

160 Flute

p

approach to recapitulation

281 Violin I

Flute

f

approach to coda

Unity in Other Works

The themes of this movement are integrated in their rhythmic aspects as well as in their underlying contours of pitch. For one, the motive of the opening theme effects a double augmentation of itself in its overall metric character. These metric implications are reinforced in secondary voices at various points in the movement, for example, the horns at measures 119–120 or measure 203 (see score).

Beyond this detail there is a striking degree of coordination among dynamics, texture, weight, and modes of articulation, all integrated with the underlying rhythmic properties of themes. The two upbeat-oriented themes are generally soft in dynamics, lyrical and legato in character, and relatively light and transparent in orchestral texture. Their opposites, the downbeat-oriented themes, are prevailingly forte, nonlegato, and often marcato or otherwise punctuated. By way of further distinction, all the downbeat-oriented themes are initiated by means of elisions with their foregoing passages. This is not the case with the two upbeat-oriented themes.

One of the more subtle rhythmic touches of the movement concerns the opening theme of the second group, restudied here. In some respects this passage suggests a downbeat character, for it establishes the tonal region of B♭ major following a less stable transitory passage. Further, it is the first measure of a series of two-measure metric groups whose subsequent harmonies are less stable than this first measure. Moreover, the new dynamic level makes a sudden contrast with the preceding passage, emphasizing its demarcation.

On a deep-structure level the opening measure of this passage is in fact a downbeat— a structural one that brings about stability through its establishment of the relative major. On a more surface level, with respect to the rhythmic character of the second thematic group, it is upbeat-oriented. The explanation of this lies in the opening measure of the theme. Although this measure establishes the tonic, it does so via a $\frac{6}{3}$ inversion, that is, on a chord position of only relative stability. Full, true tonal stability on this new center is not felt until the cadence seven measures later, when B♭ as a tonic is heard in root position.

Thus rhythmic emphasis at this point is perceived in two ways—contradictory ways at that—operating upon two different levels. The deep-structure downbeat is felt at the same point that the upbeat-oriented theme, on a more surface level, is initiated.

HAYDN'S SYMPHONY NO. 104

The first movement of Haydn's Symphony No. 104 (*London*) is unified in both its pitch and rhythmic organization, and in its tempi—the latter are discussed in Chapter 4, as are the tempi of Mozart's Symphony No. 40. Almost every theme and subsidiary idea in this movement is found to derive from a parent shape. The movement also contains a juxtaposition of leading tone and octave (tonic) as tonal centers that arises from an earlier motivic germ.

Example 38 shows the opening theme. As can be seen the theme divides rhythmically into two segments, each of which influences the rhythmic shapes of subsequent themes, listed below it. (Rhythms of the first parent segment are identified by a square bracket ⌐‾‾‾⌐ ; those of the second by a curved bracket ⌣‾‾‾ . The double curved bracket ≈‾‾‾ suggests that the short eighth-note motive relates to the following segment as a rhythmic diminution.)

The rhythm of the first motive in the opening theme (measure 18) is found in a number of subsequent themes. It has a relationship as well, though a less obvious one, to the rhythm of the opening motto in the Introduction (measure 1); the figure ♩ ♩.. ♩ ♩ in measure 1 is a variant of the rhythm ♩ ♩♩ | ♩ in measure 18. The generic relation is the more complex, perceptually, due to the function of tempo. While the Introduction is rhythmically a diminution of the Allegro figure, its statement as an Adagio results in its being heard twice as slowly as the Allegro—virtually an augmentation (**Adagio C** ♪= ♩ **Allegro ¢**). The Introduction relates to the rest of the movement in melodic and harmonic details as well as in rhythm, bearing in fragmented and disguised form aspects of the shapes that will be prominent in the following section.

Ex. 38. Haydn: *Symphony No. 104 in D Major,* **first movement**

The Concept of Unity: Analyses

The themes studied earlier in terms of rhythm are examined here for their pitch relationship to the basic shape of the opening two measures of the Allegro theme. (The second segment of this opening theme itself is seen to be derived from the first two measures.) As indicated, all of these basic pitch shapes are based upon contour inversions and variations of what amounts to a turn figure or its fragments, the latter formed of two-note groups of major or minor seconds.

Basic pitch shapes common to themes:

Unity in Other Works

The most subtle derivations of these shapes are seen in connection with a motive which, in pitch structure, is least like others in the work (though in rhythm it derives clearly from a parent shape). This rather individual pitch shape (measure 32) yields two subsequent themes in the course of phrase extensions, themes in which the parent shape is hidden by embellishments (measure 40, measure 80). (It also serves as ground material for augmentation in measures 88–91, and syncopation in measures 101–102 page 140.) A third line is also embedded in the passage at measure 80, its roots in a different source but one which, again, lies among the movement's motivic shapes (measure 21).

One function of the classical introduction was to present, often in microcosm and in disguise, those elements that would play a prominent role in a movement as it subsequently unfolded. The figure D–E–D–C♯ in the *London* Symphony is such an element, its fragmented presentation in measure 3 a case of this usage. Of the fragments that constitute this passage, the D–C♯ figure, with its unresolved leading-tone tension, is prominent from the outset and plays an important later role on several levels.

The distinctive character of this phrase is exploited motivically throughout the Introduction on differing harmonic levels (measures 9–12). The same motto, on the same pitches C♯–D, is prominent in the opening measures of the Allegro (measure 19); it acquires particular prominence here by its statement in the high register of the cellos, a sound unique in timbre and intensity. Subsequently it figures ornamentally as a pedal point (measure 33, measures 36–37); its half-step interval is a prominent melodic motive in later phrases, the chromaticism emphasized through the dynamic accents *sf*, >
(measures 40–43).

By the time the development section is reached, this motive has attained musical stature, a stature now amplified in a larger dimension by casting the D–C♯ complex as tonal poles. C♯ becomes a temporary key center, the goal of a long sequential passage (measures 124–145) in which the same motive with its prominent chromatic motto is the prime element. Recontextualization is part of this thinking. The C# minor passage (measure 145) in its first two measures reworks the leading-tone motto (C#–B#) that has its source in the Introduction; this time it is on a tonal level that by its relation to the tonic, D, is itself a part of that motto. Motive thus gives rise to theme, in turn to harmony, and ultimately to long-range tonal motion.

Unity in Other Works

Schoenberg is reported by members of his circle to have felt that entire works were probably unified by some of the elements of shape he had found within individual movements, though he never had opportunity to follow up this supposition. Very likely he was right. Many musicians have noted motivic correspondences in the late quartets of Beethoven, those within Op. 130–135 having yet further relationships among the different quartets themselves. It is obvious in Brahms's Second Symphony that the head motives of movements one, three, and four derive from the same source (as does that of movement two, but in a more subtle manner—see the opening and closing notes of the first two cello phrases: F♯, B♯, and B). Motivic relations are also projected through the tonal schemes in these movements, especially in movements one and four.

Schumann is another composer many of whose major works are unified throughout. Cyclical form, which presupposes such an inner conceptual unity, was a central feature of his output, found, for example, in the song cycles; the piano works (*Kinderscenen*, *Carnaval*, and others are in many respects cyclical); the piano quintet. The symphonies of Schumann are also organized in this manner, the Fourth and Third being excellent cases in point.[4] In both these works the motivic ideas of all their movements reside in underlying shapes or germs. All movements further relate through tempo schemata. Moreover, within the essentially sonata-form first movements of each are large-scale tonal relationships that reflect motivic shape.

That Schumann viewed the entire Fourth Symphony (D Minor) as one musical whole is clear from the score, which does not separate the work into movements in the conventional manner, allowing for performance breaks in between, but divides "movement" conclusions only by thin double lines and fermatas, suggesting just a breath in making the connections.

This attempt to achieve oneness in performance has both literal and figurative implications. The sections, such as the Romanza and Scherzo, remain by any conventional standard bona fide movements in themselves. Yet the work is literally a compositional whole in the sense that all "movements" have interconnections of motive, harmony, tempo, and dynamics.

SCHUMANN'S THIRD SYMPHONY

The Third Symphony (*Rhenish*), the last of the four to be composed by Schumann, shares the cyclical approach of the earlier D Minor Symphony. Integrated throughout are such elements as motivic shape, tonal plan, and tempo relations—all emanating from a central generic idea. The diversity in character and derivations from this central source is a striking aspect of Schumann's mature powers.

The basic pitch contour operating throughout these five movements might best be described as a $^6_4$ tonic triad, variously ornamented. As it has before, the question arises here of triad-as-norm versus triad as a unique concept. The prevalence of this shape as a basic shape and the high degree of correlation between its properties and events that evolve in numerous domains leave little doubt that for this work the shape is special, not general. The particular inverted form of the triad used, the fifth always the low point of its contour, ever prominent as a head motive, reinforces the impression of uniqueness.

Ex. 39 shows the opening theme of the first movement and the embellished triadic shape that underlies a major segment of this theme. Grouped below this are numerous themes from the following movements, their relationship to this same shape also shown. (For the sake of comparison they have all been transposed to E♭.)

Ex. 39. Schumann: *Symphony No. 3 in E flat Major*

Themes

Underlying ♮ triadic shape

Unity in Other Works

The implications of the opening theme are greater than this one shape alone. The following passages show three derived subshapes that fall into more-or-less distinct categories: the large overall line of the theme (measures 1, 367, 77, 253, 215); the interval of a fourth (bracketed in measures 1–13), so prominent as an opening head motive; and lastly a motive of three descending chromatic notes, initially C–Cb–Bb, within the opening theme (measure 10).

The overall line appears in a number of contexts within the first movement, some of which are indicated here. The line is in effect a summary of the theme itself. Its most dramatic employment comes at a point most apt for this kind of summation—the heroic horn call that appears in measure 367 shortly before the recapitulation (see derived shapes below dotted arrow).

The interval of a fourth, prominent in the opening theme of the first movement, also figures prominently as the head of almost all motives in movements two, four, and five, as can be seen from a second look at Ex. 39, where these shapes are bracketed. The opening theme of movement one also makes extensive use of the interval beyond that of a head-motive. This theme could in fact be seen paradigmatically as a series of fourths governed by a descending contour, as suggested below. The second theme of the first movement also makes use of the interval, recontextualizing through different harmonic settings those same fourths prominent in the opening theme. Fourths as motivic fragments are found throughout the first movement.

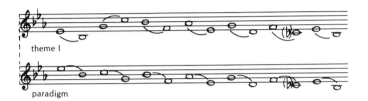

Unity in Other Works

Although the three-note chromatic motive is less obtrusive than the other two derived subshapes in the large plan of the first movement, it does appear in several ornamantal capacities.

Derivatives of chromatic motive

This same motive also plays a major role in structuring the point of recapitulation: the bass line in the phrases approaching this moment embodies the motive in measures 403–411. This explains the recapitulation on the unlikely $\frac{6}{4}$ position of the tonic, as the bass B♭ at this point is also the terminal note of the motive.[5] The same chromatic figure, relocated and inverted as A♭–A♮–B♭, also affects harmonic motion on fore- and middle-ground levels within the opening movement. See measures 51 and 399.

The boldest implementation of the relationship between motivic shape and tonal plan is found in the broad perspective of the first movement, the span from the opening measures until the return to the tonic at the recapitulation. The shape which motivates it is the overall line that derives from the opening theme itself. The tonic-dominant implication of the fourth motive E♭–B♭, though normal in the tonal motion of expositions, is incorporated in this special context as well. More striking is the remainder of this line and its deployment, the pitches G–C–B♭–A♭–G(♭)–F–E♭, as seen in the soprano line. Most of these pitches serve as temporary tonal centers, only the G♭ at measure 311 standing as a melodic point, supported by a passing E♭-minor harmony. The tonic $\frac{6}{4}$ harmony at the recapitulation is also partly determined by this linear motivic scheme. (See previous illustration.) While the bass at this point results from the chromatic motive and its termination, the extreme upper part concludes the overarching melodic motive.

The tonal plan of this development thus projects motivic shape through tonal centers. The development also reveals Schumann's proclivity for stating his musical ideas sequentially, with literal phrase repetitions placed upon different harmonic levels. The dotted phrase lines over the motivic sketches indicate these sectional parallelisms, which are here interspersed among other thematic ideas.

Unity in Other Works

The control of time in the Third Symphony serves as a further unifying agent, integrating ideas throughout the five movements by way of rhythms and tempo. The source of much of this control is (perhaps predictably) found in the first notes of the symphony's opening theme, with their ambiguous rhythmic-metric nature, $\frac{3}{4} : \frac{3}{2}$.

This aspect of the music has been discussed to some extent in Chapter 4. (See again the tempo scheme of the symphony presented in Ex. 30.) The earlier discussion pointed out that the first six measures of the opening theme, in their metric organization and in its reinforcement through orchestration, make unclear whether the music is to be perceived as $\frac{3}{4}$, moving with a pulse of one to the measure, or as $\frac{3}{2}$, where two written measures actually form one metric unit of three pulses:

The ultimate *perceived* nature of the motion is not clarified until the seventh measure, where the rhythm ♩ ♩ | ♩ ♩ | ♩ ♩ | can only be heard as $\frac{3}{4}$, moving in one. The two meters possible through this ambiguity are played upon throughout the movement, at times one version or the other explicit, at other times both possibilities implicit, as in the opening, creating situations incapable of a definitive singular interpretation. (Some of these places are discussed in Chapter 4.)

Rhythmic, metric, and tempo aspects of the entire symphony arise from this opening ambiguity. For one thing the head-motive of a fourth, prominent throughout the entire work, receives its initial emphasis through its ambiguous metrical statement in these first two notes of the opening. For another, the $\frac{3}{2}$ pole of the metrical ambiguity immediately implies that the half note—two-thirds of the $\frac{3}{4}$ pulse—is an important metric-rhythmic unit, thus establishing in the musical materials the inherent 3:2 temporal ratio that is fundamental to tempo relations throughout the symphony. (See again the discussion of this tempo scheme in Chapter 4; also its depiction in Ex. 30.)

This $\frac{3}{4} : \frac{3}{2}$ ambiguity effects a curious temporal control over the opening theme— its phrasing, pacing, and tensions, as they emerge in performance and as they relate to motivic shape. The point is illustrated below, where the opening theme is shown in its two segments, the initial one in which the $\frac{3}{4} : \frac{3}{2}$ metric is ambiguous, and the following segment in which $\frac{3}{4}$ is explicit. The pitches of the overall motivic line are so arranged that they are heard within closer time intervals in the opening segment— virtually every half note apart—whereas in the explicitly $\frac{3}{4}$ segment they are separated by the greater time interval of three half notes. Thus there is an inner temporal tension. Where the music may metrically be perceived as $\frac{3}{2}$ —a slower metric grouping—the motivic line is stated more quickly than in the following section, where the quicker metric grouping prevails. The performance implications of this fact require that players make explicit the $\frac{3}{4}$ meter at measure 7 by "quasi-waltz" agogics that move the phrase forward. Otherwise a slight time delay can result, perceptible enough for one to sense a dragging pace in the latter half of the phrase.

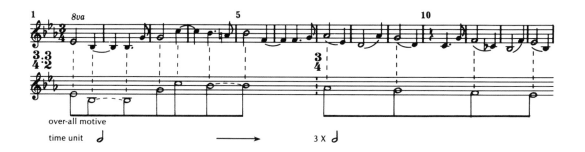

over-all motive

time unit

Other implications of the $\frac{3}{4}:\frac{3}{2}$ duality relate to the symphony as a whole, most
notably its first four movements. Some of these are suggested in the chart, which lists
themes from these movements and abstracts their rhythms. (Tempo/pulse relations
between the movements are indicated vertically.) It is clear that the rhythmic shapes
of motives in the various movements stem from common generic roots. The interrelations
in some cases are varied through metric displacements; elsewhere, through augmentation/
diminution effected by notation or by tempo/pulse relations—that is, by the assignment
of pulse to different metric values. (Both means amount to the same musical result.)

The themes of movements two and three (see p. 155) are obviously similar in rhythmic shape, though their 2:1 relation to tempo (movement three being twice as slow as movement two) masks this identity in performance. The same is true for the diminution of the eighth-note theme in movement four, in regard to its quarter-note forebear in the same movement. On the other hand, this same eighth-note theme has an identity with the opening theme of the symphony, from which it derives; both themes in fact are heard at the same tempo. Similarly the opening themes of movements one and two, heard almost contiguously at the close of the former and the start of the latter movement, move at the same tempo and are rhythmically related, their triple-meter identity somewhat clouded by metric shift. Note the prominence of the motto

♩. ♪ | ♩. , which pervades all these movements. It is heard either within the same length of time as its opening-movement statement or within double this length, by virtue of augmentation.

Finally, a further example of a unifying rhythmic pattern, one that in this case integrates virtually the entire third movement and all its thematic ideas. All third-movement themes, as indicated below, share an upbeat orientation. All share the same metric length of four beats as well (or, as in the third idea, at measure 7, a two-beat fragmentation, repeated).

The entire movement in fact is a *tour de force* on the highest artistic level, in which essentially all phrases are tailored to this prevalent four-beat length, (measures 13–14 being the one real exception). If one is unaware of this in performance it is due largely to the variety of rhythmic patterns that lie within these four-beat confines, as the previous illustration shows, and to the occasional links between phrases, or inner sub-divisions within a phrase, that Schumann provides. The first-violin line from measures 4–5 is such a link, the motives themselves lying in the winds. Measures 46–48 effect a link more complex in concept. The extended line in the violins joins the measures; the entrance of the viola imitation punctuates the two-beat mid-point of the motive; then the inner voice of the cellos subtly indicates the rhythmic point at which the second phrase unit fits. (The brackets show the underlying four-beat phrases. Some-thing of the same thinking occurs in measure 33, where slurring the ♩♩♩♩ in the last half of the measure obscures the upbeat demarcation of the phrases.)

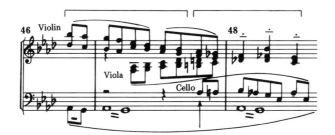

Upbeat orientations are a major aspect of the Third Symphony. In the second movement such orientations are almost the only ones to be found. There is not a downbeat coincidence of phrase rhythm and metric beat until the last two measures of the movement, so that all which precedes this point stands as its extended upbeat. Even the chordal entries of winds and violins approaching the final cadence are not rhythmic downbeats, despite their attacks on metric strong points. They fall within the third and fourth measures of the cello-bassoon phrase—upbeats still to the one downbeat of the movement, its final cadence.

Schumann's Third Symphony, though a small sample of the composer's mature works, is yet representative of his compositional thinking in many ways. Beyond the structural attributes already discussed, it further suggests an interesting kinship in musical thought between Schumann and his younger protégé, Brahms, who was to extend so many of these inclinations to their most complex reaches.

In his recognition of ambiguity as a compositional value of extensive implications; in his turning of harmony to ways that avoid the grounding pull of structural downbeats; and in his working of rhythms, both local and more extensive, to produce syncopes, metric displacements, and other avoidances of regularity within a prevalent metric, Schumann appears very much the progenitor of these musical characteristics that have been widely associated with Brahms. There is more yet to be understood of this relationship and of the influence of the older man. It would also seem that Schumann is due greater credit for his approach to rhythm. Certainly the cases studied here indicate his rhythmic devices were more than experiments, as some writers have suggested. Beneath their surface lies a sophisticated appreciation of the values for structure inherent in rhythmic complexity.

NOTES

1. Arnold Schoenberg, *Structural Functions of Harmony* (New York: Norton, 1954), p. 65.

2. It is also heard locally as a link between phrases, though in fragmented form and with no potential significance implied at the time. See the bassoon line of measures 20–22.

3. The pitch D plays a special role as both a reference point and an axis in this chromatic recontextualization. At the outset of the movement D is the local melodic focus, embroidered with the upper E♭ neighbor tone in the first theme. It serves as the same focus, and as an axis of symmetry, from measures 14–20, where the neighbor tone is inverted to C♯–D at the half-cadence. The role of neighbor tone is further amplified at the opening of the development, where D becomes the turning point by which the descending fifth settles a half step lower into the key of F♯ minor.

4. The Fourth Symphony (D Minor), though composed second in the sequence of the symphonies, was revised ten years later in 1851 and published as the final symphony.

5. The $\frac{6}{4}$ position is also a chordal condensation of the basic-shape motive.

8   AMBIGUITY AS PREMISE

Musical compositions are, among other things, products of ordered thought—thought structured by concepts, procedures, and modes of reference intrinsic to the medium. Like all manner of ordered thought, compositions are based upon initial ideas from which thinking emanates.

These ideas have been referred to in parts of this book as "premises," understood in the sense of bases, stated or assumed, upon which reasoning proceeds. Premises should not be associated here with axioms, postulates, or similar parts of a specific system of logic. Logic, in the conventional formal sense, might be applicable to some aspects of music. It is questionable, however, whether it is the appropriate mode of thought fully to encompass music as a system or as a structure.

Analyses in earlier parts of this book have elucidated different kinds of musical premises, some of which have been studied in relation to their subsequent realizations, rather than as premises alone. These realizations have been seen not necessarily as end results of a linear mode of thought—as "conclusions"—but as entities continually present, informing musical contexts in multiple perspectives.

It is useful in dealing with compositional bases to distinguish between what may simply be a frame of reference and what may truly be a premise, intrinsic and unique to a particular composition. The two often intertwine, and musical ideas may devolve from one status to the other. Yet basic differences exist between them.

Of the analytical approaches discussed so far, those concerning historical or stylistic aspects of musical language and those concerning general formal features (such as phrases, periods, sonata-form) are essentially frames of reference. They are conventions, limitations, general modes of approach—all of which exist as a background prior to any act of composition—guidelines, in effect, within which musical thinking may flow and beyond which, as we have seen, thinking may extend.

By contrast, basic shapes or musical ideas as a total concept—that which Schoenberg viewed as a *Grundgestalt*—are matters of premise. While "idea" in this sense may be molded or limited by conventions or reference frames, its musical embodiment is particular, exclusively involved with a single composition, affecting its specific events within or beyond norms, as the case may be.

This seems to be a matter of the general versus the specific—the confines within which a thought may be conceived and the unique operations of that thought itself. In this sense Schenker's analyses span both areas. His *Ursatz*, in its predictable harmonic and melodic motion, represents musical properties shared by virtually all music from the period in question—that is, it provides a reference frame or convention. Events in middle- and foreground levels reflect the unique play of ideas within the context of an individual work—a reflection, in other words, of premise.

Premise and reference frame at times interchange roles. Formal convention, for instance, can become a focal compositional premise. Schumann's Fourth Symphony in its first movement turns the recapitulation to this effect, truncating the section and abandoning conventional procedure and even prior thematic material. The results become a major feature of the movement, anomalous but intrinsically right for the piece.

It could be argued that manipulations of motive—compositional procedures which affect premises of basic-shape nature, so intrinsic to a work—nevertheless represent a kind of convention, and that the basic shape is, in other words, a compositional generalization. This is true, but a significant fact remains: conventions of form, style, and procedure are background generalities; compositional matters concerning shape involve individual works. The range and the nature of thought between the two concepts are different.

Basic shape, "idea," unity probably constitute the most pervasive premises unique to a given work (as do Schenkerian middle- and foreground concepts). Other premises can also be found. Like that of basic shape, these arise from special qualities of ideas themselves.

Whereas basic shapes are pervasive, to the extent that their properties can be generalized, these other premises offer no similar consistency. Nor for that matter are they likely to dominate formal landscapes in such large-scale ways. Their roles are subsidiary, structurally determinative in partial rather than overall ways. Because their contexts may be unique, they must be studied within their particular settings.

Ambiguity functions as such a subpremise. So do local events, such as pedal points and other configurations. So does compositional procedure itself in some cases. Nor are these elements totally divorced from basic shapes; they may be part of them, but are so perceived and used as also to play a special role in themselves. The chapters that follow examine specific instances in which premises like these function, providing not so much a "law" of their behavior as an insight into this kind of premise-influenced compositional thought.

AMBIGUITY IN BRAHMS'S SECOND SYMPHONY

Ambiguity was seen as a structural subpremise earlier in these studies, in Beethoven's *Eroica* Symphony, first movement, and in Schumann's *Rhenish* (Third) Symphony. In each case a local event of ambiguous nature exerted some specific subsequent influence upon the music. The C♯ in measure 5 of the *Eroica*'s opening theme, for example—unclear in its harmonic tendencies—initially acted as melodic appoggiatura, rising to a tonal resolution. In the parallel place in the recapitulation, however, it functioned as a D♭, resolving downwards to C and effecting a temporary new key center of F major. In the *Rhenish* Symphony, the rhythmic-metric ambiguity of the opening measures (whether $\frac{3}{4}$ or $\frac{3}{2}$) determined tempo relations for the subsequent movements.

Perhaps no composer of the period so reveled in the structural possibilities of ambiguity as did Brahms. His Second Symphony is a case in point, ambiguous properties inherent in the basic ideas of the opening movement exerting pervasive effects upon the overall structure of this and subsequent movements.

The main progenitor of these ambiguities is the cello-bass motive of the opening measures. Both its harmonic and rhythmic properties are unclear and capable of producing various viewpoints, many of which are explored as the music progresses. These viewpoints are, in fact, partial generators of the movement. The harmonic ambiguity of this motive and its effect upon rhythm have been studied to some extent in Chapter 4 (Ex. 9). The apparent lack of clarity in the opening two measures (Should they be heard as tonic or dominant oriented? Is the first measure upbeat or downbeat?) is but part of a larger harmonic plan in which the initial structural downbeat, coincident with the first true establishment of tonic harmony, occurs at measure 44. The opening is thus a long dominant-oriented upbeat, which has the effect of turning the few measures of tonic harmony in measures 5–9 into local way stations within what is a dominant-oriented passage.

None of this is clear beyond dispute. Much in fact depends upon the perspectives within which these measures are heard—perspectives of phrase length and of harmony. The richness of the passage, as with much of Brahms, lies in part in its depiction of musical ideas in these different perspectives—in other words, upon its inherent ambiguity.

Tonal ambiguity next plays a deep-structure role with respect to the second thematic group of the exposition, which seemingly appears in the mediant key of F♯ minor (measure 82). The mediant is not the ultimate key, however, for the exposition ends normatively in the dominant. The mediant is itself a tonal way station, therefore, whose structural rationale is not evident on the surface. Nor is F♯ minor itself as a tonal center always clear. Quite the contrary; the passage is tonally fluid, seemingly moving through several key centers.

The thinking behind this harmonic plan seems to inhere in the tonal implications of the opening materials. These opening ideas are twofold, the cello-bass motive of measures 1–2 and the horn motive of measures 2–5. Both motives bear the same implications, though in different ways. Both imply the harmonies I, iii, and V. As seen in Ex. 40, these are the only normative (triadic) harmonies—and potential tonal centers—lying within the note combinations of the cello-bass motive. Also they are the principal notes outlined by the horn motive, which functions in tandem with this first motive.[1]

Ex. 40. Brahms: *Symphony No. 2 in D Major,* **first movement**

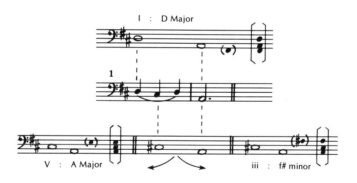

The section in F# minor is a transient one, then, using the mediant as a passing tonality on the way to V. It thus outlines by means of tonal motion the "triadicity" of D major, one of several foci of the piece. Moreover, the harmonic scheme of this second group theme, though it is heard ostensibly in the mediant, is itself ambiguous. It moves among three key centers in the course of its complete statement—the same three of I, iii, and V—further reinforcing these centers as focal points of the D major triadic shape. The large schema shows this plan. The nature of the motion is subtle; some of these key centers are clearly established, while others are more implied than stated, and implied only in passing contexts within the fluid harmonic plan.

The large overview of this passage brings out the motivic shape of the opening cello-bass line. The focal notes of this shape are clear enough, attaining prominence through their placement as extreme points of line and through their rhythmic or repetitive emphases. As the example indicates, they combine in different ways to place this motive on different tonal planes.

Rhythmic ambiguity also plays a structural role in this movement of the Second Symphony, once again stemming from properties inherent in the opening cello-bass theme. The question here is the often discussed one of whether the opening two measures of the motive are downbeat-upbeat in nature or vice versa. (This is often asked by orchestra players in terms of upbow or downbow bowings for the phrase.)

No answer is definitive for these two measures. Taken by themselves in an isolated context, the measures would logically read as downbeat-upbeat, that is, as downbeat-oriented. The first measure achieves weight by its placement on the tonic—the most stable point—and the phrase moves to a less stable dominant area. The following measures contradict this, however; measures 9–10 and 13–14, using the same motivic figure, imply the secondary-dominant progressions vi–ii and ii–v respectively, where the second measure of the figure each time is the more stable, tending to be heard as the downbeat side of the figure and turning the first measure into an upbeat.

The opening two measures, moreover, cannot be truly heard in an isolated context. While they in themselves might seem logically down-up in nature, the second measure—presumably the upbeat—announces the horn theme. By their attack and by the added texture they create, the horns give an accent or emphasis to the second measure, thus lending it a downbeat quality. This pattern is carried out in the succeeding phrases: the entrances of the horn motive in measures 6, 10, 14 all give downbeat qualities of emphasis to these measures (in each case the second measure of the cello-bass motive).

Thus there is no definitive way to hear these measures.[2] Their ambiguous qualities are exploited by Brahms throughout the movement as a basis for development. For example:

(1) In the measures preceding the first large structural downbeat (at measure 44), it is unclear how to hear the fragmented motive from the original cello-bass figure—whether down- or upbeat.

(2) As the big D major section after measure 44 develops to a climax at measure 59, the rhythmic nature of the motive is again unclear. It appears at measure 59 with great downbeat force—the resolution of a long dominant passage, further intensified by a crescendo. However, its attack is on the third beat of the preceding measure, robbing this attack of a congruent emphasis with the local metrical downbeat of measure 59 itself.

(3) The succeeding passage at measures 63 ff. further confuses the rhythmic structure: the motive combines with itself in diminution. Its first measure, in normal rhythm (measure 63), seems downbeat oriented until heard in the elision at measure 64, where a new phrase apparently begins. This new phrase is also unclear. (a) Is its first note a downbeat or an upbeat related to the previous measure? (b) Is it to be heard as $\frac{6}{8}$ or $\frac{3}{4}$? (c) Does it interconnect the diminished form of the four-note motive as it appears twice in measures 64–65, or is it to be heard as two three-note fragments of the full motive? If it interconnects the diminished form of the motive, are the first notes in each group of three eighth notes rhythmic downbeats or upbeats? The *sf* in midmeasure lends emphasis to the second statement of the group (whether the emphasis is one of accent—that is, structural—or one of stress is uncertain); however, the unstable diminished-seventh harmony at this place gives the passage an upbeat quality. The phrase is one of the most ambiguous moments in the movement.

(4) The rhythmic ambiguities discussed above are further compounded in several ways in the passage from measures 136 to 152. For one, the rhythm of the opening cello-bass motive, now heard in canon between lower and upper strings, is embodied in a new shape whose pitch contours do not resemble those of the original opening phrase (measures 136–141). Further, the initial question of upbeat or downbeat orientation with this original phrase is now more confused in the new melody. This is achieved by displacing the melody metrically, beginning it on the second beat of the measure. Brahms removes the usual metric referents by which downbeat or upbeat orientation might be judged by destroying the metric background at this point. The ♩♫ rhythm

by which this background might be perceived—in fact, from which it emanated in the motive heard just previous to this section—is now altered by ties, with the result that (a) no articulation is heard on the metric downbeat of the individual measure; (b) background metric articulations are all off the beat—syncopations that by their extensive reiteration almost begin to sound like beats themselves; (c) because the new theme rests largely upon harmonies prevalent for some time, there is engendered a sense of quasi-stability that lends the melody something of a downbeat orientation, a quality in conflict with its metric displacement to a weaker point in the measure (a measure by now unclear in itself). Even the sense of semistability is illusory, for the harmonies that create it are seventh chords, themselves in motion. Thus the passage floats, rhythmically and metrically ambiguous, its referents and normative properties all but destroyed during these 17 measures. The picture is not clarified until measure 154.

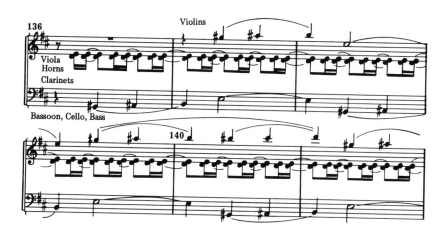

(5) Still greater uncertainty regarding the opening motive is found in the development-section stretto (measure 224). Whatever accentual property the motive had originally is further confused, since the figure is shortened to its first three notes only. (The descent of the fourth, with its agogic emphasis, is now missing.) The overlapping entrances of the stretto also alter the picture. The fourth entrance (measure 226), uncomplicated by overlaps and entering on a dissonant, unstable harmony, has the quality of a powerful upbeat, further emphasized by the weight of the full orchestra attack on the following measure. However, the unstable seventh chord on this following measure conflicts with the metrical and textural weight on this beat to make yet more unclear its downbeat or upbeat quality.

The following phrase (measures 230–233) reflects the same paradox,
and its successor (measure 236), with its motivic diminutions, shares ambiguities similar
to the diminutions seen earlier in measures 63–65.

These are but some of the many reflections of the ambiguities within this opening
motive, as it is treated throughout the first movement. Virtually every statement of the
motive illuminates these properties in a different fashion. There seems only one place
where this motive is stated with its rhythmic character clear and unenigmatic. Ap-
propriately enough this occurs at the closing segment of the coda—that moment in the
movement's action where D major has once more been achieved, where tonal repose has
brought a sense of relaxation and stability to the music. It is here (measure 477) that
the opening cello-bass motive is heard with its first measure—the tonic measure—unequivocally downbeat-oriented (measures 475–482).

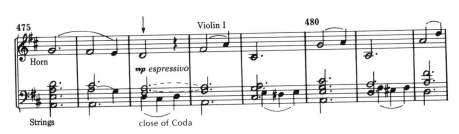

While the rhythmic and harmonic ambiguities of this movement generate many local
features of interest, and in this sense serve as one among several sets of compositional
premises, these same ambiguities are turned to larger purposes of musical design. We
have already seen how harmonic ambiguities serve to establish the tonality of D major—
the central harmonic focus of the work—through the extensive elaboration of this key
and its satellite harmonic areas. Rhythmic ambiguity also serves a broader design: by
disguising and in several ways deemphasizing rhythmic downbeats, the music in its
longest spans is kept continually on a quasi-upbeat footing, with few points of stability.
As a result the forward motion of the music is constant, pushing toward the end of the
movement and its final resolution, which is compounded of all musical elements—
rhythmic, harmonic, textural, dynamic. Forward motion is relieved at some places—
carefully chosen ones that are structurally important junctures. We have seen one, the
opening downbeat at measure 44, which turns the initial 43 measures of the movement
into a large dominant-oriented upbeat. A second place is the arrival at F♯ minor (iii),
in measure 82, to initiate the second group. A third is the close of the coda, the return
to D major already discussed (at measure 477).

It is characteristic of Brahms that the beginnings of the coda (measure 447) and of
the recapitulation are not points of repose. The coda begins on a false cadence. The

recapitulation is disguised, its precise moment of articulation uncertain, but lying between measures 298 (see trombone 1) and 302.

The repose achieved in the exposition, when the music settles into its dominant region during the second group, is also not total. The dominant harmony is established on the third beat of the preceding measure, thus diminishing its potential force by robbing it of congruence with the metrical downbeat at measure 156. Further, the harmony on V is announced in $\frac{6}{3}$ position.

This sense of forward motion through the avoidance of clear-cut structural downbeats is a salient feature of Brahms's compositional technique, found throughout his music. It accounts for much of the apparent metrical and rhythmic confusion that is so often encountered in his scores, where attacks that seem qualitatively strong (downbeats on large-scale or local levels) are placed upon metrically weak beats.

The second movement of this symphony is another excellent example of avoidance of clear-cut downbeats. Its opening theme begins in a rhythmically strong manner but on the weakest beat of the measure; cadences likewise occur largely on weak beats; resolutions of harmonic tensions are often only partial, closing upon more stable chords but upon inverted positions of these chords, so that a degree of tension and irresolution is retained. Other structural downbeats, such as the second group at measure 33, are anticipated before the metrical downbeat, thus weakening their effect. The one unequivocal downbeat is found at the final measure of the movement, all that precedes it serving on one level or another as its prolonged anacrusis.

Unity

Although the focus of this chapter is not upon matters of unity, it is worthwhile pointing out some unifying features in this symphony. The basic pitch shapes common to all movements have been touched upon earlier and are illustrated here (see chart in Ex. 49).

First movement

Second movement

(Transposed to D Major)

Third movement

Fourth movement

It is notable that they underlie ideas not only within individual movements but among all movements; the entire work is an integrated whole. The first and last movements, whose themes are variants of one another, generally outline the same key centers in their tonal explorations, these parallel functions further enriching the symmetry of the symphonic design. (See again note 1 in this chapter.)

The rhythmic figures in the design of themes within the first movement are themselves derivations and permutations of a basic shape. Further relevant to this movement's

Thematic source   Derived rhythmic shapes

thematic materials is a secondary chromatic motive derived from the sequential statements of the original cello-bass figure in measures 59–64. This secondary motive is actually the essential chromatic shape underlying the passage at measures 59–64. The derived motive generates a number of harmonic progressions later in the music, such as the passages shown in the large schema and others throughout the movement.

We have seen how in the *Eroica*'s first movement the derived motive E♭–D♭–C, whose roots lie in the early three-note chromatic figure, serves as an important element in demarcating major segments of the movement—turning points of the forms, so to speak, such as the transition to V for the second group, the beginnings of the developments, recapitulation, and coda. The derived chromatic shape in the first movement of Brahms's Second Symphony serves much the same purpose. It directly precedes a number of major turning points, most of which are shown in the schema. They include: (1) the establishment of the mediant as the initial point for the second group, following measures 78–82; (2) the arrival at the dominant as the closing tonality for the exposition, following measures 114–118; (3) the beginning of the development, following upon the passage from measures 173–179; (4) the return to I as the ultimate locus of stability (where the opening motive is finally and unequivocally heard as downbeat-oriented), following the passage from measure 455, with its chromatic bass line; (5) the final statement of I at the close of the movement, following the passage from measure 497.

There is a further place at which this chromatic shape helps to forecast, if not demarcate, a significant point in the movement. The means, however, are more subtle. This is the long approach to the recapitulation, a section that actually begins at measure

246, where the first of a series of pedals upon D and A in the timpani introduce emphases upon the chief points of the tonality ultimately to be reestablished. Throughout this passage of some 55 measures a chromatic motive appears four times, each phrase sounding against a bass on one or the other of the pivotal tonal points of D or A. The form of the chromatic motive at these places is not the simple and direct ascending line seen in previous instances. Nor is its role exactly similar, for in the earlier cases it serves as a secondary line in bass or soprano, a counterpoint against more prominent melodic parts. In this case it constitutes the primary melodic line. About its origins, however, there can be little doubt: it is the retrograde, or symmetrically reversed form, of the original ascending chromatic line at measures 59 ff., the line that serves as the progenitor of the derived chromatic shape.[3] (See large schema.)

The connection between tonic and mediant keys (D major–F♯ minor) in the first movement is partly established through their mutual tones F♯ and A. The oscillation between the two chords/keys has been seen as the structural underpinning of the second group (see derived rhythmic shapes) and also of the opening motive (Ex. 40). A similar relationship among other tonal centers is used in the first-movement development as a means of transitory modulations, some of these shown in the schema for measures 258–270 and measures 190–202.

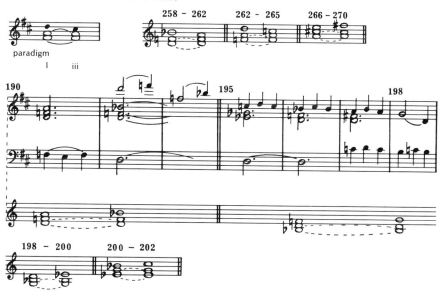

Finally, interconnections of tempo further unite all movements of the symphony, as indicated here:

Brahms: *Symphony No. 2 in D Major*

I. $\frac{3}{4}$ **Allegro non troppo**   II. $\frac{4}{4}$ **Adagio non troppo**   III. $\frac{3}{4}$ **Allegretto grazioso (Quasi andantino)**   IV. ¢ **Allegro con spirito**

♩. = ♩ = ♩ = 𝅝

[2 : 3 : 2]

Tonality and Motion

This discussion provides a picture of Brahms's use of harmony, rhythm, and structural downbeats to effect the forward motion of the first movement. We have shown how certain of the central points of articulation—structural downbeats on broad middle-ground levels—are in some ways frustrated or robbed of their ultimate power by features of imbalance. This imbalance is created by such means as less than fully stable positions of the harmony articulated at these points; by articulation a beat before the metrical downbeat of the measure, thus avoiding rhythmic and metric congruence; and by false cadences. Other downbeat articulations, on the other hand, are unambiguous and strong.

What now becomes clear is the structuring of these focal articulations on two levels—levels distinguished by their complete or less-than-complete force of statement and, concomitantly, by their clarity or their ambiguity. All these features are deployed to the overall purpose of a measured, graded unfolding of the tonality of D major, such that the tensions inherent in this unfolding are controlled and kept in check from one end to the other of the total span of the movement.

The movement contains two places only where D major as the central tonal focus is stated clearly, unambiguously, and with the power of unobstructed structural downbeats. Appropriate to the form, these points are at either end of the movement, framing all that transpires between. The first place is the statement at measure 44, to which all that precedes is an extended upbeat. The other is at measure 477, the moment in the coda where the original motive is obviously downbeat oriented and where the music finally achieves tonal repose.[4]

These two points serve as poles—rhythmic, tonal, and harmonic—marked by ultimate stability and finality. The most significant major points of structural articulation that lie between these poles are handled in ways that diminish their stability to some extent, with the result that forward motion is maintained at these points and stasis avoided.

Thus the settling into A major, as the key of the second group, is partly weakened in force through its arrival a beat before measure 156, heard as dissynchronous with the metrical downbeat and further placed upon a $\frac{6}{3}$ inversion. (The parallel place in the recapitulation, measure 424, is treated in similar fashion.) The next point of arrival, the start of the development (measure 183), is articulated upon a false cadence. The demarcation is further obscured by the statement of the cello-bass motive a measure earlier, its relationship to the horn figure and its ambiguous upbeat-downbeat orientation unchanged from the opening measures of the symphony.

The recapitulation—the next major point of demarcation—is likewise disguised in typical Brahmsian fashion. Also obscured, through a false cadence, is the initiation of the coda at measure 447.

By contrast, several structural downbeats are clear. All of them, however, lie in some manner or other upon weaker or less salient tonal points in relation to the parent tonality of D major. A balance in tension is thereby maintained: though the rhythmic force of these articulations is strong, their harmonic position with respect to D major is correspondingly weak. Salient points of change are rendered oblique through ambiguous foreground treatment; tonally oblique points of change are salient in their announcement. A duality of balance between forces thus exists. Forward motion, as a result, is unimpeded.

Thus the statement of F# minor at measure 83 is strong, but F# minor is only the mediant way station moving toward V. What occurs within F# minor is unstable. Measure 118 is a powerful downbeat that initiates the dominant region, but it does so in tangential fashion, essentially sitting upon V of V before the (less clear) settling into V at measure 156.[5]

The derived chromatic motive that presages all these points of articulation now appears as something of a mediator, or connecting link, between these two levels of articulation. It is the one constant element common to announcements that are functionally strong but unclear, or clear but functionally less strong.

AMBIGUITY IN BRAHMS'S INTERMEZZO, OP. 118, NO. 2

Ambiguities like those seen in the Second Symphony are found in much of the music of Brahms. Invariably they serve structural purposes on several levels of design. Among the Op. 118 piano pieces are typical examples. The Intermezzo, Op. 118, No. 2, in essence an ABA form, builds its outer sections with the interesting harmonic feature that the tonic—although evident and never unclear as far as the tonal orientation of the piece is concerned—is never heard as a point of rest until the closing measures of these outer sections. Its common role is that of anacrusis, passing chord, or as a bass that implies tonic harmony although chords heard over it are of other roots. The presence of the tonic is generally inverted and unstable.

Thus A major is established by implication rather than by direct statement until the closing measures of the outer sections, when the music "arrives" home. Here again, as seen in the Second Symphony, the harmonic implications are rhythmic as well. The initial point of true repose, or structural downbeat, in this music is not found until the close of the first section, when the tonic explicitly arrives. All that precedes is, on the largest scale, its upbeat. (By contrast, the middle section begins downbeat oriented, but in a weaker tonal region—stating clearly the local key center of F# minor.) Segments of these features are found in Ex. 41, the various tonic chords arrowed.

Ex. 41. Brahms: *Intermezzo in A Major,* **Op. 118, No. 2**

1. The notes outline the tonic triad, D–F#–A. Once again the question arises whether this shape reflects the most commonplace norm of the tonal system or whether it is intrinsic to the music at hand.

The criteria for this point have been discussed in Chapter 6, devolving upon the consistent, repetitive deployment of patterns and shapes defined by the triad. While the present analysis does not go extensively into these questions, there is evidence enough in the opening movement of the Second Symphony to confirm the unique uses of these triadic shapes by even a cursory view. Note, for example, the continual outlining of the third-fifth (and lower fifth) scale-degree shape in the main motives of the movement (horn motive, measure 2; second group, cello, measure 82; violin 1, measure 118; cello-bass, measures 136 ff.).

The entity of D major is in a somewhat special way the focus of the entire work, its "creation" achieved through the exploitation and exploration of the tonality in a large and varied number of ways. The materials of the last movement—variants of those in the first movement—emphasize D major as a shape. So do the tonal levels of subsidiary sections in movement four (I, iii [measures 170 ff., 206 ff., 221 ff.], V, [vi]), again paralleling the structure of the first movement. (In movement one, vi serves as the key in the recapitulation for the restatement of second-group material originally heard in iii; the classical transposition of second-group material down a fifth in recapitulations is maintained.) In movement four, the key centers outline the pitch levels of the opening theme, thus introducing (briefly) C# minor (measures 184 ff.) and B minor (measures 189 ff.), as well as the centers already mentioned.

The first and fourth movements are thus variants of one another, framing through D major both ends of this large symphonic structure. The D major triad in the trombones that closes the symphony (five measures from the end of the last movement) can be heard as an ultimate codetta to the ultimate coda—the statement, in clear and simple form, of what has been established by complex means throughout the work, the tonality of D major.

2. From a performance viewpoint, the most efficacious decision is probably to consider the opening measure of the piece an upbeat, leading to a (local) downbeat on the second measure with the entrance of the horns. The price paid for this decision, however, is the peculiar imbalance created by a downbeat on the unstable $\frac{6}{4}$ position of the tonic at measure 2.

Ultimately this is no problem since the first true downbeat, structurally speaking, occurs with the tutti at measure 44. This fact dictates its own performance demands, however; the phrasing of the opening 43 measures must have the quality of a sustained upbeat breath. Moreover the downbeat at measure 44 is a soft entrance, demanding an attack—especially in the trombones, horn, and bassoons—that will give emphasis to the D major chord at this low dynamic (the trombones are scored *pp*) without any "hard" sense of accent, almost a "leaning" onto the note. The structure works with the orchestra in this nuance. The sense of significant downbeat is felt with the statement of D major itself; players have only to support this built-in feeling. Further emphasis is not needed.

3. The motive also bears a general but less exact resemblance to the figure

introduced early in the development (cf. oboe, measures 187 ff.). The two shapes differ primarily in the contour of each three-note figure within the four measures of the melody. More significant, the earlier figure is diatonic; the one under study, chromatic.

4. This frame for the movement is striking in its symmetry—the initial upbeat of 43 measures and the closing downbeat (from m. 477) of 47 measures.

5. The parallel statements of both these moments in the recapitulation are handled in similar fashion.

9

OTHER EXAMPLES OF PREMISE

Ambiguity in Brahms's music played more than a specific role in particular pieces. Its presence was pervasive throughout his works; it became virtually a part of his style. One finds such a generalized stylistic use of ambiguity rarely in earlier classic-romantic music. It is present, though, in the music of Brahms's contemporaries and later romantics—those who, like Brahms, were exploring the harmonic resources of tonality to their farthest boundaries. Wagner's "Tristan" chord is a famous example.[1]

Other kinds of musical premises (or, more accurately, subpremises), seen in the following pages, do not play such generalized roles. They arise from the unique contexts of individual pieces and consist of some aspect of the music adopted, as its working-out demonstrates, as a partial basis for structure. As these compositional bases lack a general character or methodology, they can be recognized only in their specific contexts. A sampling of such cases follows.

LOCAL EVENT AS PREMISE

Mozart's Piano Concerto in A Major, K. 414

A local musical event may evolve as a subpremise, some aspect of its properties generating subsequent features of structure. Mozart's Piano Concerto in A Major, K. 414, provides a good example, the pedal point in the initial measures of the first movement acting as such a premise (Ex. 42). This tonic pedal on A becomes a distinct aural event by the second measure, where it dissonates against the dominant harmony. Harmonic clashes like this are by no means unique in Mozart's music. However, this pedal point seems to have achieved a salient structural character, for similar pedal points function throughout the concerto.

Other examples within the first movement are also found in Ex. 42. Virtually all the significant thematic ideas of the movement share this feature. Moreover, the entire development is so structured that a pedal point is present in the upper voice of all passages, the predominant portion focusing around C♯. This pedal also serves as the common tone for the abrupt modulation from a C♯ chord (V of F♯ minor) to A major at the recapitulation (see arrow at measure 190). In addition, what has been true of pedal points in the exposition is reiterated throughout the recapitulation. The entire movement is thus marked by the conspicuous deployment of pedal points.

Ex. 42. Mozart: *Piano Concerto in A Major,* **K.414, first movement**

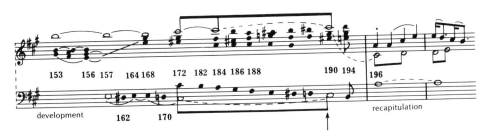

The pedals in this first movement are essentially of three kinds: (1) dissonant non-chord tones, like the sustained A of the opening four measures; (2) common tones among alternating harmonies, such as the dominant pedal in the I–V progression at measure 17–21, and (3) tones either sustained and/or implied through local, ornamental voice-leading. The latter is the case in the long C♯ pedal that predominates in the development, sustained for 13 measures from measures 172–184 and then further implied through ornamentation of the upper voice until its return at measure 190.

Pedal points are not limited to the first movement alone; they are a hallmark of the entire concerto. A sampling of thematic ideas from the second and third movements follows. In all of these excerpts pedals are prominent features of the texture, functioning for the most part as common tones within basically I–V or I–IV contexts—ornamented versions in some cases.

Third movement

Several issues arise from this discussion. For one, it can be questioned whether any of these pedal points are in fact significant to the music, since they are for the most part such ordinary events—common tones in tonic-dominant progressions, for example, or, at the most extreme, conventional dissonances of tonic versus dominant.

The question of their significance relates to the contexts of the work itself; the answer lies in their frequent, recurrent, and consistent pattern of appearance. It would be entirely possible, and is in fact common, to build harmonic progressions such as those found in this concerto without constructing them so that pedals—particularly common-tone pedals—are sustained for such lengths of time. This was not done, however; the sustained tones are unique to these contexts, clearly a deliberate, aural feature of the texture.

A second and more interesting issue is the control these pedals exert over the music, and the demands they consequently place upon performance. We have seen that forward motion in tonal music depends largely upon the intertwined functions of harmony and rhythm, and that rhythm in its large dimensions rests upon the upbeat-downbeat, unstable-stable inflections of harmonic tension and resolution.

Because of the pervasive presence of pedal points in this concerto, there is relatively little real or structural harmonic motion in the large (and thus there is restricted rhythmic motion as well). The pedals are made possible by (and, conversely, they make possible) the limited harmonic activity of local tonic-dominant, or tonic-subdominant, interchange and ancillary ornamental chords. A glance at the themes of the first movement shows how restricted the large-scale activity is among these ideas.[2]

The development section of the first movement is a further case in point. It focuses around the pedal B and its upward motion to C♯, which constitutes the full extent of the structural activity in the upper voice. Around these two tones are built the limited harmonic activity of I–V–I in E major and V–i–V in F♯ minor. Much the same sort of limited activity is found in the following movements.

This concerto has long been known among pianists as problematic; it is difficult as a whole to sustain in performance. The foregoing discussion illuminates this problem: it is not a matter of compositional weakness, but one of recognizing the inherent nature of the music and working with rather than against this nature in shaping an approach to performance. In effect, because of the restricted real, or structural, harmonic-rhythmic motion, a performance must focus upon and sustain the long phrases created by this relatively static structure. If details of the moment—of individual measures or motives—are concentrated upon more than large-scale line, the static property of the concerto will be reinforced, a property so much a built-in presence that it does not need, in fact cannot withstand, further emphasis.

Brahms's
Intermezzo,
Op. 117, No. 3

The last of the three intermezzi in Brahms's Op. 117 cycle of piano pieces is another example of a local event serving as a partial premise, generating subsequent aspects of the music. The event itself is a focal, rather than a minor, aspect of the piece in this case.

The initial and concluding sections of this ternary form are of interest here. Each is built of two parts, an initial and consequent motive, the latter always heard in virtually unchanged form—in effect a "foil" to the opening motive. It is this opening motive that serves as the generative premise. In each of its appearances the head of the phrase is harmonized in a different manner. This harmonic recasting in fact seems the raison d'être for the continual recurrences of the opening phrase.

Both motives of the opening section are shown in Ex. 43. Both are, in fact, built of the same basic shape—the span of a minor third, filled in by diatonic steps. The different harmonic and rhythmic casts of the consequent phrase effectively mask this fact. The schema below measures 10–15 shows the underlying relationship.

Ex. 43. Brahms: *Intermezzo*, **Op. 117, No. 3**

The subsequent recastings of the primary head motive are schematized as they occur sequentially throughout the piece. The illustration also reveals another principle operative in the music: the presentation of the motive in successively more complex harmonizations. Its initial statement is the simplest possible—the unaccompanied motive itself. Following this the obvious tonic-dominant aspects of the motive are made explicit, its subdominant implications treated in the next appearance. These constitute the versions found in the opening section.

The preparation for the return initiates the first of the more complex, chromatic harmonizations, though in itself this statement is not extreme, adding only the raised sixth to the tonic chord at measure 81. The returning A section introduces secondary dominant harmonizations that entail chromatic alterations, and the short coda climaxes this procedure by the most extended such harmonizations of the piece (VI–II–V–i), with their concomitant chromatic complexities.

Other Examples of Premise

Despite the prevailing *sotto voce* character of this work—dynamics louder than *p* are few—the music has built-in tensions that are almost guarantors of sustained performance. They reside in the inherent harmonic tensions of the plan just discussed. Thus the climax of the music is its coda, where the most complex of the recurrent motivic harmonizations is found. Its climactic character is perceived without the reinforcement of dynamics; the level, or intensity, of sonority here, as in most of the piece, is largely one of suppression.[3]

PROCEDURE AS PREMISE

It seems by now axiomatic that any feature in a compositional matrix has potential structural import. In realizing this import it fulfills a role as premise to some degree. We have seen the extent to which shape fulfills this role, as well as the consequences that can emanate from local events. Musical procedure can play a similar role.

As with most analytical distinctions, that of procedure is not clear-cut or separate from other musical elements. Obviously a procedure cannot be put into effect without utilizing specific musical materials, in most cases those of local nature. The distinction, then, is largely one of perspective—whether the focus is upon idea itself, that is, the nuclear shape or event, or upon the course of action by means of which idea may be transformed.

The point is illustrated by the examples that follow, which move from less to more complex cases of procedurally influenced thought. The first concerns the Mozart Piano Sonata in F, K. 332, whose initial movement reveals the relatively simple, indeed normative, procedure of phrase repetitions.

Mozart's Piano Sonata in F Major, K. 332

The procedure of phrase repetitions in the first movement controls the flow of almost all the important ideas presented in the exposition, as well as the opening idea of the development, as illustrated in Ex. 44. As can be seen, each of these phrase repetitions is marked by some degree of ornamentation—of pattern, texture, dynamics—or by some other means of variation, extending as far as the alteration of modality in some cases.

Ex. 44. Mozart: *Piano Sonata in F Major*, **K.332, first movement**

development

Other Examples of Premise

The procedure plays an important structural role at the recapitulation, where the dominant preparation is minimal. The repeated motive, this time carried to four statements—twice the number of repetitions earlier prevalent—serves as a counterbalance to the spare harmonic preparation. At the same time the repetitions place melodic focus upon the pitch E, turning it to its leading-tone capacity—a further counterbalance to the limited harmonic preparation that underlies the passage (measures 124–134).

Mozart's Symphony No. 29 in A Major

Imitation, as procedure, is a structural premise in the two examples that follow. In the first, the opening movement of the Mozart Symphony No. 29 in A Major, K. 201, almost all important phrases within its exposition are marked by imitative responses in other voices (see Ex. 45). The development is also based largely upon imitations. These imitations range from small fractions of a theme, as in the second group at measures 37–41 to canonic writing, as in the *forte* statement of the opening theme, measures 13–17. Elsewhere the imitation is exclusively rhythmic, rather than melodic, as in the duet between strings at measure 45. What is true of material in the exposition is similarly true of its reappearance in the recapitulation, where the same procedures are retained.

Ex. 45. Mozart: *Symphony No. 29 in A Major,* **K.201, first movement**

development

Imitation as a procedural premise thus pervades the entire first movement, achieving the climactic point of the music through its ultimate extension, in the coda. Here it results in a four-voice stretto, with closely spaced entrances that make this section the most complex set of imitations in the entire movement—the fulfillment of a premise underlying all that has gone before (measures 189-192).

Other Examples of Premise

This coda seems to be an instance where compositional logic and its demands override other requirements, even practical ones of performance. The stretto in this coda is difficult to perform with clarity. Imitative parts overlap each other in range. Subsidiary lines, such as that of the second violins, further complicate the texture by voice-crossings, resulting in what is for Mozart a dense thicket of sound. All this seems secondary to a structural design—the elevation of imitation to its most significant compositional level in the movement.

Beethoven's *Eroica* Symphony

The last movement of the *Eroica* Symphony presents an enigma in its form on which the above discussion sheds some light. The movement begins, after a short introduction, as a theme-and-variation form in the conventional classical pattern. The initial variations retain the two constants that are distinguishing features of the classical approach—constant phrase lengths (in this case, repeated eight-measure segments), and the general harmonic plan of the theme.

This pattern underlies the theme itself and the first three variations that follow. What poses an interesting question, with consequences for the rest of the movement, is the direction the music takes after the close of the third variation—from measure 108 onward. Variation III is extended beyond its close by nine measures in a modulation to C minor. What follows where the fourth variation might be expected, at measure 117, is a fugato which abandons the constant phrase lengths and harmonic plan that mark the earlier variations. From this point on the movement becomes in part one of development, the phrases "free" both in length and in harmonic plan, by contrast to the strict and controlled framework within which the earlier variations were contained. The line between "development" and "variation" in these passages is hazy at best. Only in two other places do "strict" variations return in the movement—at the *Poco andante* of measure 349 and in the section that follows this, at measure 381.

From the extension of the third variation onward, then, the movement changes character because of its formal disposition, moving from the mold of the classical variation, a form whose future behavior is in several respects predictable, to the less determinate freedom of a quasi-development/variation approach.

What elements in this music motivate the change in orientation? This question calls into consideration a number of matters, some only generally related to the movement. For one, there is the intrinsic fine line that always exists between variation and development, a point Schoenberg suggested in his statement that all music is in a state of "developing variation." All variation is a species of development; conversely, all development consists of varying in some manner the nature and character of original material. What distinguishes variation as a formal classical approach is its retention of the two thematic constants discussed earlier—constant phrase lengths and harmonic plan of the theme. It is this fine line that Beethoven crossed here and elsewhere, as did his successors.

A second and less tangible point concerns the sense of forward motion and the accretion of musical tension that lend drive to any movement. While these are properties of all good music, the way they are engendered in strict variation form is especially interesting. For many elements are absent here that might contribute to this sense of forward drive and that are freely handled in pure development—such as varied phrase lengths, motivic fragmentation, harmonic plan, modulations. Yet an accumulation of musical tension does exist within variation form. One senses a principle that guides the change in character from one variation to the next. Variations cannot successfully be interchanged, nor can just any variation follow in random fashion from another. Whatever affects this sequential ordering is certainly related to the matter of accrued intensity, though the *how* and *where* may differ with each piece.

Beyond these general questions, two specific aspects of musical procedure serve as premises early in this movement. Both bear upon the departure of the "fourth variation" from the classical variation mold. The procedures are imitation and the successive diminution of rhythmic values.

Imitation as a procedural premise is established within the statement of the theme itself. (Ex. 46). Here the repetitions of the eight-measure phrases are marked by canonic dialogue between strings and winds (measure 20). The principle is further employed in

Ex. 46. Beethoven: *Symphony No. 3 in E flat Major,* **fourth movement**

variation I through the imitations of the counter-motive between cellos and first violins (measure 44). The premise is also evident in variation II, with the three-part imitations in the lower strings (measure 59). While variation III has more of a generalized contrapuntal texture than one marked specifically by imitation, imitative procedure is present at the tail of the variation theme (measures 91–95, oboe 1—violin 1). Significantly, it is this tail motive that is used to extend the variation toward the forthcoming sections of free development.

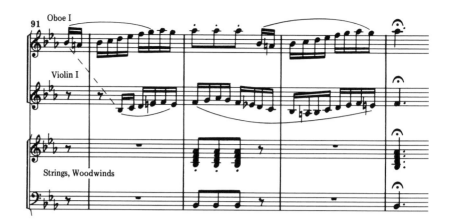

Concomitant with imitation as a procedural premise throughout the theme and the opening three variations is a second procedural premise, the introduction of progressively diminished rhythmic values. In its opening statement the theme exerts one impulse to the measure—in essence, a half-note pulse (measure 12). One effect of the canonic imitation that follows is to double this pulse rate—now two quarter-note (sub-)pulses (though the notation is more ornate). (See again measure 20.) With variation I the rate again doubles to eighth notes (measure 44), is further diminished to triplet eighths in variation II (measure 59), and ultimately reduces to sixteenths in variation III (measure 76).

The two procedural premises of imitation and rhythmic diminution drive the music to a critical point by the end of variation III. Motion and accrued intensity are by now inherent musical factors, exerting further demands for fulfillment. How are these to be achieved? To introduce rhythmic values smaller than sixteenths is impractical; they would be unplayable at the tempo that governs the movement. To extend imitations to progressively greater complexity within the strict variation framework would be equally impractical. One or two such constructs might be feasible, but the procedure obviously could not continue until the conclusion of the movement without excessively complicated results. (The musical demands at this point place the denouement a long way off.)

Extension of these prior procedures is thus not feasible by the end of variation III; a change in direction is required. Yet a change must not abandon the inner logic by which the movement has so far progressed.

The solution is the fugato that initiates "variation IV." The imitative principle is retained, and rhythmic diminutions, while not carried to greater extremes, preserve their prior forms. Thus the direction and manner of application of these procedures are deflected; the procedures themselves, as structural rationales, are sustained. A by-product of this solution is the altered form of the music, at variance with the classical precedents with which it began. After variation III the movement becomes a free form, guided and restricted only in a general way by the earlier premise of strict variation form; it is shaped henceforth by other limits and directions imposed by the composer's imagination.

There are practical consequences of this fact. As a result of the departure from convention after variation III and the later brief return to conventional variation procedure, the movement is "framed" by two points of stability: those two places where standard variations are found. Both of these are also rooted firmly in the tonic. (The brief coda is a third such place.) Virtually all that lies outside these points is unstable tonally and unpredictable in terms of development—the latter constituting a procedural correlate of instability.

These facts must be taken into account in shaping a performance of this movement of the *Eroica*, for the sectionalization of the music in its largest dimensions is contingent upon them. The perspective that emanates from these premises also sheds light upon the opening introductory measures. In their voice-leading these measures are essentially a large harmonic elaboration upon the leading tone D, which ultimately resolves to the tonic at measure 12, prior to the theme. In another sense these measures initiate the instability that surrounds the two E♭ standard-variation segments—a foretaste, in the opening measures, of things to come.

1. The question whether this chord is an altered secondary dominant in the key of A or whether its origins lie more in tonally directed chromatic ornamentation is an interesting one. See (among others) William Mitchell, "The Tristan Prelude: Techniques and Structure," *The Music Forum* I (1967): 162–203.

2. There is a larger amount of activity within the few phrases that follow these themes, but they are of short duration. The consequent phrases in fact provide the contrast of greater harmonic activity that the music needs in order to sustain interest.

3. Though Ravel's *Rapsodie Espagnole* is removed in style and era from this Brahms piano piece by some distance, its opening movement is based upon much the same musical premise, namely, varied harmonizations of a reiterated musical figure. As in the Brahms piece, the Ravel figure descends over the 3–2–1 scale degrees, though it is carried a step further to end on the leading tone. (The leading tone, that is, if the figure is heard in D minor. The piece implies D as the central tonal focus but hovers ambiguously around other tonal centers.)

Ravel's harmonic practice had fewer of the restraints of conventional tonal syntax than did Brahms's, with the result that the former's range of harmonization is broader. The conceptual thinking behind the two pieces, however, has interesting points in common.

The basic Ravel figure follows, together with a sampling of the harmonizations with which it is set within the opening movement. (The figures ②, ②+ 5, and so on refer to rehearsal numbers in the score, and to the number of measures following the rehearsal number.)

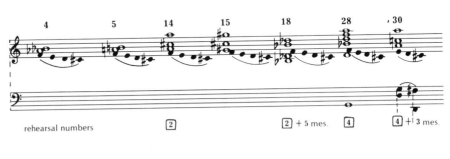

Structure and Premise: Analyses

V OTHER PERSPECTIVES

10

Analysis imposes a disparity of treatment, indeed of perception, between the spatial and the temporal in music, a disparity supported by both the graphology and the terminology of analysis itself. For analysis is largely static—dividing, studying in terms of component parts. Its terminology is compatible with this and is likewise oriented toward isolable study. When kinetic aspects of music are described—rhythmic motion, for example—the description is removed some degrees from the actuality of the event itself.

Perhaps it cannot be otherwise, in view of the nature of motion and of a language largely incapable of direct correspondence in its description of motion. The older school of physics and, before this, metaphysics faced a similar problem with kinetic studies, exemplified by Zeno's paradox of the arrow in motion. A more comprehensive mathematic was needed before kinetics could be studied without distorting basic properties of motion. Music to date lacks such a calculus.

The graphology of music also suggests stasis, since the two-dimensional musical space it portrays is largely independent of time. Its vertical dimension portrays aspects of height-depth, register, and contour with a direct correspondence to their vertical properties. The horizontal dimension is more complex. Many observations within it are indeed spatial, concerned with such aspects as lengths, beginnings, closure. Time in these instances is presumed, but largely as a qualifier—that is, as a continuum within which events take place. It is the spatial properties of these events that receive clear focus.

Horizontal notation also represents the temporal, as in matters of rhythm and meter. The representation does not provide a one-to-one correspondence, however, nor can it, as the dimensions of time and space do not lend themselves to such a compatible and direct visual representation. Rhythmic and metric notation really constitute a "time-line" representation, not only removed in degree from the real thing, as with any notation, but removed in domain as well.

All of this indicates a contradiction that is probably irreconcilable, between an art form of which time is an essence and an analytic viewpoint that is essentially static, independent of time. In the absence of a kinetic methodology for analysis, one capable of communicating the dynamics of musical motion directly, is there some way to bring these two polar views into rapprochement?

Allied with kinetics is another matter—the chronometry of musical statement. As a work unfolds in time it reveals, in progressive stages, quanta of information about itself. At times the process of revelation itself seems a partial generator of that energy which must be resolved to achieve final closure. What principles govern this timed, controlled release of information?

The durational nature of these questions suggests that their answers lie within the rhythmic domain of time—specifically, in the large-scale aspects of temporal segmentation and proportioning that represent the ultimate temporal control of music.

We have seen earlier that in classic-romantic music rhythm in the large is intimately intertwined with large-scale harmonic progression. In the tension-and-release principle of structural harmonic progression lie the deepest levels of structural articulation—thesis and arsis, structural up- and downbeat. Thus, if a work unfolds temporally through some principle of control, the source of that control would seem to be large-scale harmony, with its correlated rhythmic inflection.

This suggests, among other things, how close to the primal source of musical energy were Schenker's musical perceptions. It is true that Schenker's studies paid relatively little attention to rhythm in the conventional sense of foreground pattern. However, this foreground pattern concerns the surface, or presence, of musical events rather than the deep structure that controls larger dimensions and directions. On these deeper levels, Schenker's ideas are very much in tune with rhythmic reality, for it is here that structural rhythm is articulated.

The rate, even the manner, by which a piece unfolds varies in each case. One generalization seems applicable, however: namely, that harmonic progression on middle- and background levels exerts basic control over both the unit of information imparted and the duration of the phrase within which this information is imparted. This is particularly true with respect to linear ideas such as motives and melodies. Classic-romantic music tends to deal largely with single ideas, or with sets of ideas, at any one time. The durational periods within which these are stated rest upon these harmonic/rhythmic factors.

The point is illustrated by way of the first movement of the *Eroica* Symphony (see large schema). Level *A* of the example presents a harmonic sketch of the middle-ground level (derived from Schenker[1]) of the exposition section as a point of departure, suggesting as well the deeper, quasi-*Ursatz* levels of the section that are largely concerned with harmonic motion. At the same time the various segments of the exposition—its opening thematic group, transition, second and closing groups, the small "coda" at its close—are indicated.

Further simplification is found in level *B,* where harmonic motion is reduced to skeletal functional outlines. It is here that the rhythmic proportioning of the exposition is shown, controlled by this harmonic motion. The figures in heavy-face type indicate the overall duration of each section in measures, while subsections of inner activity within a segment, such as those of the closing group, are indicated in light-face type. Level *B* also reveals the structural emphases of up- and downbeat inherent within these phrases, the harmonies marking arrival points of large periods.

An attempt has been made in level *B* to indicate durational proportions by conventional rhythmic notation. (These proportions must be understood as approximate only; existing means of notation do not allow precise proportions without ungainly complications.) It is notable that the opening group and transition are roughly equivalent in duration (44 and 38 measures), and that the second thematic group is roughly half this length (26 measures, somewhat over half the median 41-measure length of the other two sections). This relationship has been suggested with a half-note duration for the second group, and so forth through the exposition.

There is a further significant correlation in this picture: the most prominent themes of the exposition are those introduced at major points of harmonic articulation, indicated generally as whole, half, or quarter notes on level *B.*

Level *C* of the graph is designed to suggest how large-scale harmonic-rhythmic proportioning controls the presentation of thematic material in the exposition. This is the principle, in other words, that governs the timed release of thematic information. This is suggested on level *C* by indicating themes and motives treated in each long

In Search of the Compositional Dynamic

phrase. It is significant that each of these themes is delimited in its entrance and exit from the scene by structural harmonic points: either of resolution or way stations—passing harmonies—within progressions. These control points are indicated by the dashed vertical arrows between levels *A, B,* and *C.*

Were this graph carried further into the movement its details would be different. In the development section the rate of structural harmonic activity on middle-ground levels would be more rapid and would extend to more distantly related tonal areas. Concurrently the thematic material treated in these phrases would be more dense per unit of time. In some cases more than one motive would have to be shown as treated simultaneously, as in the case of measures 186–193, where the motives ♩♪ | ♩ ♩ | and ♫ ♪ are codeveloped. These differences are virtually predictable; they simply underscore the well-known characteristics of development sections. In similar fashion the recapitulation and coda would reveal their particular and different characteristics.

The basic principle remains operative throughout these sections: both the delimitation of material and durational confines within which material is treated are controlled by structural harmonic motion—motion that is rhythmic in the deep-structure sense. This harmonic-rhythmic motion also controls the phrasing scheme. It integrates thematic ideas with balances and contrasts of texture, dynamics, and other secondary features to emphasize and articulate all large phrases. One aspect of these details has been studied earlier in the *Eroica,* the use of texture and register to articulate major points of segmentation.

The control exerted by the deep-structure harmonic-rhythmic plan is counterbalanced by a further element, one that affects the forward motion of a given movement. That element is the formalism of procedure established by style and tradition. For example, the relative instability created by the motion to V of V in the *Eroica* transition (levels *A* or *B*) is resolved when the dominant arrives at measure 83. Were this resolution the sole arbiter of motion, and concomitantly of length, the movement might well be shorter than it is, for this goal is attained by measure 83. However, the exposition extends farther, the dominant region remaining its tonal focus for close to another 80 measures until the section closes. This extended length is dictated by the formalisms and procedures of so-called sonata-form—the need to state other thematic material such as second group, closing group, closing codettas. It seems that a fine balance continually serves as a control between the inner energies and action of a work—the drives, themes, tensions integral to its materials (its psyche, so to speak)—and the formalized procedures of an era or style, which to some extent determine the manner whereby these inner features may be stated.

The balance between these poles swings one way or the other in a given work, or at a particular moment within a work (for instance, in an extended coda or a truncated recapitulation), depending upon inner demands. The poles themselves probably constitute the two most far-reaching elements of formal control. Of the two, the active pole—that arising from internal demands—seems the deeper source of a compositional dynamic.

NOTE

1. See Heinrich Schenker, *Der Freie Satz* (Vienna: Universal, 1935), Appendix, Plate, p. I, 1–2, Fig. 6.

11 EPILOGUE

The music on which these studies are based has been limited in its historical era, national source (the German-Viennese tradition), and abstract nature ("absolute" music), providing a model of restricted but coherent characteristics from which deductions can be drawn with minimal exceptions. These deductions may be applicable to music beyond the confines of this model—to some extent, for example, to the middle and late baroque. This era had its own codified compositional practices. One often has the impression, however, that the ear of the best of baroque composers was striving toward aspects of tonal control that the harmonic-tonal practices of the classic-romantic era brought to such highly developed lengths.

The model used here may also be a point of departure for tackling structural problems in later music, perhaps through our own era, whose major composers—Schoenberg, Webern, Bartók, Hindemith, among others— were deeply influenced by tradition. Contemporary music has not had a highly developed system of tonal relations upon which to rely for broad aspects of coherence. It has been forced to find substitute elements to compensate for features of a system no longer viable.

Our view of rhythm in contemporary music, as a case in point, might benefit from criteria used in these studies. One senses in much twentieth-century music that large-scale rhythmic articulation, with its heavy and light structural pulses, has features in common with romantic music. Yet articulation is achieved without the aid of a conventional harmonic syntax and the coherence that this once provided. How, then, is it achieved? What factors compensate for the absence of prior tonal contexts?

The present studies suggest a point of view toward composition reminiscent of Aristotle's idea that the form of the statue resides a priori within the material, awaiting its revelation by the sculptor. This seems almost a paradigm of compositional thinking: a musical idea, once conceived, has a variety of possible manifestations; it is the composer's obligation to realize these and to give them concrete form. Perhaps it is an indication of the greatest talents that they are so in tune with their material that even its most unusual manifestations, unified by only tenuous surface qualities, are perceived and brought to light.

Within this duality of variety-within-unity lies the ultimate meaning of formal fulfillment, a process that in essence has only tangential relation to conventional notions of form. When a work has fully exploited the possibilities inherent in its basic ideas, it has completed itself and must end. It may do so in general consistence with certain formalized procedures such as harmonic progressions and cadence, but the compositional obligation of final closure ranks foremost at these moments. To continue beyond the point of satiety risks redundancy or the inclusion of extraneous material. To conclude at the appropriate moment, and thus to preserve internal consistency, can result in an outward form deviant from convention. Consistency may in fact explain formal uniqueness.

Thinking of this sort may have lain behind Schoenberg's criticism to his students, related by a number of them in their writings, that a theme in their works-in-progress had not yet realized itself. For composition to Schoenberg, and to many others, was the revelation of "idea," idea in the sum total of its embodiments and implications.

The prevalence of scientific thinking in the past few decades has had its effect upon musical theory, nurturing a development that has moved along positivistic lines, dealing almost exclusively with objective data. The natural focus of such positivism is structure, and musical theory has developed its own brand of structuralism, though not one specifically correlated with current formalized theories of structuralism. Thus music has been preoccupied with models, paradigms, syntax, transformations, and the like. Even information theory has been drawn upon as a source.

This positivistic approach has been in part a reaction against the subjective fantasizing about "content" that was current at the end of the romantic age in music. Nor could aesthetics be of much help in the effort to understand musical content—not beyond the point, at least, where it was recognized that expressive meanings in a work of art are incapable of translation into any other medium, that they are intrinsic, perceptible, and comprehensible only in their own terms. Attention then turned elsewhere, toward the study of those aspects of music that could be dealt with and communicated in terms of words, that is, toward the objective data of the medium—its sounds, harmonies, rhythms, accents—which in organized form meant musical structure.

Musical structuralism has thus become the predominant mode of discussion within the field of musical theory. Other approaches to content, particularly those concerned with affect or expression, have been consigned to the passé. The nonverbal aspects of these approaches and the inability to discuss them with clarity or precision make them unproductive topics and at times embarrassing ones.

While the value of the structuralist approach is beyond question, it is unrealistic to think that it answers all the relevant questions about music. It is widespread experience that much of the power of musical communication lies within the domain of the ineffable and nonverbal—call it affect, expression, gesture, or whatever. Significant as structure may be, it is not all. If this other domain is valid, which seems beyond question, then theory must find a way to deal with it, if theory itself is to cope fully with the phenomena of music. The question is how to find such a way. Certainly a return to the subjectivities of the past is not the answer.

A number of approaches suggest themselves. For one, much structuralist thought has concerned itself with musical forms built by means of the objective data of the medium—pitches, rhythms, themes, motives, key systems. It may be, however, that the affective aspects of music do not lie directly within this perspective. We have seen in our earlier discussion, for example, that time in music, for meaningful demarcation, depends upon many varied degrees of emphasis. We have also seen that emphases are not purely intellectual or cerebral in nature, but rather are physical, bodily experiences. Further, the physical in music is intimately related to the psychological. The discussion of pulse as related to tempo touched upon this fact, though there is much yet to be explored. For instance, current evidence indicates that biological time-clock mechanisms, of which so much has been heard in recent years, may operate upon many time spans, the diurnal-nocturnal variety so familiar to jet-plane travelers being only the most familiar but not necessarily the most significant. The psychologist John Cohen, writing about this as long ago as 1966, pointed out that there is evidence for the existence of more than one localized pacemaker in the body, in fact even within a single cell and, further, that in the central nervous system rhythms may occur independently of external periodicities. Thus inner clocks may be set to work with great reliability by an initial alternating stimulus or even by a single stimulus, provided it is powerful enough.

Such triggering effects are readily linked with highly sensitive phases in the development of an organism, taking us into the realm of "imprinting" or single-trial learning, which appears to characterize the early development of the human baby as well as the young in various other species, and which relates to the successful timing experiences in the life of the growing child.[1]

The relevance of this evidence to the musical experience of tempo is obvious, though its implications are extensive and complex. Moreover, physical and visceral bodily experience, of which tempo is just one musical aspect, is generally recognized as a correlate of emotional experience. This may as well be true of the spectrum of feelings in music as it is in broader realms of life, though the nature of this experience, its description, and development leave much yet to be investigated.

Secondary elements in music also play a role in expression and meaning. Many properties of musical ideas lie as much beyond their pitch and rhythmic structures as within them, involving such matters as timbre, articulation and inflection, intensity, manner and degrees of emphases, quality or sense of motion. No shape can exist in musical reality—that is to say, in real time—without embodying these secondary elements, all of which are central to gesture. They are the properties "behind" the printed notes, so to speak, properties that a score is incapable of communicating. Yet all these properties inhere deeply in the psychological content of ideas. A theme may be "developed," for example, by inversion or fragmentation, that is, by textbook notions of musical procedures. The sensory and psychological properties in which such a theme is clothed may also develop, however—may be amplified in degree, altered, modified. In the latter may lie much of the communicative content of the ideas, suggesting development on a different, if not deeper, level.

This aspect of development is a prime feature of the music of Gustav Mahler, seen clearly in his symphonies, the scherzos of the First and Fifth being cases in point. In each of these movements waltzes serve as musical foci (or, more superficially, as "themes"). What is so powerful in the movements is not the presence of such ideas but their treatment. Waltzes initially introduced in the most elegant Viennese manner are transformed into visions of the demonic—bitter, ironic caricatures of their former selves. Tempi increase almost to headlong rushings; elegant articulations turn into harsh and heavy accents; sweet, characteristic waltz harmonies give way to bizarre dissonances; stateliness and control move toward disorganization and chaos. The music at its height seems an analogue of a schizoid, if not paranoid, state. No performance of these scores can be successful unless these transformations are controlled in their degree and rate of change. Yet our theoretical treatment of music has not at this time a methodology for quantizing these musical properties in any precise fashion.

In a less frantic but equally significant way, two variation works studied earlier rely in a deep-structure sense upon controlled use of secondary musical elements. They are Brahms's Variations on a Theme of Haydn (the orchestral version) and Schumann's Symphonic Etudes. Recall that in each, variations fall into groups distinguished by elements of articulation (legato or marcato), sense of motion (broadly phrased or short, choppy statements), dynamics (relative softness or loudness)—all operating in tandem with the more obvious aspects of thematic treatment. Thematic treatment in these scores may be the objective level on which musical thought is revealed; these other elements reside on a different level, one more subtle, less precise, but of psychological import.

This discussion, while not concerned with affect in so many words, is clearly relevant to the area of expression, meaning, emotion, or whatever other terms may be invoked in the honest, imprecise, and often vain attempt to grapple with the elusive nonverbal aspect of music. What becomes clear at this point is that affect, however we may describe it, and structure are in truth two sides of the same coin. Structure can be seen among other ways as the mechanism whereby musical affect, once stated, is carried forward, expanded, developed, and ultimately resolved in conclusion. A broadened theoretical perspective might embrace both affect and structure, but in quantifiable and controllable terms, rather than by abstractions alone.

We have become aware in recent years of a potential contribution to theory offered by linguistics. Music has many elements in common with language, both possessing such elements as syntactical structure, connotative meanings, aspects of grammar, and transformation. Most attention so far has been paid by musical theorists to the objective, structural aspects of both media and to the parallels to musical structure that may lie in linguistic theory, which has itself emanated from a positivistic approach.

Another approach may also be useful, one that focuses more upon the inflectional than the syntactical aspects of the two media. Both language (particularly spoken language) and music are inflected structures. In both structures coherence, segmentation, and partition of thought are communicated through inflection. Moreover, many alterations of meaning can only be revealed in language through inflection. Irony and sarcasm are two obvious examples ("Brutus is an honorable man . . . "). Context conditions such remarks, yet their ultimate conviction is imparted through inflection. Even in written language this would seem to hold, the mind and the ear supplying a sense of inflection to the printed word.

Other forms of emphasis also condition meanings in spoken languages. The phrase "I love you," for instance, has a normative sense unless some special context obtrudes. Modify it by emphasis to "*I* love you" or "I love *you,*" give to it different articulations, and more complex meanings are implied.

Current linguistic theory accounts for such situations, in small dimensions such as those above, in terms of presupposition and focus, or of old information and new or contrasting information. Emphasis provides the key to such interpretation. Linguistics seems not to have dealt with the question fully on broader levels of discourse. Yet the problem is intrinsic to thought on all levels. Certainly a participant in a discussion, intent upon making a point, will modulate his voice (graduate his emphases) by infinite degrees over a long stretch of dialogue, equivalent perhaps to several paragraphs or more.

Should this procedure and its modifications of meaning not be grist for the linguist's mill? If so, music may hold some clues (at the same time linguistic specification of this process may be suggestive for performance theory). For music is not only an inflected structure, molded and controlled, like language, by emphasis. Music must itself control emphasis throughout the course of an entire musical movement, if not an entire multi-movement work. In such a process, all manner of musical ideas must be graduated in emphasis such that their proper levels of significance within the whole are imparted to the listener. Failure to achieve this stratification of emphasis, or any unnecessary ex-aggeration of detail, contribute to disunity and can destroy the organic coherence of a work.

The thrust of this discussion is the need for a new and broader frame of reference for theoretical inquiry in music. Musical structuralism has made significant contributions during its development over the past three or four decades and doubtless has more to yield. One can almost forecast, however, the nature of further structural work, as it will in large part track down more data and trace further implications along lines already drawn.

Structuralism has not, however, and probably cannot deal with the kinds of questions concerning affect and expression discussed here, for it is limited in its operative assumptions to the handling of primarily objective musical data. We may be ready for another of those shifts of perspective whose need arises on an almost cyclical basis in theoretical inquiry. Some possible avenues for such a shift have been suggested in these pages.

The discussion also suggests that this inquiry may require an interdisciplinary approach, encroaching as it does upon such areas as aesthetics, linguistics, psychology, and biology. This would seem to be one of those interesting junctures in thought where the exclusive pursuit of data intrinsic to one field alone cannot yield the kind of knowledge that is sought. Intellectual polygamy, or a limited engagement, if not outright marriage, might prove a worthwhile trial.

NOTE

1. John Cohen, "Subjective Time," *The Voices of Time*, ed. J.T. Fraser (New York: Braziller, 1966), p. 258.

Appendix A   SCHOENBERG'S STUDIES OF MOTIVE, MOTIVE-FORMS, AND
DEVELOPING VARIATION

Schoenberg's detailed studies of motive, motive-forms, and the process of developing variation are found in various of his essays, notably the ones in *Style and Idea* (New York: Philosophical Library, 1950), and in his pedagogical books, *Models for Beginners in Composition* (New York: G. Schirmer, 1943), *Preliminary Exercises in Counterpoint*, ed. and foreword by Leonard Stein (London: Faber & Faber, 1963), and *Fundamentals of Musical Composition* (New York: St. Martin's Press, 1967). The latter three books are steeped in the music of the common-practice era and were written with the express purpose of imparting to students the musical concepts and the compositional methodology of this period, which Schoenberg considered essential to musical understanding in general. He explains in the Preface to *Models* (Syllabus, p. 3) that he found his method successful in communicating this basic compositional thinking even to students who had no desire or ability for musical creation. Partly because of this approach, perhaps, we find his concepts in these three books quite carefully explicated, even if on an elementary level.

In the Glossary to *Models* (pp. 15 ff.), Schoenberg explicates the meaning and functions of motif and variation:

Motif is a unit which contains one or more features of interval and rhythm. Its presence is manifested in its constant use throughout a piece. Its usage consists of frequent repetitions, some of them unchanged, most of them varied. The variations of a motif produce new *motif-forms*, which are the material for continuations, contrasts, new segments, new themes, or even new sections within a piece. Not all the features are to be retained in a variation; but some, guaranteeing coherence, will always be present. Sometimes remotely related derivatives of a motif might become independent and then be employed like a motif.
Variation is that kind of repetition which changes some of the features of a unit, motif, phrase, segment, section, or a larger part, but preserves others. To change everything would prevent there being any repetition at all, and thus might cause incoherence.
Obligations of the motif derive from a tendency or inclination inherent in a motif by which it aims at developing variation. *Obligatory forms* are those in which the tendency of development has not been "neutralized." [A further passage with musical examples shows how constant neglect of an interval within a musical figure neutralizes the obligations of this basic interval, making the figure finally nonobligatory.]

In *Fundamentals of Musical Composition* (pp. 8–9), a later and more extensive book than *Models*, Schoenberg once again writes of these matters, repeating some of the above points and expanding upon them:

Even the writing of simple phrases involves the invention and use of motives, though perhaps unconsciously. Consciously used, the motive should produce unity, relationship, coherence, logic, comprehensibility and fluency.
The *motive* generally appears in a characteristic and impressive manner at the beginning of a piece. The features of a motive are intervals and rhythms, combined to produce a memorable shape or contour which usually implies an inherent harmony. Inasmuch as almost every figure within a piece reveals some relationship to it, the basic motive is often considered the 'germ' of the idea. Since it includes elements, at least, of every subsequent musical figure, one could consider it the 'smallest common multiple.' And since it is included in every subsequent figure, it could be considered the 'greatest common factor.'

However, everything depends upon its use. Whether a motive be simple or complex, whether it consists of few or many features, the final impression of the piece is not determined by its primary form. Everything depends on its treatment and development.

A motive appears constantly throughout a piece: *it is repeated*. Repetition alone often gives rise to *monotony*. Monotony can be overcome by *variation*.

Use of the motive requires variation.

Variation means change. But changing every feature produces something foreign, incoherent, illogical. It destroys the basic shape of the motive.

Accordingly, variation requires changing some of the less-important features and preserving some of the more-important ones. Preservation of rhythmic features effectively produces coherence (though monotony cannot be avoided without slight changes.) For the rest, determining which features are more important depends on the compositional objective. Through substantial changes, a variety of *motive-forms*, adapted to every formal function, can be produced.

He goes on to examine in more detail what constitutes a motive (pp. 9 ff.):

Any rhythmicized succession of notes can be used as a basic motive, but there should not be too many different features.

Rhythmic features may be very simple, even for the main theme of a sonata. A symphony can be built on scarcely more complex rhythmic features. The examples from Beethoven's Fifth Symphony [given in the book] consist primarily of note-repetitions, which sometimes contribute distinctive characteristics.

A motive need not contain a great many interval features. The main theme of Brahms' Fourth Symphony, though also containing sixths and octaves, is . . . constructed on a succession of thirds.

Often a contour or shape is significant, although the rhythmic treatment and intervals change . . . .

Every element or feature of a motive or phrase must be considered to be a motive if it is treated as such, i.e. if it is repeated with or without variation.

Treatment and Utilization of the Motive

A motive is used by repetition. The repetition may be exact, modified or developed.

Exact repetitions preserve all features and relationships. Transpositions to a different degree, inversions, retrogrades, diminutions and augmentations are exact repetitions if they preserve strictly the features and note relations.

Modified repetitions are created through variation. They provide variety and produce new material (motive-forms) for subsequent use.

Some variations, however, are merely local 'variants' and have little or no influence on the continuation.

Variation, it must be remembered, is repetition in which some features are changed and the rest preserved.

All the features of rhythm, interval, harmony and contour are subject to various alterations. Frequently, several methods of variation are applied to several features simultaneously; but such changes must not produce a motive-form too foreign to the basic motive. In the course of a piece, a motive-form may be developed further through subsequent variation.

In a further chapter of the book, Schoenberg deals with a higher level of composition, that of connecting motive-forms. Here again he states his conviction that compositional unity arises from relationships among properties of these motive-forms. These relationships may lie in different domains of the work; what is more, such relationships themselves may constitute a significant type of basic shape. Thus he suggests that "common content, rhythmic similarities and coherent harmony contribute to logic. Common content is provided by using motive-forms derived from the same basic motive. Rhythmic similarities act as unifying elements. Coherent harmony [defined in a footnote as deduced from the practice of the period from Bach to Wagner] reinforces relationship"

(*Fundamentals*, p. 16). In another passage he speaks of regularity, achieved through motivelike repetitions of "motive of the harmony" and "motive of the accompaniment," which contributes to unity and comprehensibility (p. 16).

Later in the same chapter, in illustrating how phrases may be built, Schoenberg demonstrates ways of elaborating upon a basic motive-form. These methods provide insight, from another vantage point, into his concept of basic shapes and the ways in which they underlie successive events in a work. The descriptions in fact virtually summarize Schoenberg's procedures for developing musical ideas, as illustrated by continual examples throughout *Fundamentals* and *Models*. They are illustrative as well of basic-shape concepts elucidated by Schoenberg in analyses of classical works. (See the study of Beethoven's Fifth Symphony [*Style and Idea*, p. 200] and Brahms [in the essay "Brahms the Progressive," also in *Style and Idea*], as well as the analysis of basic shapes in Beethoven's Piano Sonata, Op. 10, No. 1, by Schoenberg's disciple Josef Rufer.[1])

In these procedures for building phrases, a large number of phrases are produced out of one basic motive. Some of them might be used to begin a theme, others to continue it, others as material to meet other structural requirements such as contrasts and subordinate ideas. In certain cases the original form is varied by adding ancillary notes, though all the notes of the basic motive are retained. In other cases the rhythm is preserved, producing closely related motive-forms in spite of changes in interval and direction. Combined with transpositions to other scale degrees, Schoenberg points out, this procedure is often used in traditional music to produce entire themes. In such cases each note of the melody is either a harmony note or a nonchordal note that corresponds to one of the established conventional formulas.

More far-reaching variations are produced by combining rhythmic changes with the addition of ancillary notes, as well as with changes of interval and direction. By rhythmic shifting and rearrangement of features, further material is produced for the continuation of extended themes and for contrasts. In working out all these derivatives of a motive, the composer warns, it is important that the results have the character of true phrases—of complete musical units (*Fundamentals*, pp. 16–17).

Later in the *Fundamentals*, discussing the construction of themes, Schoenberg points out that the preservation of original rhythm allows extensive changes in melodic contour, preserving unity in slow tempi and comprehensibility in rapid tempi. He also mentions, though does not amplify, a seemingly important point: that distantly related motive-forms, in which certain features may be preserved despite the variation of others, may sound incoherent.

The construction of themes is further developed in another chapter of the *Fundamentals* (pp. 58–62). Schoenberg observes that "the order of motive-forms is conditioned by the requirements of comprehensibility and musical logic. Thus, repetition, control of variation, delimitation and subdivision regulate the organization of a piece in its entirety, as well as in its smaller units" (p. 58). The circumstances that produce the different aspects of a basic motive—its variations and developments—derive from such considerations as variety, structure, and expressiveness. In the higher forms of construction, such as the sentence, the statement of an idea starts at once a kind of development as well. As the driving force of musical construction, development leads to remotely varied motive-forms, which in masterpieces has given rise to a great variety of structures. (Musical examples from this chapter illustrate how Schoenberg saw the variations and underlying shapes of motive-forms in themes from the great works. See *Fundamentals*, pp. 61, 68.)

Intimately linked with the concept of a basic shape in Schoenberg's thinking was the companion process of "developing variation." Through this process successive themes and other events in a work derive from the germs initially present in earlier ideas. All such ideas, however, are seen as manifestations of the underlying "idea," or basic shape.

Schoenberg explained the process of developing variation briefly in *Style and Idea* and by way of example showed the derivation of themes from a basic germ in the first movement of Beethoven's Fifth Symphony (*Style,* pp. 199–200). He dealt with it again in the chapter on "Motive" in *Fundamentals* (p. 8), where he stated:

Homophonic music can be called the style of 'developing variation.' This means that in the succession of motive-forms produced through variation of the basic motive, there is something which can be compared to development, to growth. But changes of subordinate meaning, which have no special consequences, have only the local effect of an embellishment. Such changes are better termed *variants.*

He refers to the same point in the *Preliminary Exercises in Counterpoint* (p. 155) and briefly in *Models* (Syllabus, p. 3, paragraphs 6 and 7).

NOTE

1. Josef Rufer, *Composition with Twelve Notes Related Only to One Another*, tr. Humphrey Searle (London: Rockliff, 1954), pp. 38–45; musical illustrations in Appendix, pp. I–II.

The intensive discussion of the *Eroica* Symphony in Chapter 6 indicates that, in the first movement of this work at least, the relationships between certain temporary key centers (those chromatically and anomalously related to the tonic) and the modulatory processes that establish these temporary centers appear to be manifestations in the large-scale pitch structure of similar pitch relationships found in the opening theme (in the basic shape of the movement). This observation raises the question whether such relationships between thematic motives—chromatic ones in particular—and key centers and modulations are unique to the *Eroica,* or whether such structural interrelationships were a basic part of Beethoven's musical thought. This question is investigated here. The evidence points consistently toward the latter conclusion and strengthens the impression that for Beethoven the influence of basic shapes was multidimensional.

Sonata-form first movements are examined here in middle-period Beethoven works in three major areas of his output: the symphonies (Second through Eighth), string quartets (Op. 57 through 127), and piano sonatas (Op. 14 through 81a). The point of inquiry is whether, in movements that contain chromatic elements as part of their basic pitch shape, this chromatic shape is subsequently reflected in the movement in terms of patterns of modulation and key relationships. Conversely, in movements whose basic shapes do not contain such chromatic elements, are there no, or significantly fewer, such relationships?

The evidence strongly suggests a positive conclusion in both cases. In virtually every instance in which Beethoven's initial themes contain a striking chromatic element, this shape is manifested in the large as described above. In many of these cases the composer highlights the initial thematic chromaticism dynamically (as in the *Eroica*) by such means as a crescendo, diminuendo, or *sf*, as if to denote its significance at the outset. In contrast, those movements whose thematic shapes are fundamentally diatonic have markedly fewer modulations or key relations that conform to this chromatic pattern.

The modulations in these chromatically influenced works are basically of two types. In one type, the key centers themselves reflect the chromaticism of the thematic motive, in a manner similar to the minor tonal centers C–C♯–D of measures 178–194 of the *Eroica.* In the second type, the pitches of the chromatic motive (sometimes transposed, inverted, or occasionally permuted) will be found as an upper or bass line distributed over a wide expanse of musical time, in much the fashion of a far-flung Schenkerian middle-ground voice-leading line. Certain of these pitches will determine the harmony (or temporary key center) by serving as chord roots. Others will serve as other notes of the temporary key (such as third, fifth). In all cases, the prevalent harmonic-tonal complex results from the influence of these pitches. (An example in the *Eroica* is the bass line of the development, outlining the basses and/or key centers B♭–B♮–C–C♭–B♭ .)

While the correlations between chromatic elements in themes and modulatory patterns are clear in these works, it is worth noting the varied characteristics of these chromatic elements as they appear in Beethoven's themes. They are prominent aspects of initial melodies in cases like the *Eroica* or the Second Symphony; on the other hand, in a work like the Piano Sonata, Op. 14, No. 2, they are seemingly unimportant neighbor tones; in Op. 31, No. 1, similarly unimportant passing tones.

The extent to which related modulations appear is also quite varied among these works. In some cases, like the *Eroica*, modulatory patterns and key relations are highly significant factors in the formal design. In other pieces, such as the String Quartet in F Minor, Op. 95, while these relations are present, the chromaticisms of the opening theme are treated more extensively in melodic lines than in the overall design of tonality. All of this points up a hardly surprising fact: that Beethoven's imagination was immensely varied, and the ways in which he explored the ramifications of his musical shapes differed from work to work, rarely falling into stereotyped repetitions—a not inconsiderable index of creativity.

The consistency of these correlations indicates the multidimensional implications for structure that basic shapes bore for Beethoven. The harmonic progressions in many of the development sections that follow also exemplify the contention about tonality that Schoenberg outlined in his *Structural Functions of Harmony:* within a tonal work there is only one tonality—the original key. All other keys of the work are not "separate" keys but are chord centers related to the tonic either closely or by varying degrees of remoteness. Seen in the perspective of the entire work, these temporary centers are in effect chords within a large-scale progression initially emanating from and returning to the tonic. Indeed this is the exact description of Beethoven's procedures, particularly in his developments, whether his temporary centers are those of conventional progressions such as secondary dominant chains, or the chromatic progressions so consistently motivated by his thematic shapes of similar character.

STRING QUARTET IN E MINOR, OP. 59, NO. 2 (FIRST MOVEMENT)

This is one of several Beethoven openings in which the second thematic statement is on the Neapolitan chord (others being the String Quartet in F Minor, Op. 95, and the *Appassionata* Sonata). In this case the Neapolitan statement itself and the half-step relationship it establishes with the first phrase (E–F) are important aspects of the basic shape (Ex. B1). (The relationship is extended upward two more degrees in the following measures, measures 3–13, through F♯ to G.)

Ex. B1. Beethoven: *String Quartet in E Minor,* **Op. 59, No. 2, first movement**

This half step appears in numerous melodic and harmonic capacities in the following measures: the Neapolitan chord is prominent in the runs of measures 16–17 and 24–25; half steps in the bass motivate the rather brusque harmonic progressions of measures 49–50 and 53–55, as well as the more extensive progression from measure 58–64. Moreover, the chromatic harmonic progression of the transition section, between first and second groups, is permeated by this interval in the voice leading (see schema for measures 25–31).

The effect of the half step upon modulations and temporary key centers is seen throughout the development section. Early in the section (measures 78–84) the music progresses upward through the key centers of B minor and C minor, the upper voice hinting at a further extension that does not in fact occur. Shortly afterward (measure 91–107) a similar progression moves through the key centers of B♭ minor, B minor, and C major. Subsequently, with the music temporarily settled in A minor (measures 111–127), the Neapolitan relation to B♭ is exploited; and from measure 127 the return to the tonic key of E minor, in anticipation of the recapitulation, is effected by chromatic modulations motivated by the rising bass line. Finally, the transition to the repeat of the development and recapitulation prior to the coda (measures 209–212) juxtaposes somewhat starkly the major key centers of E and E♭—curiously, the inverse of the Neapolitan relationship basic to the opening theme.

STRING QUARTET IN E♭, OP. 127 (FIRST MOVEMENT)

The chromatic element in the basic shape of this movement, which develops into a significant formal element for the larger structure, is the seemingly unimportant, graceful set of three notes (B♭–B♮–C) that connect the repeated statements of the Allegro opening theme (See Ex. B2, measure 10). Reference to the score will reveal that the figure is reiterated a number of times as it links phrases between measures 7–22. Its first appearance is earlier still, in a subtly disguised form in the Introduction, measures 5–6. It recurs in diminution during the extension of the opening group (measures 27–34).

Ex. B2. Beethoven: *String Quartet in E flat Major*, **Op. 127, first movement**

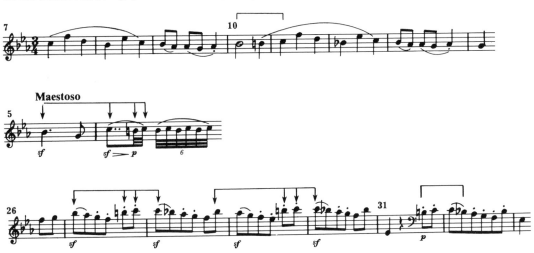

The larger formative role of this motive is in part connected with the unusual form of the movement itself. Note that the slow Maestoso section recurs twice after the Introduction, each time establishing a change of key or mode. It reveals the overall soprano line that prevails from the establishment of the second group in measure 41 until this final Maestoso. The pitches are those of the chromatic motive in the basic shape. As can be seen, they are determinative of the key centers other than the tonic that are most important to the movement's structure, namely G minor, G major, and C major. In the first two instances the pitches B♭ and B♮ affect the mode of the key; in the last, the pitch C is the root of the key itself.

Note also that the same motive B♭–B♮–C is the background line of the upper voice that guides the harmonic progression (measures 125–133) toward the tonicizing of C at measure 135.

FOURTH SYMPHONY (FIRST MOVEMENT)
Measures 5–6 of the opening phrase in the introductory Adagio contain a minor second, G♭–F, which assumes significance later in the movement as part of the basic shape (Ex. B3). Its potential import is implied dynamically in these measures by the swell. The set of notes is expanded one degree further to include the two half steps E–F–G♭ within the following two measures. It is essentially this three-note motive, related by half steps, that generates modulations in the development section of the forthcoming Allegro.

Ex. B3. Beethoven: *Symphony No. 4 in B flat Major,* **first movement**

Beethoven does not wait until the Allegro to expand harmonic implications of this motive. From measure 13 on, the harmony moves upward by half steps through a series of chromatic progressions, utilizing all the while this thematic idea. The schema shows a condensation of these measures. Note that the temporarily sustained harmonies reveal in several ways the two-half-step motive in the voice leading of the upper part.

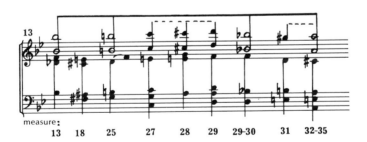

The half step appears numerous places as a melodic motive, though this fact is tangential to the present discussion. Not the least of these appearances is in the extension of the second group in the Allegro (measure 121).

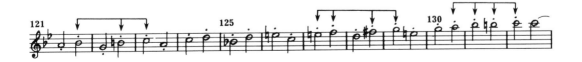

It is in the development section that the richest exploitation of the half-step motive is seen in its harmonic implications. The section is rather lengthy and traverses a number of temporary key centers, remaining in some of them a relatively long time. Measures 187–305 reveal that these temporary centers are in fact chords within a large-scale progression, rather than key centers, though their sustained duration lends to many of them a seeming tonal stability. This is the salient point—the harmonic progressions and resultant passing modulations of the development are directed largely by the voice-leading of the upper part, which itself expresses the three-note, two-half-step motive seen in the Adagio.

SECOND SYMPHONY (FIRST MOVEMENT)

The musical procedures in this movement are similar in several ways to those of the Fourth Symphony just studied. The aspect of the basic shape that motivates modulations in the development is again a half step and, as in the preceding work, it first appears in the Introduction as a fragment of a longer line. (In this case it is the half step D♯–E in measures 2–3.) (See Ex. B4.) Also, as in the Fourth Symphony, this half-step motive directs these harmonic progressions and passing modulations by virtue of its embodiment in an important voice-leading line. This time, however, the line is in the bass.

Ex. B4. Beethoven: *Symphony No. 2 in D Major*

The chromatic notes D♯–E first appear in the Introduction with no particular designation of their future import, though in measure 3 the hidden appearance in an inner voice of the same notes is marked by a swell. This motive generates activity in the following restatement of the theme (measure 5) through the chromatic embellishments in the bass line and the *sf*, which this time denotes the original set of two notes.

(The chromaticism established here in the bass turns out to be a compositional premise of consequence in the musical events that follow.) Further progressions, motivated by half-step voice leading as seen above, follow in the Introduction (measures 8–12, 19–23, 29–33).

The transient modulations and harmonic progressions in the development section are of two types: (1) conventional chains of secondary dominants and (2) chromatic progressions. Both are seen in the harmonic sketch of the development (measures 138–215). The former are indicated as black-note chords with stems, connected by beams, and are of minor concern here (though local chromatic motives are denoted). The latter are seen as whole-note chords with no stems.

As can be seen by the brackets, these chromatic progressions are largely directed by the chromatic motion of the bass line. They derive from the half-step motive of the Introduction and from similar progressions in the Introduction, which themselves emanate from this motive. Much of the melodic development from measures 184–198 also highlights the chromaticism of this motive.

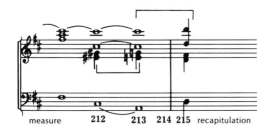

measure **164** **165** **166** **167** **168** **169** **170** **182**   **190**   **194**   **198**

measure   **212**   **213** **214** **215** recapitulation

**PIANO SONATA
IN G MAJOR,
OP. 14, NO. 2
(FIRST
MOVEMENT)**

The half-step neighbor-tone aspect of the opening theme, often chromatic, is a salient feature of the basic shape in this movement. It features prominently in all the themes, the principal ones shown in Ex. B5. Note that the basic thematic shape, as well as the neighbor tones in question, underlie these themes.

Ex. B5. Beethoven: *Piano Sonata in G Major,* **Op. 14, No. 2**

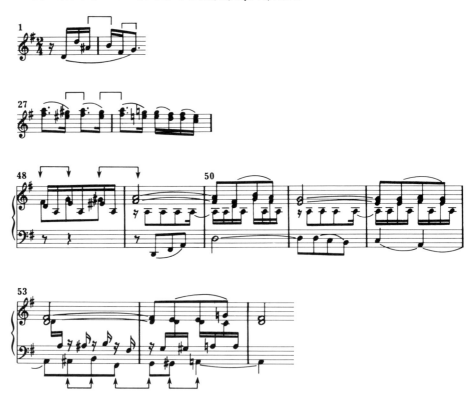

Melodic and thematic appearances of this half-step figure are numerous throughout the movement, as even brief study will reveal. Not the least dramatic of these is the suspended passing tone, prolonged by a fermata, which presages the recapitulation and concludes a long string of neighbor-tone figures (measures 122–125).

Middle-Period Beethoven

The effects of this half-step figure upon key relations and modulations in the development are several. There are two instances in which temporary key centers are contiguous, their roots a half step apart. These occur at measures 65/82 (G minor/A♭ major) and measures 100/124 (E♭ major/D major). This latter case marks a special nuance: the E♭ center introduces what turns out to be a false recapitulation, though at its onset it has the earmarks of a true one (save the wrong key), complete with fermata and pause beforehand to articulate its statement. Five measures later the music moves down to D, which serves as an extensive dominant preparation in anticipation of the true recapitulation at measure 126.

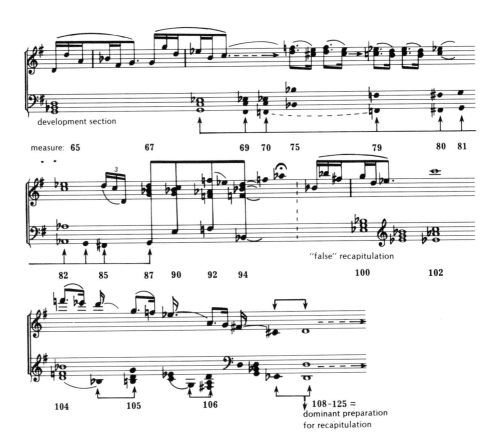

In a more pervasive manner the half-step motive is prominent in the bass line during much of the development. It is the means by which the transient modulations and others as well are effected (measures 65–108). The half steps are bracketed, and secondary dominant progressions are stemmed and beamed.

PIANO SONATA IN G MAJOR, OP. 31, NO. 1 (FIRST MOVEMENT)

We have already seen how in Beethoven's musical thinking unusual events that occur early in a movement have larger implications that are fulfilled later in the work. Thus the half steps E♭–D–C♯ in the *Eroica*, the Neapolitan statement of the second phrase of the String Quartet in E Minor, Op. 59, No. 2, the chromaticisms of the Fourth Symphony introduction—all generate subsequent events of significant formal design. To be sure, some events like these may turn out to be inconsequential, even mere whim. The indications are, however, that they often portend more.

Thus the opening of the G Major Sonata, Op. 31, No. 1, signals an alert, for the second statement of the first theme occurs abruptly in F major, ♭VII, a remote key. One immediately wonders why.

The answer lies in the same line of thought that has been discussed in the previous pages: the relationship among keys is part of a larger formal design, emanating from a motivic element of the basic shape. A curiosity about this example, however, is the fact that the strange key relations are found in the exposition and recapitulation to a more striking extent than in the development.

The motivic fragment within the thematic shape that generates this activity is the three-note sequence of half steps D–D♯–E, passing in such rapid and seemingly unimportant fashion in the opening measures (Ex. B6). Similar half-step embellishments, some of them chromatic, are found in the subsequent themes, as shown in measures 66–70 and 98–102. The embellishment figure grows still further in importance in numerous ways, such as the extension of the opening theme from measures 30–39, the extension of the second thematic group (measures 96), the clash of E♭ versus D in the long dominant preparation prior to the recapitulation (measures 182–185), and other passages.

Ex. B6. Beethoven: *Piano Sonata in G Major,* **Op. 31, No. 1, first movement**

The relation of the curious statement on ♭VII of the opening theme can be understood in the light of this three-note chromatic figure. For the tonal level on F is itself part of a larger design structured by this figure. The F of measure 12 is complemented by the F♯ of measure 54, thus completing the figure: G (beginning)–F–F♯. That Beethoven attached great significance to this F♯ is evidenced in several ways. It marks the focal point for the first truly structural modulation, which sets up the key for the second group. (Indeed, the F♯ also determines that the key of the second group is the unconventional key of B major—III—rather than that of the dominant.) Its appearance is heightened by its contrast to G, the tonic, which from measure 35 until measure 54 (the F♯) has been extensively tonicized. Further, the establishment of the F♯ is punctuated by a dynamic accent.

Thus the motivic pattern is completed by the F♯, and in turn the key of III (B major) is determined as the tonal center for the second group. With the knowledge of hindsight, other events on a more localized level can be seen as fitting in with this design. For example, the pattern G–F♯–F is heard in measures 1–12. The same pattern, on the pitches E–E♯–F♯ (measures 64–87) reinforces the modulation onto the F♯, as seen in the phrases that follow this event (measures 55–63). And the repeated cadential figure

I–V–I that occurs so often throughout the exposition now seems a reinforcement, albeit truncated, of this structurally important half step (measures 10–25).

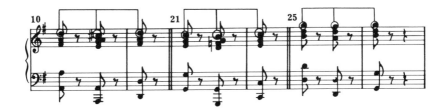

Modulatory patterns in the development section are for the most part along conventional lines, the half-step motive, as mentioned earlier, exerting little influence here. The motive is the means by which two transient changes are effected, however, as shown in measures 134–150.

A final point of interest concerns the modulation by means of which the second group is introduced in the key of E major—VI—in the recapitulation. Here again the three-note succession of half steps operates. The note ultimately determinative of harmonic direction is the D♯ in the chord on B in measure 210, which inflects the music toward the key center of E major (measures 205–210). The set of pitches E–D–D♯ are of ultimate importance here, heard in the inner voices of the harmonies.

The examples studied up to this point have illustrated situations in which minor seconds, often a chromatic aspect of a basic shape, exerted rather far-reaching influences upon subsequent key relations and transient modulations in the rest of a movement, frequently though not exclusively in its development section. The Seventh Symphony in A Major is offered here by way of contrast. The underlying shapes of its themes are fundamentally diatonic, and indeed the key relations and transient modulations within the movement are for the most part along conventional, nonchromatic lines. There are, however, two chromatic aspects of the thematic materials, admittedly less impressive in their prime state than the other ideas of the work. They are influential upon subsequent key relations, though their influence, seemingly in proportion to their initial thematic importance, is less than other, more conventional factors.

These two chromatic aspects (half steps) appear in separate parts of the movement, namely the Introduction and the subsequent Allegro. The most noticeable is the embellishment figure in grace notes that occurs three times in the opening Allegro theme (Ex. B7). The other is the chromatic bass line that is less thematic than it is a

Ex. B7. Beethoven: *Symphony No. 7 in A Major,* **first movement**

secondary, accompanying line to the melodic ideas of the opening ten measures of the Introduction (see schema of measures 1–10). This opening bass pattern is seen again in the phrase that follows the opening, from measures 15–22. Its inversion, furthermore, guides the ascending harmonic progression in the sequences from measures 32–40 to measure 48 and, ultimately, to the establishment of the dominant pedal E upon which the Allegro begins.

As mentioned earlier, these two figures are less noticeable as thematic components and less significant, formally, in the particular relationship under study than other elements of the basic shape. They do exert some effect upon harmonic progressions and modulations, however, as can be seen in measures 108–122 (see schema). In some

of these cases, such as at measure 171 and in the coda phrase at measures 383 ff., the progression clearly derives from the grace-note motive that is itself prominent at these

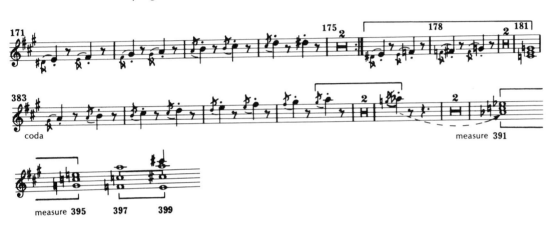

places. The specific influence of this motive is less apparent in the other examples, where the general presence of half steps in bass and soprano lines is a more pervasive factor.

PIANO SONATA IN F MINOR, OP. 57 (FIRST MOVEMENT)

The *Appassionata* Sonata, like the Op. 59, No. 2 quartet and the Op. 95 quartet, opens its first movement by stating the opening theme on the Neapolitan harmony following the initial statement in the tonic. In the *Appassionata*, as in the Op. 95 quartet in the same key, the Neapolitan harmony has an influence on the harmonic progressions of subsequent themes, as well as on larger harmonic-tonal schemes.

The half-step relationship established by the chords of these two opening statements in the *Appassionata* is also seen as a secondary melodic motive at several places in the exposition (Ex. B8, measures 3, 11, 15). It also appears as a feature of the transitional ideas leading to the second thematic group (measures 24, 30). The above covers only some of the appearances of the interval as a motivic unit, but is sufficient to establish its import in the design of the music.

Ex. B8. Beethoven: *Piano Sonata in F Minor,* **Op. 57, first movement**

One effect of the initial Neapolitan harmony is its recurrence as part of the harmonic schemes of both the second and closing themes, appearing toward their cadential portions (measures 40–45 and 51–54). The first influence of the motive upon modulations

occurs in the transition to the second group. In this instance the key scheme itself is not unusual, but the manner in which it is effected is. Thus in measure 23 the music moves abruptly from V in the tonic key of F minor to V of III in order to prepare for the second group. The modulation is not gradual, as tradition dictated, but is created by the sudden shift of the outer voices of the chords in opposite directions by half steps.

The pattern by which this modulation takes place—namely the motion of leading voices by half steps, turns out to be the dominating principle by which transient modulations take place in the development. This includes a similar procedure at the inception of the coda in measures 205–206. The pattern is consistent throughout the movement. The structural influence upon modulations of the half-step motive is found in the voice-leading of prominent lines, rather than in the juxtaposition of particular tonalities.

development starts

POSTSCRIPT

The foregoing analyses cover only some of the cases in middle-period Beethoven—even in the genres of works selected for study—in which relationships operate between chromatic thematic motives and modulatory schemes. They do seem sufficient, however, to indicate that such occurrences are not accidental.

The examples show some of the varied ways in which these relationships are found. The reader may wish further to examine first movements in works like the Fifth Symphony, in which the chromatic extension of the second theme affects harmonic progressions in the development; Op. 95; Op. 53; or Op. 81a, a particularly interesting case, where the "*Le-be-wohl*" motive, itself diatonic, undergoes chromaticization and ultimately compression in the development and, through voice leading, generates highly chromatic progressions. Beethoven's works in other genres (violin or cello sonatas, trios, concertos) doubtless contain other examples.

What is striking in these analyses is the high degree of correlation between chromatic elements in thematic shapes and their effect in directing chromatic modulations later in the same movements. Equally striking in Beethoven's music of this period is the minimal amount of such modulations in works where chromatic shapes are absent from the thematic ideas. Thus there seems to be a causal connection between the chromatic design of theme and the tonal scheme.

BIBLIOGRAPHY

Abraham, Gerald. *A Hundred Years of Music.* London: Duckworth, 1964. Chicago: Aldine, 1964.

"Analysis Symposium." *Journal of Music Theory* 10 (1966): 20-52. Articles by Howard Boatwright and Ernst Oster.

Babbitt, Milton. "Remarks on the Recent Stravinsky." *Perspectives of New Music* 2, no. 2 (Spring–Summer 1964): 35-55.

———. Review of Felix Salzer's "Structural Hearing." *Journal of the American Musicological Society* 5, no. 3 (Fall 1952): 260-265.

———. Review of René Leibowitz's Schoenberg and his School." *Journal of the American Musicological Society* 3, no. 1 (1950): 57-60.

———. "Set Structure as a Compositional Determinant." *Journal of Music Theory* 5 (April 1961): 72-94.

———. "Some Aspects of Twelve-tone Composition." *The Score*, June 1955, pp. 53-61.

———. "Twelve-tone Invariants as Compositional Determinants." *Musical Quarterly* 46 (April 1960): 246-259.

———. "Twelve-tone Rhythmic Structure and the Electronic Medium." *Perspectives of New Music* 1 (Fall 1962): 49-79.

Backus, John. "*Die Reihe:* A Scientific Evaluation." *Perspectives of New Music* 1, no. 1 (Fall 1962): 160-171.

Barford, P. "*Urphaenomenon, Ursatz* and *Grundgestalt.*" *Music Review* 28, no. 3 (1967): 218-231.

Barnett, David. *The Performance of Music.* New York: Universe Books, 1972.

Beach, David. "A Schenker Bibliography." *Journal of Music Theory* 13 (1969): 2-37.

Beeson, Roger. "Background and Model." *Music Review* 32, no. 4 (1971): 349-359.

Berger, Arthur. "New Linguistic Modes and the New Theory." *Perspectives of New Music* 3, no. 1 (Fall-Winter 1964): 1-9.

Berry, Wallace. *Form in Music.* Englewood Cliffs, N.J.: Prentice-Hall, 1966.

Boretz, Benjamin. "A Note on Discourse." *Perspectives of New Music* 4, no. 2 (1966): 76-80.

Boulez, Pierre. *Boulez on Music Today.* London: Faber & Faber, 1971. Cambridge, Mass.: Harvard University Press, 1971.

Brindle, Reginald Smith. *Serial Composition.* London: Oxford University Press, 1966.

Brinkmann, Reinhold. "Arnold Schoenberg: Drei Klavierstücke, Op. 11." *Studien zur früher Atonalität bei Schoenberg.* Wiesbaden: Franz Steiner, 1969.

Carter, Elliott. Letter to the *New York Times.* Music page, Sunday, 20 October 1968.

Clifton, Thomas. "Training in Music Theory: Process and Product." *Journal of Music Theory* 13 (Spring 1969): 38-63.

Cohen, John. "Subjective Time." In *The Voices of Time,* edited by J.T. Fraser, pp. 257-275. New York: Braziller, 1966.

Cone, Edward T. "Analysis Today." *Musical Quarterly* 46 (April 1960): 172-188.

———. "Beyond Analysis." *Perspectives of New Music* 6, no. 1 (Fall-Winter 1967): 33-51.

———. Communications to the Editor. *Perspectives of New Music,* 1, no. 2 (Spring 1963): 206-210.

———. "Music: A View from Delft." *Musical Quarterly* 47, no. 4 (October 1961): 439-453.

———. *Musical Form and Musical Performance.* New York: Norton, 1968.

———. "Stravinsky: The Progress of a Method." *Perspectives of New Music* 1, no. 1 (1962): 18-26.

Cooke, Deryck. *The Language of Music.* London: Oxford University Press, 1959.

Cooper, Grosvenor, and Meyer, Leonard. *The Rhythmic Structure of Music.* Chicago: University of Chicago Press, 1960.

Craft, Robert. "The *Rite of Spring:* Genesis of a Masterpiece." *Perspectives of New Music* 5, no. 1 (1966): 20-36.

de la Motte, Diether. *Musikalische Analyse, mit kritische Anmerkungen von Carl Dahlhaus.* 2 vols. Kassel: Barenreiter, 1968.

Ferguson, Donald N. *Music as Metaphor.* Minneapolis: University of Minnesota Press, 1960.

Fletcher, Grant. *Rhythm—Notation and Production.* Phoenix: author's publication, 1969.

Flothuis, Marius. "Forma Formans." *Sonorum Speculum* 41 (Winter 1969): 3-6.

Fokker, Adriaan D. "Wherefore and Why?" *Die Reihe* 3 (1968): 68-79.

Forte, Allen. *Compositional Matrix: Monographs in Theory and Composition.* Baldwin, N.Y.: Music Teachers National Association, 1961.

———. *Contemporary Tone-Structures.* New York: Teachers College, Columbia University, 1955.

———. "Exact Tempi in the Brahms-Haydn Variations." *Music Review* 18 (1957): 138-149.

———. "Schenker's Conception of Musical Structure." *Journal of Music Theory* 3, no. 1 (April 1959): 1-30.

Foss, Lukas. Remarks from a panel discussion. *Newsletter* of the American Symphony Orchestra League, August–October 1968, p. 11.

Gerhard, Roberto. "Apropos Mr. Stadlen." *The Score* 23 (July 1958): 50–57.

Goodman, Nelson. *Languages of Art: An Approach to a Theory of Symbols.* Indianapolis: Bobbs-Merrill, 1968.

Gould, Glenn. *Arnold Schoenberg, A Perspective.* Cincinnati: University of Cincinnati, 1964.

Hermann-Benger, Irmgard. *Tempobezeichnungen.* Tutzing: Schneider, 1959.

Hiller, Lejaren A., and Isaacson, Leonard M. *Experimental Music.* New York: McGraw-Hill, 1959.

Hindemith, Paul. *A Composer's World.* New York: Doubleday Anchor Books, 1961.

Hsu, Dolores Menstell. "Ernst Kurth and his Concept of Music as Motion." *Journal of Music Theory* 10, no. 1 (1966): 2–17.

Kassler, Michael. "Toward a Theory That is the Twelve-Note-Class System." *Perspectives of New Music* 5, no. 2 (Spring–Summer 1967): 1–80.

Katz, Adele T. *Challenge to Musical Tradition.* New York: Knopf, 1946.

Keller, Hans. "Britten: Thematic Relations and the 'Mad' Interlude's Fifth Motif." *Music Survey* 4, no. 1 (October 1951): 332 ff.

———. "The Chamber Music." In *The Mozart Companion*, edited by H.C. Robbins Landon and Donald Mitchell. London: Faber & Faber, 1965. New York: Oxford University Press, 1956.

———. "Functional Analysis: Its Pure Application." *Music Review* 18 (1957): 202–206.

———. "K. 503—The Unity of Contrasting Themes and Movements," Part I, *Music Review* 17 (1956): 48–58; Part II: 120–129.

———. "Knowing Things Backwards." *Tempo* 46 (Winter 1958): 14–20.

———. "Strict Serial Technique in Classical Music." *Tempo* 37 (1955): 12–24.

Kolisch, Rudolf. "Tempo and Character in Beethoven's Music." *Musical Quarterly* 29 (1943): 169–187, 291–312.

Komar, Arthur. *Theory of Suspensions.* Princeton: Princeton University Press, 1971.

Krenek, Ernst. "Extents and Limits of Serial Techniques." *Musical Quarterly* 46 (April 1960): 210–232.

———. "Tradition in Perspective." *Perspectives of New Music* 1, no. 1 (Fall 1962): 27–38.

Kurth, Ernst. *Grundlagen des linearen Kontrapunkts: Bachs melodische Polyphonik.* Bern: Haupt, 1917.

———. *Musikpsychologie.* Berlin: Hesse, 1931.

———. *Romantische Harmonik und ihre Krise in Wagners "Tristan."* 2d ed. Berlin: Hesse, 1923.

———. *Die Voraussetzungen der theoretischen Harmonik und der tonalen Darstellungssysteme.* Bern: Haupt, 1913.

Langer, Suzanne. *Feeling and Form.* New York: Scribner, 1953.

———. *Philosophy in a New Key.* New York: Mentor Books, 1951.

La Rue, Jan. *Guidelines for Style Analysis.* New York: Norton, 1970.

Leibowitz, René. *Schoenberg and His School.* Translated by Dika Newlin. New York: Philosophical Library, 1949.

Leichtentritt, Hugo. *Musical Form.* Cambridge, Mass.: Harvard University Press, 1951.

Lewin, David. "A Study of Hexachord Levels in Schoenberg's Violin Fantasy." *Perspectives of New Music* 6, no. 1 (Fall–Winter 1967): 18–32.

———. "A Theory of Segmental Association in Twelve-Tone Music." *Perspectives of New Music* 1, no. 1 (Fall 1962): 89–116.

Ligeti, Gyorgy. "Pierre Boulez." *Die Reihe* 4 (1960): 36–62.

Lockwood, Lewis. "The Autograph of the First Movement of Beethoven's Sonata for Violoncello and Piano, Op. 69." *The Music Forum* 2 (1970): 1–109.

Mann, Thomas. *The Story of a Novel.* Translated by Richard and Clara Winston. New York: Knopf, 1961.

Martin, Richard M. "On the Proto-Theory of Musical Structure." *Perspectives of New Music* 9, no. 1 (1970): 68–73.

Martino, Donald. "The Source Set and Its Aggregate Formations." *Journal of Music Theory* 5 (November 1961): 224–273.

Mendel, Arthur. "A Brief Note on Triple Proportion in Schuetz." *Musical Quarterly* 46, no. 1 (January 1960): 67–70.

———. "A Note on Proportional Relationships in Bach Tempi." *The Musical Times*, December 1959, pp. 683–684.

———. "Some Ambiguities of the Mensural System." In *Studies in Music History*, edited by Harold Powers, pp. 137–160. Princeton: Princeton University Press, 1968.

Meyer, Leonard. *Emotion and Meaning in Music.* Chicago: University of Chicago Press, 1956.

———. *Music, the Arts and Ideas.* Chicago: University of Chicago Press, 1967.

Mitchell, William. "Schenker's Approach to Detail." *Musicology* 1, no. 2 (1946).

———. "The Tristan Prelude: Techniques and Structure." *The Music Forum* 1 (1967): 162–203.

Mozart, W.A. *The Ten Celebrated String Quartets*. Edited by Alfred Einstein. London: Novello, n.d.

Nelson, Robert U. *The Technique of Variation*. Berkeley: University of California Press, 1948.

——. "Webern's Path to Serial Variation." *Perspectives of New Music* 7, no. 2 (1969): 73-93.

Newlin, Dika. *Bruckner, Mahler, Schoenberg*. New York: Kings Crown Press, 1947.

O'Connell, Walter. "Tone Spaces." *Die Reihe* 8 (1968): 34-67.

Oster, Ernst. "Register and the Long-Scale Connection." *Journal of Music Theory* 5 (1961): 54-71.

Perle, George. *Serial Composition and Atonality*. Berkeley: University of California Press, 1963.

——. "Theory and Practice in Twelve-Tone Music: Stadlen Reconsidered." *The Score* 25 (June 1959): 58-64.

Powell, Mel. "A Note on Rigor." *Perspectives of New Music* 1, no. 2 (Spring 1963): 121-124.

Quantz, Johann Joachim. *On Playing the Flute*. Edited and translated by Edward R. Reilly. New York: Free Press, 1966.

Ratz, Erwin. *Einführung in die musikalische Formenlehre*. Vienna: Osterreichischer Bundesverlag für Unterricht, Wissenschaft und Kunst, 1951.

Redlich, Hans F. *Alban Berg*. New York: Abelard-Schuman, 1957.

Reich, Willi. *Schoenberg: A Critical Biography*. Tr. Leo Black. London: Longman Group Ltd., 1971. New York: Praeger, 1971.

Reik, Theodore. *The Haunting Melody: Psycho-Analytic Experiences in Life and Music*. New York: Grove Press, 1953.

Reti, Rudolf. "Duothematicism in the Evolution of Sonata Form." *Music Review* 17 (1956): 110-119.

——. *Thematic Patterns in Sonatas of Beethoven*. Edited by Deryck Cooke. London: Faber & Faber, 1967. New York: Macmillan, 1967.

——. *The Thematic Process in Music*. London: Faber & Faber, 1961. New York: Macmillan, 1951.

Riemann, Hugo. *Analyses of Bach Well-Tempered Clavier*. Translated by J.S. Shedlock. London: Augener, n.d.

——. *Handbuch der Musikgeschichte*, vol. 2, part 3. Leipzig: Breitkopf & Härtel, 1913.

——. *Kleines Handbuch der Musikgeschichte*. Leipzig: Breitkopf & Härtel, 1908.

Robbins Landon, H.C. and Mitchell, Donald, eds. *The Mozart Companion*. London: Faber & Faber, 1965.

Rochberg, George. "The Harmonic Tendency of the Hexachord." *Journal of Music Theory* 3 (November 1959): 208-230.

——. *The Hexachord and Its Relation to the Twelve-Tone Row*. Bryn Mawr, Pa.: Theodore Presser, 1955.

Rosen, Charles. *The Classical Style*. London: Faber & Faber, 1971. New York: Viking, 1971.

Rudolf, Max. "Storm and Stress in Music." *Bach* (The Quarterly Journal of the Riemenschneider Bach Institute) 3, nos. 2, 3, and 4 (1972): 1-28.

Rufer, Josef. *Composition with Twelve Notes Related Only to One Another*. Translated by Humphrey Searle. London: Rockliff, 1954. New York: Macmillan, 1954.

Sachs, Curt. *Rhythm and Tempo*. New York: Norton, 1953.

Salzer, Felix. *Sinn und Wesen der abendländischen Mehrstimmigkeit*. Vienna: Saturn-Verlag, 1935.

——. *Structural Hearing*. 2 vols. New York: Dover Publications, 1962.

——. "Tonality in Medieval Polyphony." *The Music Forum* 1 (1967): 35-98.

Schenker, Heinrich. ["Beethoven's *Eroica* Symphony."] *Das Meisterwerk in der Musik*. Vol. 3. Munich: Drei Masken Verlag, 1930.

——. *Ein Beitrag zur Ornamentik*. Vienna: Universal, 1908.

——. *Five Graphic Analyses*. Introduction and glossary by Felix Salzer. New York: Dover, 1969.

——. *Der Freie Satz*. Vienna: Universal, 1935 and 1956.

——. *Harmony*. Edited and annotated by Oswald Jonas. Translated by Elizabeth Mann Borgese. Chicago: University of Chicago Press, 1954.

——. ["Mozart's Symphony No. 40."] *Das Meisterwerk in der Musik*. Vol. 2. Vienna: Drei Masken Verlag, 1926.

——. "Organic Structure in Sonata Form." Translated by Orin Grossman. *Journal of Music Theory* 12 (1968): 164-183.

Schindler, Anton. *Biographie von Ludwig van Beethoven*. Münster: Aschendorff, 1971.

Schoenberg, Arnold. *Fundamentals of Musical Composition*. New York: St. Martin's Press, 1967.

——. *Harmonielehre*. 3d ed. Vienna: Universal Edition, 1922. English translation, *Theory of Harmony*. Translated by Robert D.W. Adams. New York: Philosophical Library, 1948.

——. *Letters*. Edited by Erwin Stein. Translated by Eithne Wilkins and Ernst Kaiser. London: Faber & Faber, 1964. New York: St. Martins Press, 1958.

——. *Models for Beginners in Composition*. New York: G. Schirmer, 1943.

——. *Preliminary Exercises in Counterpoint*. Edited and foreword by Leonard Stein. London: Faber & Faber, 1963. New York: St. Martins Press, 1964.

———. "Problems of Harmony." *Modern Music* 11, no. 4 (May–June 1934): 167–187.

———. *Structural Functions of Harmony.* New York: Norton, 1954.

———. *Style and Idea.* New York: Philosophical Library, 1950.

Sessions, Roger. *The Musical Experience.* Princeton: Princeton University Press, 1950.

Stein, Erwin. *Orpheus in New Guises.* London: Rockliff, 1953.

Stockhausen, Karlheinz. "How Time Passes." *Die Reihe* 3 (1959): 10–40.

Stravinsky, Igor. *Poetics of Music.* Translated by Arthur Knodel and Ingolf Dahl. Cambridge, Mass.: Harvard University Press, 1947.

———. Review of Joseph Kerman's "The Beethoven Quartets." *New York Review of Books,* 26 September 1968, pp. 4 ff.

Stuckenschmidt, H.H. *Arnold Schoenberg.* Translated by Edith Temple Roberts and Humphrey Searle. New York: Grove Press, 1959.

Thayer, Alexander Wheelock. *Life of Beethoven.* Revised and edited by Elliott Forbes. Princeton: Princeton University Press, 1964.

Tovey, Donald Francis. *A Companion to Beethoven's Pianoforte Sonatas.* London: Associated Board, Royal Schools of Music, 1951.

———. *Essays in Musical Analysis.* 6 vols. London: Oxford University Press, 1935–39.

———. *The Forms of Music.* New York: Meridian Books, 1956.

———. *The Mainstream of Music and Other Essays.* New York: Meridian Books, 1959.

Travis, Roy. "Directed Motion in Schoenberg and Webern." *Perspectives of New Music* 4, no. 2 (1966): 85–89.

———. "Tonal Coherence in the First Movement of Bartok's Fourth String Quartet." *The Music Forum* 2 (1970): 298–371.

Treitler, Leo. "Musical Syntax in the Middle Ages: Background to an Aesthetic Problem." *Perspectives of New Music* 4 (Fall–Winter 1965): 75–85.

Vetter, Walther. "Sinfonia Eroica, Betrachtungen über Beethovens Ethik." *Die Musik* 14, no. 3 (Vienna: 1914): 1.

Walker, Alan. *An Anatomy of Musical Criticism.* London: Barrie & Rockliff, 1966.

———. *A Study in Musical Analysis.* London: Barrie & Rockliff, 1962.

Webern, Anton. *The Path to the New Music.* Edited by Willi Reich. Translated by Leo Black. Bryn Mawr, Pa.: Theodore Presser Company, 1963.

Wellesz, Egon. *Arnold Schoenberg.* Translated by W.H. Kerridge. London: Dent, 1925. New York: Da Capo Press, 1969.

———. *The Origins of Schoenberg's Twelve-Tone Technique.* Washington, D.C.: Library of Congress, 1958.

Westergaard, Peter. "Toward a Twelve-Tone Polyphony." *Perspectives of New Music* 4, no. 2 (Spring–Summer 1966): 90–112.

———. "Webern and Total Organization." *Perspectives of New Music* 1, no. 2 (Spring 1963): 107–120.

Youngblood, Joseph E. "Style as Information." *Journal of Music Theory* 2 (April 1958): 29–35.

Zaslaw, Neal. "Mozart's Tempo Conventions." *Report of the International Musicological Society, Copenhagen, 1972.* Copenhagen: Wilhem Hansen, 1973.

ACKNOWLEDGMENTS

Grateful acknowledgment is hereby made for permission to quote from the following copyrighted material:

The Classical Style by Charles Rosen; copyright 1971 by Charles Rosen. Reprinted by permission of The Viking Press, Inc., New York and Faber and Faber, Ltd., London.

Boulez on Music Today by Pierre Boulez; copyright 1971 by Pierre Boulez. Reprinted by permission of Faber and Faber, Ltd., London.

Composition with Twelve Notes Related Only to One Another by Josef Rufer; original edition published by Max Hesses Verlag, Berlin, 1952; English version copyright 1954 by Rockliff Publishing Corp. Ltd., London. Reprinted by permission.

Der Freie Satz by Heinrich Schenker; copyright 1935 by Universal Edition A.G., Vienna. Reproduced by permission.

Klavierstück, Op. 33b, by Arnold Schoenberg; copyright 1932 by Arnold Schoenberg. Used by permission of Belmont Music Publishers, Los Angeles, California 90049.

String Quartet No. 4, Op. 37, by Arnold Schoenberg; copyright 1939 by G. Schirmer, Inc. International copyright secured. Used by permission.

Begleitmusik zu einer Lichtspielscene, Op. 34, by Arnold Schoenberg; copyright 1930 by Heinrichshofen's Verlag, Wilhelmshaven. Used by permission.

Rapsodie Espagnole by Maurice Ravel; copyright 1908 by A. Durand & Fils, Paris. Used by permission.

INDEX

242　　　Index